MAKING SAINTS

MAKING SAINTS

Religion and the Public Image of the British Army, 1809–1885

Kenneth E. Hendrickson III

Madison • Teaneck
Fairleigh Dickinson University Press
London: Associated University Presses

Associated University Presses
440 Forsgate Drive
Cranbury, NJ 08512

Associated University Presses
16 Barter Street
London WC1A 2AH, England

Associated University Presses
P.O. Box 338, Port Credit
Mississauga, Ontario
Canada L5G 4L8

The paper used in this publication meets the requirements of the American National Standard for Permanence of Paper for Printed Library Materials Z39.48–1984.

Library of Congress Cataloging-in-Publication Data

Hendrickson, Kenneth E., 1965–
Making saints : religion and the public image of the British Army, 1809–1885 / Kenneth E. Hendrickson, III.
p. cm.
Includes bibliographical references and index.
ISBN 0-8386-3729-9 (alk. paper)
1. Great Britain. Army. Chaplain's Dept. 2. Great Britain. Army—Chaplains—History—19th century. 3. Great Britain. Army—Public relations—History—19th century. 4. Soldiers—Great Britain—Conduct of life—History—19th century. 5. Militarism—Great Britain—History—19th century. I. Title.
UH25.G7H46 1998
306.2′7′0941—dc21 97-14917
CIP

PRINTED IN THE UNITED STATES OF AMERICA

Contents

Acknowledgments

I would like to express my thanks for the kind direction and assistance I received from the following people: Professor Jeff Cox, University of Iowa; Professor R. J. Q. Adams, Texas A&M University; Professor John W. Osborne, Emeritus Rutgers University; and Professor Hew Strachan, Edinburgh. I also greatly appreciate the cooperation and guidance offered by: Major Margaret Easy, Royal Army Chaplains' Department; staff at the National Register of Archives, at the Public Records Office in Kew, and at the Rylands Archive. I could not have completed the project without the generous efforts of the University of Iowa library staff, especially those in the Inter-Library Loan office so ably presided over by Mr. Keith Rageth. Lastly, I reserve a special thanks for Professor James Burk, editor of *Armed Forces & Society* and Professor Peter Dennis, editor of *War & Society* for their kind permission to reprint here material that appeared in their journals.

Chapter 6, "A Kinder, Gentler British Army," is reprinted from *War & Society*, volume 14, number 2, (October, 1996).

Chapter 7, "Winning the Troops" is reprinted from *Armed Forces & Society*, volume 23, issue 4, (Summer 1997).

Introduction

Popular British militarism of the sort that astounded observers of war mania in 1914 was not born of the travails of South Africa or the Edwardian competition with Germany. It was instead the fruit of the greatest victory won by the Victorian army: carrying the ramparts of British social respectability. Historians have yet to explore fully the story of the Victorian British army's integration into the mainstream of civil life. The salient social history on the topic is at least twenty years old, while more recent histories have tended toward issues of politics and administration.[1] Discussions of the growth of army popularity have focused on a common set of explanatory factors: the advent of a civil police force; the Crimean War experience; and reforms of army life, particularly after 1868 under Lord Cardwell.[2] Until very recently, the social power of British Christianity has had only limited place in narratives concerned with political-administrative issues or the confrontation between popular classes and state authority. Such interpretations have fallen respectively on the right and left sides of the historiographical spectrum, dealing either with the high politics of Parliament and government ministries or with forms of class conflict in nineteenth-century Britain. In either of these schools of thought, the force of religion (if appearing at all) is frequently explained as either a tool of the establishment, or not the realm of serious politics, or merely a manifestation of a popular culture.[3]

It is the contention of this study that the popularization of the British regular army at home and the (perhaps unsought) notable late-Victorian increase in militarism resulted from a thoughtful and long-term policy. This development of policy itself hinged upon a realization of the power of Christian religion to link the army to civil society. Leaders within the army, concerned clergy and laity outside of it, as well as successive members of governments all took the case of Christian religion in the army as a serious measure of the overall quality of the troops and the efficacy of the leaders over them.[4] Furthermore, there existed a coherent, traceable pattern of development whereby army religion became a major vehicle for the integration of the army into civil society. In short, any examination of the social role of the Victorian military and general attitudes toward military endeavor demands a rethinking of the assumptions of political and military histories. To get at issues of empire and militarism, we must return to a serious consideration of religion as religion, and not as a sociological expression of something else, in nineteenth-century British society.

The conventional view of the development of the nineteenth-century British army has been that of an institution moribund after the glorious moment of Waterloo. Only after forty years and the disasters and humiliations of the Crimean War did the army awaken to a dramatic and pressing need for reform. The development of religious life among the troops and of any serious concern for the moral conditions of soldierly life has likewise been dated to the winter of 1854–55.[5] In fact, for many years before the war with Russia, the British army, slowly and piecemeal, often through experimentation, reformed itself from within, and in the varied fields of supply, weapons, tactics, strategy, as well as morale and discipline.[6]

Prior to Crimea the army had at least a twenty-year history of religious reforms. Through trial and error at first, military and civilian authority had hit upon a scheme of limited religious pluralism by the close of the 1830s. This pluralism in principle also existed in various army stations, significantly flawed, however, by the extensive practice of contracting local civilian clergy to perform religious services. After his appointment as principal chaplain in 1844, George Robert Gleig combined the principle of pluralism with activist leadership to make meaningful religious practice a central part of army life.

As late as 1842, while the Chaplains' Department still languished under the control of conservatives, the practical commitment of the army to the religious instruction of its men remained of a low order. That year, the estimates included only £11,000 for religious instruction for the entire army at home and abroad.[7] Nearly all of the money went to repay services performed by civilian clergy, with small sums dedicated to sundry items like religious literature and officers' pew rents. In all, the Chaplains' Department budget represented 0.18 percent of the general army estimates.[8]

In the summer of 1844, Gleig immediately set about reversing the current trends in his department. Over the next three years, he secured the appointments of five active chaplains to the forces.[9] Small as this accomplishment was, it nonetheless reversed fourteen years of a policy that relied upon only civilian clergy and the recall of retired chaplains in the event of a campaign. Moreover, by 1848, Gleig had increased the budget for his department by over 60 percent. For 1853, the last full year of peace before Crimea, Gleig's budget was nearly double that of 1842, both in absolute size and relative to the general estimates.[10] Over the same decade, he increased the number of home military stations with paid clergy from 102 to 141, or by 72 percent.

By 1846 Gleig had War Office agreement that all newly constructed barracks would have chapels and schoolrooms.[11] The schoolrooms, meant primarily for the secular instruction of both personnel and their dependents, nonetheless contributed to Gleig's overall vision of a moral army. Through the schooling of recruits, he hoped not only to benefit from what he believed to be the general civilizing effects of education, but also to enhance his religious reforms by increasing soldier literacy as a prelude to religious indoctrination and Bible reading.[12]

After Crimea, public attentions to the army were short-lived. Indeed, by late 1856, the debate about military performance in the Ukraine had become an internal matter for the army. The Mutiny in India revived popular attention to military matters, but the case differed significantly from that of Crimea; issues of Christian versus non-Christian, European versus non-European, and the general stability of the empire predominated over more tactical concerns of military standards and practices. By 1860, the army was off the front pages, and stayed that way until Gladstone's ministry of 1868 and the reforms of his secretary for war, Cardwell.

During the intervening eight years, while reforms within the army lost their charm as media events, Gleig worked to maintain the expanded budget he had been awarded during the crises. Estimates for 1858, the year the army returned to building a body of regular commissioned chaplains, gave Gleig nearly £37,000, over twice the amount of his pre-war money. By 1863, the amount was up to £46,000 and constituted 0.33 percent of the total expenditure on the army.[13] This represented a relative doubling over 1842 of the army's commitment to the Chaplains' Department, and a quadrupling in absolute numbers. Though Gleig retired in 1875, military budgets, even under his ineffectual successor, Claughton, reflected the same level of spending. Rising with the general increases in army spending, the budget devoted to divine service remained roughly 0.34 percent of yearly military costs, and did not dip significantly below £60,000 from 1882 to the close of the century.

Personnel increased with the increase in money. At the start of war in Crimea, the Chaplains' Department had only five active chaplaincies. This small contingent represented a victory in principle over the army's older system of contracting clerical services, but five chaplains alone could not serve the needs of the whole army or even of one strenuous campaign. In 1858, Gleig secured, through Palmerston's resort to a royal warrant, an establishment of twenty-five regular, commissioned chaplains, including Roman Catholics and Presbyterians.[14] By 1868, the year the War Office reached a compromise with the episcopate in the form of the Army Chaplains' Act, Gleig's establishment had grown to over eighty active-duty chaplains.[15] Numbers of chaplains remained steady at this amount throughout the rest of the century and until after the South African War, 1899–1902.

Growth of the department under Gleig also brought an expansion in representation for denominations other than the Church of England. Before 1850, Roman Catholic priests in England, Scotland, and Wales officiated services for soldiers in only twenty-two stations. In 1858 that number increased to over forty, and had by 1868 risen to over eighty. In Ireland in 1850, only ten stations offered the services of a priest. By 1858, nearly fifty did so, the number thereafter remaining stable. Presbyterians likewise benefited, but less dramatically because their numbers were significantly smaller than the Catholics'. Nonetheless, whereas Presbyterians in England, Scotland, and Wales had only five chaplaincies in 1850, they had twenty-five after 1858. In Ireland they increased from three to ten, and held these gains through 1868.[16]

In the same decade, relative numbers of men in each denomination held roughly steady at 59,000 Catholics, 21,500 Presbyterians, and about 3,500 Wesleyan Methodists, who had gained the privilege of their own category in 1862. By choice, however, their chaplains did not accept official commissions until 1903. Only the Anglicans declined in absolute numbers, from 124,000 in 1861 to roughly 110,000 by 1868. No other denomination seems to have gained by the Anglican decline, with the difference appearing instead in a corresponding drop in the total strength of the army.[17] Catholics and Presbyterians did not decline in absolute numbers until a few years later, in the 1870s, but again this corresponded to a general reduction in the army.[18] By percentage of total troop strength, the major denominations remained at similar levels relative to each other through the 1880s. After 1886, however, Irish recruiting fell off while the army expanded with English recruits. Until the First World War, Catholicism in the army declined from 20 percent representation to 14 percent. Anglicans benefited, climbing from 61 percent in 1879 to 70 percent by 1913. Wesleyans and Presbyterians held their positions at roughly 5.5 percent and 7.5 percent, respectively. Congregationalists, Baptists, other Protestants, and Jews combined never amounted to more than about 2.5 percent, or 5,500 men, in the pre-war era.[19]

Clearly then, from the 1840s the army and government made systematic efforts to rehabilitate the moral and religious life within the ranks. The origins of this movement predated Crimea. The publicity generated by that war aided Gleig's drive, but did not cause it or carry it to its culmination. Rather, this policy developed over time. It illustrated the contemporary consensus that the institutional Christian churches indeed defined a publicly acceptable moral standard and were the chief instruments of its dissemination. Previous efforts to describe the development of popular nationalist consciousness and support for the army and empire have often missed the centrality of religion to that process. That bias has somewhat eroded in the last few years.

Recently, Linda Colley has taken up the theme of religious allegiance in the formation of the British nation.[20] She contends that a particular Protestant identity rooted in the established Church of England played a key role in the development of a popular national consciousness. Likewise, she cites the British experiences of the wars against the French Revolution and the Napoleonic Empire. Particularly in the light of the ancient British enmity for Catholic France, these experiences proved indispensable to the birth of modern Britishness. Colley in part measures national identity by exploring the popular will to defend Crown and home against French aggression. Eighteenth-century wars with France, and most importantly the crusade against Napoleon, created a popular awareness of Protestant Britain; the Catholic "other" provided enough external pressure to forge British unity. But this militant Protestant identity, she argues, did not long outlive Napoleon. Catholic emancipation made that impossible. After 1829 (and 1832) and the loss of a national Protestant identity, British nationalism increasingly defined itself in secular forms of government and the British capacity for reform and improvement.

Thus, parliamentary reform, arguments over democracy, and

the antislavery crusade became the hallmarks of British goodness. But Colley's case must not be overstated. Public Christianity did not fade. True, a strictly Protestant identity was harder to maintain. However, the public Protestant identity adapted to the new multidenominational environment to reemerge as a more encompassing Christian self-identity, particularly potent in the empire. Britain in Europe had for years identified itself as Protestant; Britain in the world continued to define itself as ostentatiously Christian.

As Colley suggested, the history of the social transformation of the British army through its religious identity is indeed an important part of the total history of British religion and society. Taken together, "other Protestants" constituted a major portion of the British public, yet non-Anglican denominations gained representation in the army relatively late in the nineteenth century. Only Roman Catholicism and Presbyterianism managed to achieve official recognition prior to the action in the Crimea. Wesleyan Methodism, for example, had to wait nearly twenty years more. However, the unrecognized presence of Nonconformist troops within the army, the hope of earning state approval by serving perhaps the arch representative of state authority, and a desire for general social recognition of their worth brought forth Nonconformist leaders who promoted a synthesis of military virtues and Nonconformist conscience.

Historians generally accept the universal antimilitarism of nineteenth-century Nonconformity. Despite the undoubted strength of such a sentiment across many Nonconformist congregations, the case for a religious soldiery found midcentury champions in popular Nonconformist leaders and authors, both at home and in colonial missions. They reconciled traditional Nonconformist suspicion of empire with Victorian imperialism by turning to the figure of the Christian hero. By searching the army for believably pious soldiers, they successfully revived a crusader image, not popularly hailed in Britain since the seventeenth century. This time, the focus was not on "Protestant," but on the conflict between Christian and "other."

A pattern emerged between 1857 and 1885 (and was secure by that date) for the national adulation of British status and power. Its basis was a martial Christian identity at first pinned upon a few heroic exemplars, then connected to the institutional army at large. The chronology of this pattern derived from the careers of two of the greatest Christian hero figures: General Sir Henry Havelock (d. 1857 at Lucknow, India) and Major General

Sir Charles George Gordon (d. 1885 at Khartoum, Sudan). By 1885, the year Gordon died, public belief in the Christian soldier-hero was deep and complete. People did not require much in the way of rigorous fact, which explains the cult surrounding Gordon despite his quirky character. Appearances and assumptions were enough because people already accepted the seemingly commonsense notion that Britain produced not just heroes, but morally superior Christian heroes. Thus, the stories of Havelock and Gordon close this narrative.

In 1815, the British public supposed the army to be a band of murderous thugs and drunkards whipped into shape only by the strenuous efforts of great men like Wellington. By 1885, the curious figure of Charles Gordon could immediately and easily slip into the robes of Christian martyr splendor, standing as proxy for the moral force of the army at large. The story of how the British army went from rabble to crusaders begins with the century that witnessed Britain's greatest imperial triumphs. It begins, simply enough, with serious and sober men doing the commonplace work of running an army.

MAKING SAINTS

1

The Royal Army Chaplains' Department, 1809–1825

Even around the time of the glorious victory at Waterloo, popular British patriotism focused upon home defense forces like the militia and upon individual heroes like Sir John Moore, Admiral Nelson, or the duke of Wellington.[1] The regular army rank and file remained a pariah group, very much on the outside of social life. In the eighteenth century the army had become the pet instrument of the monarchy, under the Hanoverians acquiring an unsavory reputation as a mercenary police force. Throughout the second half of the century, the army repeatedly proved to be the mainstay of executive power in Great Britain. More than the magistracy, more than the yeomanry, the regular army served the Crown as the single most effective resource against civil unrest and popular agitation.[2]

This role of mercenary enforcer made the soldier a particularly unpopular man. Officers fared little better. Many of them were aristocrats who attracted the public scorn and fear directed toward the arrogant, unjustly privileged elite they were. The atrocious conditions of army service in the eighteenth century meant that only the most desperate characters would ever enlist.[3] It was no help that judges frequently offered criminals time in the army in lieu of prison sentences or exile. By 1800 the public viewed soldiers as desperate, vicious men lorded over in draconian discipline by arrogant and bellicose aristocrats.

Within the army, the officer corps maintained similar attitudes toward enlisted men. Wellington, whose opinions dominated the officer corps at least until the 1840s,[4] disdained the men of the other ranks. He believed the average British soldier to be a degraded creature who required brute discipline to make him conform and perform.

In the late 1820s, when Wellington opposed the reduction of corporal punishment in the army, he argued,

> the man who enlists into the British Army is, in general, the most drunken and the worst man of the trade or profession to which he belongs, of the village or town in which he lives. There is not one in one hundred of them who, when enlisted, ought not to be put in the second or degraded class of any society or body into which they may be introduced; and they can be brought to be fit for what is called the first class only by discipline. . . .

which in this context meant flogging or the threat of it.[5] Elsewhere he wrote, "Would nothing but corporal punishment answer the purpose [of enforcing discipline and the orders of courts martial]? I know of nothing which could produce the same effect."[6] The general contempt of the duke and his officer corps for the enlisted man, and the suspicions and hostility toward soldiers among society in general, accounted for the shoddy treatment of British soldiers. Even in the case of spiritual care, so important to contemporary debates about social policy, the army prior to the 1840s approached its responsibilities to enlisted personnel in a perfunctory manner.

Before the 1840s, army chaplains themselves did not appear to consider the souls of soldiers worth more than some venal jobbery. The chaplaincy could not in the first half of the nineteenth century point to much of a service record. By 1796, the quality of regimental chaplains had degenerated so badly that Pitt's government secured a royal warrant to abolish them. Thereafter, the government attempted to rebuild a reformed system. Before abolition, most army chaplains rarely attended the troops to which they were nominally attached. Out of their salaries they hired deputies to travel with the units, and the results were as variable as might be expected. Some regimental chaplains made no effort at all to tend to religious duties, using their commissions purely as financial investments.[7] With the new system, the government hoped to counter such practices by appointing chaplains only at the brigade level, instead of providing one for each regiment. Local civilian clergy, who supposedly would have only the interests of piety and decorum at heart during their occasional meetings with soldiers, could be hired by commanding officers to attend to the needs of smaller detachments of troops.[8]

Under the reforms of 1796, John Gamble became the first chaplain general. He was a logical choice: he served as chaplain to the commander in chief, the duke of York,[9] in 1794, and was one of the only chaplains to attend his unit during the early years of war with France. As chaplain general, Gamble was supposed to provide some measure of administrative coherence over the army chaplains. More basically, he had to get some of them to go into the field. He failed. Upon his retirement in 1809, the War Office started all over again with yet another campaign against absenteeism.[10]

By this time, the abuses of the regimental system that died in 1796 had reappeared among the brigade chaplains. Absenteeism among them remained endemic. Since chaplaincies had remained salable commissions, they were still basically sinecures for the absentee clergy who held them. The War Office decided to rework the entire system from scratch "to ensure the real and efficient discharge of Duty on the part of all Chaplains."[11]

The new system attempted to answer the most common complaints from field commanders. The officers claimed absentee chaplains wasted money and were administrative inconveniences. The new procedure worked as follows: first, Horse Guards revoked all existing appointments of brigade chaplains, as well as those to garrisons, forts, and stations. Brigade and garrison commanders, who had personally controlled the sale of chaplaincies under their commands, lost that right of sale. This itself was a significant break with army traditions. Under the systems of replacement and supply that prevailed in the British army into the nineteenth century, unit commanders could sell officer commissions in their regiments. They also frequently made stoppages of enlisted men's pay and allowances before passing the remaining money to the soldiers for uniforms and food. This paternal control constituted an important augmentation to the pay of commanding officers, which they considered a right.[12]

Under the 1809 reform, a separate corps of chaplains, for use anywhere with the army, would replace the individual appointments.[13] Current chaplains providing character references attesting to good conduct to the archbishops of Canterbury and York and the bishop of London could reenter the new establishment. Authority over all future appointments would also reside with the prelates, the military abdicating control to the ecclesiastical hierarchy. From this time until the 1840s the army did not really control or even much concern itself with the officials ministering to the troops. This change resulted in an essentially civilian and poorly organized system of army religion for the next several decades.

From 1809 until the mid-1850s, fewer and fewer chaplains were commissioned officers. Much more often the army used civilian clergy whose "parishioners" happened to include soldiers. This divorce of the church and army helped to foster the army attitude that religious care for the troops was merely an adjunct to army function; discipline and morale relied upon brute force and coercion rather than on the spiritual and mental well-being of the troops. The system also fit with regular army practice in most areas of service and support. The British army contracted for its logistical needs, as when it relied upon civilian canteens in garrison. It therefore seemed consistent in 1809 to design a system of religious administration that would rely primarily upon local civilian clergy and upon ecclesiastical administration.

At the same time, the 1809 changes damaged religious life in the army because civilian ministers, given the general social attitude toward the military and given the slack attitudes of most officers toward arranging weekly church parade, rarely took seriously the notion of soldier piety. Instead, civilian preaching to locally stationed army units was usually perfunctory, even hostile. Thus emerged a self-perpetuating cycle: the army passed off the religious care of its soldiers to civilians, thereby making religious discipline of any sort alien and of a decidedly secondary nature to the troops; civilian ministers paid to perform religious services to the troops did little more than go through the motions because the army as a whole so clearly lacked any credible basis for civilized religious expression. The effect of the whole was to perpetuate the public image of the army as a moral wasteland populated by degenerate men without scruples and without religion.

With the memo of 1809, the government also tried to regularize the salaries and terms of service of army chaplains, a reform aimed mostly at the former practice of hiring out curates. Under the new system the government hoped to prevent endemic chaplain absenteeism in a few simple ways. First, accepting a chaplaincy entailed making a minimum commitment to serve for eight years. Pay was contingent upon the presence of the chaplain with his brigade, not allowing for a curate or any other substitute. Full pay for active chaplains would be 16 shillings per day with a half pay (retired salary) of 5 s. per day available after the eight years service. At the end of the first hitch, a chaplain could retire, go into inactive reserve, or submit in writing his intention to remain on active duty. If he chose the latter, he remained liable to all the original conditions of good conduct and residency with his unit, but also increased his retired pay by 1

d. per day per year beyond eight served. He could do so until he accrued a maximum retired pay of 10s. per day. Inactive reserve chaplains likewise extended their service, but were to be called upon only for specific campaigns. Their benefits increased only for any active service performed, not for merely staying in the reserve. The rules included certain other guarantees: full pay for the first eight years, even if the chaplain were demobilized before the full term; guaranteed minimum one year full pay if activated from reserve, regardless of how long he actually saw active duty.[14]

In this manner, an establishment of only twenty-five chaplains entered into active service with the army. The system relegated all other religious services to local clergy contracted by the commanding officer and remunerated service by service.[15] While church service might have been a centerpiece of morality and discipline in the army,[16] in reality commanding officers and local clergy viewed it with indifference or as a harassing inconvenience. Local clergymen could be persuaded to cooperate only with offers of pay. Commanding officers added religious services to their other "informal" pay bonuses. All the vouchers that recorded the performance of clerical services passed through commanders, affording them ample opportunity to make stoppages out of money destined for religious service remuneration.[17] These were the minimum necessary inducements to get most clergy and officers to take even cursory interest in the religious practices of the troops.

Most critics agreed upon the necessity of creating universal standards for military clergy. Yet, in keeping with the spirit of the 1796 changes, the regulations did not establish exclusive army authority over these chaplains. Control over appointments was shared with the three highest ecclesiastic authorities of the Church of England: the archbishops of York and Canterbury and the bishop of London. The army's own authority in the field, the chaplain general, merely recommended candidates to the prelates. During discussions about the new system in 1809, Prime Minister Perceval[18] had even contemplated evading the army altogether. He suggested that the War Office transfer the appointment of the chaplain general to the prerogative of either the archbishop of Canterbury, the bishop of London, or possibly both.[19]

Neither Palmerston, who was secretary of state for war from 1809 until 1828, nor the duke of York, the commander in chief, pursued that notion. But the next year, when time came to appoint a new chaplain general, the War Office chose the Reverend

John Owen rather than a regular military chaplain.[20] Owen appeared to be a good compromise between the Anglican black and the military scarlet because he did have military experience. From 1784 to 1793 he had been an East India Company garrison chaplain at Calcutta, Bengal. There he helped secure a change in East India Company organization that made military chaplains in India accountable to the commander in chief, instead of merely to local unit commanders. He campaigned with the British army in Holland during the disasters of 1799–1800, and from 1808 to his promotion in 1810, served as senior chaplain to the forces in Spain and Portugal.[21] Unfortunately, his rule as chaplain general marked a period of quiet mediocrity. He held the post mainly as a sinecure until he died in 1824, apparently for some years before then incapacitated by senile dementia.[22]

Finally, the regulations of 1809 did nothing to address the complexity of an army drawn from three distinct kingdoms, each with (de facto, at least) an established church. For example, the original scheme revoked all fort and garrison chaplaincies granted prior to 1809 because the War Office deemed them to have degenerated into sinecures. However, protests from the General Assembly of the Church of Scotland gained the restoration of the garrison appointments at Edinburgh, Fort George, and Stirling.[23] Rather than wrestle with the question of the different establishments in the different kingdoms, the army contented itself with attacking the eighteenth-century tradition of absenteeism and dismantling its own administration of chaplains. It left alone constitutional questions relative to establishment. This policy offered the short-term benefit of allowing army officials to ignore entirely the recognition of such "difficult" groups as Presbyterians outside of Scotland and Roman Catholics in general.

After Waterloo, the British army began the task of demobilization. Successive governments between 1815 and 1830 dedicated themselves to reducing inflated wartime budgets. The army was no exception to this rule of economy, although the stand-down found no support from Wellington.[24] He thought the army too small as it was. When he was in government between 1827 and 1830 he tried to appease the Whigs by presenting them with reduced spending estimates while yet following his own course of bolstering troop strength. This strategy required him to root out all "unnecessary" spending. But of course, the prejudices of the commanders determined the necessity of an expense. Wellington and his secretary of state for war, Hardinge,[25] both complained that the Chaplains' Department roster of the 1820s and 1830s was bloated with half-pay officers who could not be recalled to duty. Yet in 1827, when Wellington was approached by an anonymous lieutenant colonel offering a scheme to reduce the army pay estimates for the regular officer corps by reducing those half-pay lists, Wellington demurred. He answered that he would look at the plan, but that "I have come to the conclusion that the thing cannot be done."[26]

Despite an apparent double standard, the high command resolved to reduce the Chaplains' Department. As chaplaincies emptied through death or became inactive when chaplains went on half pay, the army simply refused to appoint new staff chaplains.[27] Horse Guards instead instructed commanding officers to rely upon civilian clergy in the neighborhood of their posting, and to remunerate them out of a special pay allowance dedicated to that purpose. The establishment of army chaplains subsequently declined in the next twenty years. The spread of the civilian contract system only exacerbated the already uninspired and perfunctory nature of religious services in the army. Moreover, with each retirement or vacancy in the ranks of the staff chaplains, the army further removed itself from the administration, even the basic concern, for the spiritual care of its own troops.

Between 1825 and 1844, few military observers questioned this breach. Certainly the eighteenth-century officer corps had not been particularly noted for its religious fervor, and this attitude carried over into the post-Waterloo army. Despite the political successes and increasing influence of Evangelicals in British society after the Napoleonic Wars, the impact of vital religion on the army was delayed and minimal.[28] The prevailing mood among the officers remained that of disdain for overt religiosity favoring rather perfunctory allegiance to the Establishment.

In 1823, Captain Thomas Atchison and Lieutenant Francis Dawson, both of the Royal Artillery, were stationed in Malta. On 10 August they were ordered, as a diplomatic gesture, to take part in a Roman Catholic Mass, at which they were to fire salutes in honor of the Host. Atchison applied in writing in advance to be exempted from the proceedings, because he believed the Catholic Mass to be "idolatrous" worship. Some three months later, Atchison found himself charged with insubordination, disobedience, and neglect of duty. Dawson, who had simply refused to participate, faced similar charges stemming from the same incident.[29]

At their combined trial, each officer made a religious defense, arguing that as members of the Church of England, and as officers sworn to defend that faith, they could not participate in liturgies of the Church of Rome. Atchison retained a reasoned tone, arguing that the Mass did not relate to his military responsibilities, citing his prior application for exemption, his commander's apparent acquiescence, and the unusual length of time between the incident and the preferment of charges. Dawson pressed his religious case much more vigorously, taxing the court with Scripture reading, quoting Anglican anti-Catholic sermons, and making rather romantic declarations of his duty to his Protestant sovereign. When the court repeatedly warned Dawson to stick to the facts of the case at hand, he cited his Protestant conscience and withdrew from his own defense.[30]

The tribunal found both Atchison and Dawson guilty of the charges against them. Both men lost their commissions, along with hopes of retiring on half pay or of recovering the value of the commission by sale. Justifying the decision to convict and explaining the penalty later approved by Horse Guards during the appeal, the court chided both officers for their religious enthusiasms. A British officer ought not to take his religion so seriously that it interfered with the execution of direct orders. In the opinion of the tribunal, "an officer ought not entertain religious beliefs contrary to the performance of duty."[31] The court did not accept the official Anglican rejection of "popery" as an excuse for a British army officer to disrupt the chain of command. Better to acquiesce in the matter of a Catholic Mass than to disturb the smooth operation of the military machine. That the military court willingly destroyed the careers and finances of two of its own amply illustrates the low opinion the tribunal officers held of religious fervor. Although Atchison had twenty years good service prior to the incident, he never recovered from the verdict. He spent the rest of the 1820s petitioning to reverse the decision, or at least to win leave to sell his lost commission. He never succeeded.

In the early 1800s, the army remained alienated from British society at large, due mostly to the soldierly reputation for brutal, godless existence; soldiers, like the abject urban poor, were simply beyond the pale of decent life. In subsequent years, however, various leaders did come to realize the importance of army moral reform. Particularly they discovered the civilizing effects of religious practice and religious social respectability, which helped to make the army more acceptable to society. In the early nineteenth century, several factors yet prevented the army from making that leap: its recent employments enforcing domestic order; the cycle of terrible service conditions attracting the lowest type of recruits, which perpetuated official attitudes behind the terrible conditions; the duke of Wellington; antireligious attitudes and jobbery among the officers; a weak and pathetic chaplains' corps.

The army needed some jolt to break the traditions of administrative practice and attitude. Only thus could emerge some possibility of and, more importantly, public credibility in the basic decency of army life. In the first instance, the army in the 1820s benefited by a tulmultuous legal recognition of its own denominational plurality. Official Anglican establishmentarianism deadened religious activity in an army with large numbers of Irish Catholic and Scots Presbyterian soldiers. This first "jolt" proved to be just that confrontation between English designs for an "established" army and the reality of a multinational, multidenominational rank and file.

2

The Breakdown of the Old Establishment

Official disdain army religion hit a nineteenth-century low in 1830 when Wellington and Hardinge decided to reduce the entire Chaplains' Department. In the official notice dated 26 March, Hardinge tersely informed Chaplain General Robert Hodgson[1] that, "it having been deemed expedient from motives of economy, and those only, to discontinue the appointment of Chaplain General to the Army . . . it becomes my duty to make this officially known to you."[2] Hardinge thanked Hodgson for the "zealous and able manner" of his service, but made dissolution of the office retroactive to 25 December 1829. Hardinge's genteel assurances to Hodgson were sham. For years the relationship between the two men had been tension punctuated by confrontation.

Wellington and Hardinge eliminated the post of chaplain general in 1830, largely because of Hodgson's insistent efforts to expand the chaplaincy.[3] Palmerston as secretary for war and, later, Wellington and Hardinge had constantly steered Hodgson toward filling his manpower needs by activating chaplains from the reserve. Hodgson frequently tried to use new chaplains and thereby expand his total staff. Between January 1827 and his removal in March 1830 he fought his superiors several times on this issue.

In December 1827, the British sent an expedition to the Portuguese civil war. Hodgson balked at using the half-pay list to supply chaplains. He wanted new men of his own choosing. In June of 1828 he again fought with Hardinge, this time over the creation of a new chaplain to serve at Mauritius.[4] In November of that year, Hardinge rebuked Hodgson for the bloated budget of the Chaplains' Department. Contrary to army fiscal policy, the department maintained "no less than 17 Army Chaplains on half-pay, while there are only 15 on full-pay, and in addition . . . there are a great many reduced and retired Chaplains whose services cannot be made available to the public."[5]

Finally, in August 1829 Hodgson attempted to prevent Hardinge from abolishing the garrison chaplaincy at Fort George, Scotland. The garrison body there had fallen from a Napoleonic wartime high of over two thousand to just two hundred. The secretary wanted to send these troops to a local parish church, whose minister would perform the additional duties for £68 per year. The current garrison chaplain earned £158. This last episode finally convinced Hardinge to reduce the office of chaplain general. He managed this in only three months, for the chaplaincy apparently had no champions in government. The new, restructured office of the principal chaplain was designed to be a powerless and inexpensive clerk's post.

Bristling confrontations with superiors explained Hodgson's dismissal, but not the destruction of his department. But Hodgson had done more than upset Hardinge. In his few years as chaplain general, he destroyed the constitutional balance among the different denominations by exacerbating competition between the churches of the different kingdoms. His efforts to secure exclusive rights for Anglican clergy at all stations in the three kingdoms opened up denominational squabbling, which forced army administration to pluralize religion among the troops, a move liable to political as well as financial embarassments. Prior to 1826, though the War Office received some pay petitions from nonAnglican clergy, Palmerston had simply ignored the requests. Non-established clergy only bothered to petition for pay at all because of the disorganization and inconsistency of the system. Since Waterloo, the War Office had allowed commissioned chaplaincies to diminish through death and retirement, without making any new appointments. The army planned to make up the deficit by purchasing the services of civilian clergy, ideally for less than the cost of salaried army chaplains. Ministering to the troops became a public venture, with a relaxed army chain of command.

With no firm leadership in the field, and without the exclusion of civilian opinion that strict army command entailed, contending denominations began to compete, appealing to the secretary of state at war for privileges. At first Palmerston simply resisted. After Hodgson's tenure, successive war secretaries had to take a case-by-case approach to applications by heretofore unrecognized denominations.[6]

In July of 1825, calling himself an "Independent minister,"[7] I. B. M. Crea of the Church of Scotland wrote to the War Office requesting pay. He had conducted worship services for the

Twenty-sixth Foot "Cameroonian" Regiment, stationed at Tralee, County Kerry, in Ireland since November of 1824. By his own account his duties included baptizing children, visiting sick soldiers in the hospital, and performing regular Sunday services. He believed he had generally "contributed to the very orderly conduct of the 26th." Moreover, he had performed these works under "the burden of the added hardships of a Protestant minister in a Roman Catholic country."[8] Now he wanted compensation at the rates offered to established officiating clergy. Unfortunately for him, though he was a minister of the Church of Scotland, he was not in Scotland, but Ireland. While Crea had performed respectable service to the Twenty-sixth, and had the apparent confidence of the commanding officer, he acted in Ireland as a Dissenting minister. Palmerston therefore dismissed his claim, noting on the back of Crea's letter, "Pecuniary allowance is not granted by the public for duties performed to the troops by any clergyman but those of the Established Church." Adhering strictly to this rule, Palmerston in 1825 also rejected the claims for officiating allowances made by Episcopal clergymen ministering to troops in Perth and Edinburgh.[9]

Likewise, at the start of the new year, Palmerston decided to withdraw the government allowance to Catholic priest Father Joseph Murray. Murray had a special right at King's General Hospital at Phoenix Park to tend to Roman Catholic soldiers there.[10] However, at the start of 1826, King's became a general hospital. Therefore, when Murray applied for his "usual quarterly compensation,"[11] he was denied. Palmerston's reasoning was as strict and simple as it had been with Crea. He noted on Murray's letter, "Cannot be continued; this Hospital being now placed upon the footing of a General Hospital must become subject to the same Rules and Regulations as other General Hospitals and no pecuniary allowance is made by the public to Clergymen of any other persuasion than the Established Church."[12] The government solution to the problem of a multidenominational army, a solution in which army leadership concurred, was to ignore the existence of the problem. Palmerston stood on a simple assertion granting legal rights to the established churches only. There existed no recognized precedent, he argued, for any other procedure than the favored one of "three kingdoms, three churches."

Owen, who as chaplain general for 1809–24 shared nearly the same tenure as Palmerston, never raised an objection against the propriety of adhering to a strict establishment rule. After all, Roman Catholic and Presbyterian troops were not prohibited access to their own ministers, with the gross exception that Presbyterian soldiers stationed outside of Scotland had to attend Church of England services. If non-Anglican troops wanted their own services (and got permission from commanding officers to attend them), and if local clergy would provide them, it was all to be a private affair. The government interested itself only with the official faith(s).

Despite this official freedom, favoritism dominated the system. Anglican priests who took on additional duties for troops stationed in their neighborhoods received an emolument. After 1810 this pay was standardized: £1.1 for any additional service (beyond those regularly scheduled) in the parish church attended by fifty or more soldiers; 15 s. for any additional service after that; 5 s. for hospital visits requiring travel of three or fewer miles and 10 s. for hospital trips farther away.[13] In no kingdom did Roman Catholics enjoy such regularized pay. Presbyterians could collect only in Scotland. The problem was not official refusal to acknowledge the efforts of all clergy concerned with the troops. Rather the problem was a very narrow definition of what constituted religious liberty, and a traditional tendency to equate the public good with Anglican religion only.

The issue that finally shattered the old system arose not because of protest against this monopoly by the Church of England, but rather because of anomalies in the rules of establishment themselves. The basic point in contention centered upon the theological and liturgical differences between the Church of England and the Church of Scotland. Despite the fact of significant divisions of belief and practice between the two, each reigned supreme in its own territory as the established church of state. That meant however that Anglicanism, the Anglicanism that the London government regarded as established, was merely "Dissent" in the kingdom of Scotland. English officials like Robert Hodgson of course regarded the Scots Presbyterians as the outsiders. Apparently, however, this did not apply to the English in Scotland. Anglican churchmen (and Scottish Episcopalians) who had anything to do with the army in Scotland found it difficult to watch Anglican troops march off to Presbyterian services just because that form was established.

In the fall of 1826, Hodgson exposed the anomalies when he began campaigning for the rights of Anglicans stationed in Scotland. He wanted to guarantee them subsidized Anglican services rather than to submit them to the Presbyterians. He pressed Palmerston for a decision in August when he made a test case of some English dragoons stationed near Edinburgh. The local Episcopal church was, he wrote, "totally incapable of receiving [the soldiers]." The dragoons faced the alternatives of attending a Presbyterian chapel, of bringing in a Presbyterian minister (since under the rule only such could be offered pay in Scotland), or of foregoing services altogether. None of these options suited Hodgson. Either he would gain satisfaction from Palmerston or take the matter to the duke of York, commander in chief.[14]

When Palmerston remained obstinate, Hodgson first tried to win him over by arguing that Englishmen ought to have superior rights. Security demanded it. "An exception may properly be made in favour of members of the Church of England which might reasonably be refused to persons of another persuasion. . . . Where soldiers are really attached to the doctrines and formularies of our Church it is impolitic and unwise to endanger that attachment by forcing them to other places of worship, or at all events, so far to weaken it, as to make them indifferent to what doctrines they hear or in what place they attend."[15]

Palmerston still refused to budge, and Hodgson finally decided to go over his head. In correspondence with an ally, one Dr. Russell of Leith, he developed a technical argument based upon Russell's knowledge of the legal history of the establishment. Russell believed that the Episcopal Church in Scotland was more than a "Dissenting church." He argued that it was in fact equal. He went on to question whether it would be "advantageous to expose all the cavalry in the United Kingdom to the risk either of becoming Dissenters in their mode of worship, or of disregarding the religious duties in which they are compelled to engage."[16]

The tone of argument was clear. Russell knew his prospective audience. He had the military credentials of thirteen years as Episcopal chaplain at Piershill Barracks near Edinburgh. The whole letter sounded the military alarm, and Hodgson simply passed it along in toto to Wellington, at this time commander in chief. The arguments about security, the discipline of the troops, Russell's fear of "confusing" the soldiers who might have to confront the perplexity of a multiple establishment, all seemed calculated to appeal to Wellington's prejudice concerning the best interests of the army. Taking no chances, Hodgson also pressed the case upon Lord Goderich,[17] prime minister since August of 1827 and first lord of the Treasury.

The immediate result for Hodgson was victory, as achieved in two new Treasury regulations concerning payment of officiating clergy. Coming from Treasury, the changes were likely secured by the influence of Goderich. However, Hodgson's effort to involve Wellington at least succeeded in preventing any obstruction from him. The first new rule, issued 9 November 1827, stated that "whenever practicable," Anglican clergy should be secured to perform religious services for English troops stationed in Scotland. The second, issued 10 January 1828, amended the first: the fifteen "Scotch" regiments[18] when in Scotland could have at all times access to Presbyterian ministers, but must attend the established church when stationed in Ireland or England.[19] This was just, so ran the logic, because Anglican priests could perform any service required by a Presbyterian, while Presbyterians were forbidden by doctrine to engage in some liturgical practices of the churches of England or Ireland.[20] English regiments anywhere in the United Kingdom could get an Episcopalian minister to officiate services for them. Individual soldiers could always apply to attend services of their own faith, but the government recognized no responsibility to make such available or to offer any financial support.[21]

Therefore, the original steps to break with a rule of strict establishment for religious services in the army were taken not with a view toward greater liberty of conscience for the troops, not in hopes of enhancing the spiritual existence of the soldiers, not even with the initiative or approval of the government secretary charged with the direction of such matters. Palmerston always opposed tinkering with the strict establishment rule because meddling was liable to expose the War Office to applications from all denominations for money, thereby increasing demands upon the budget.[22] This in fact is what happened.

Hodgson, on the other hand, had demanded the new ruling because he believed in the supremacy of the Church of England over all other denominations in the United Kingdom. He was open to the idea of paying for Presbyterian services to Scots troops outside of Scotland. However, if the government refused on grounds of economy or establishment law, so be it. But Hodgson could never agree that Anglican troops might likewise have to compromise. He justified this double standard "because it must be exceedingly grating to the conscientious feelings of English soldiers to be forced contrary to all previous usage into places of worship where not only the forms of Divine Service differ essentially from their own, [but] doctrines, it may be, are inculcated which the Church of England does not acknowledge as true."[23] Apparently, Scots and Irish troops could not tell the difference. Hodgson somehow believed that other denominations, the Church of Scotland in particular, would accede to the special needs of Anglican troops; that the War Office could hereafter, if it so desired, hold the line against applications for Presbyterian ministers while granting those for Anglican clergy at all times and places. He did not even consider the position of Roman Catholic (mostly Irish) troops, except to say that permitting Catholic soldiers to attend Catholic priests privately did not bear on the question. "Theirs is not a religion established by law. It is tolerated and most wisely tolerated without control or limitation but a marked difference is with great propriety made by allowing no payment to its ministers for their services to the troops."[24]

Hodgson obviously believed in his legal arguments but he ignored the realities of the army of his day. In 1830 Irish Catholics comprised 42.2 percent of the infantry and the army recognized no fewer than fifteen "Scotch" regiments out of an establishment of ninety-eight. Of those fifteen, eleven were actually majority Scottish, but that still represented nearly six thousand men, not to mention Scots Presbyterians scattered throughout other units.[25] Who would expect such large minorities not to resent Hodgson's open favoritism? And if the men did not care, would the same be true of the representatives of the excluded churches? How much did the rank and file worry about Hodgson's manipulations of enforced religious practice? How long did officials of the other churches accept the double standard?

No useful records on soldiers' religious practice exist for the British army in the nineteenth century. Attendance at services was mandatory, and the denominational affiliation of each man subject to his ignorance, indifference, and the whims of his superiors. By analogy, it is possible to speculate on soldiers' attitudes. In the first third of the nineteenth century, membership in the Church of England, here determined as equal to the number of communicants at the great festivals of the church calendar, wallowed in a mire of sluggish growth. Between 1800 and 1830, Church of England membership in Britain increased by only 81,000 compared to 389,000 for Nonconformists and 121,000 for Catholics in the same period.[26] These very general figures, admittedly taken from the population at large and not the army, nonetheless indicate a general lack of enthusiasm for the Church of England, even during a period of healthy growth for other denomintations.[27] Given this overall public attitude, the army's indifference to all religious issues in this era, the hostility to religion for the troops among the officer corps, and specific evidence concerning troop behavior,[28] it is unlikely that Hodgson's efforts meant much to the rank and file. In the 1820s Hodgson's concerns reflected more the general civil politics of religion than a religious movement within the army.[29]

At the time, then, popular religion among the troops did not play a role in Hodgson's designs, nor did it change as an immediate result of them. Clerical and political competition among the denominations within the army was another matter. The changes made in 1827, while ostensibly securing Anglican rights, had also given Presbyterians a basis of general legal recognition within the army. Indeed, it was not long before the Presbyterians began attempting to expand their newly guaranteed access to "Scotch" units. In February of 1829, Reverend M. Mitchell, a Presbyterian minister officiating for troops stationed at Newry, Ireland, requested pay for the services he performed. Hodgson actually assisted the case. He had already secured money for Anglicans in Scotland, and with this in his pocket, he felt liberal enough to aid the claims of Presbyterian troops stationed in Ireland.[30] However, the rules Hodgson had secured in January 1828 stipulated only that officiating clergy could be had for Scots regiments in Scotland. Anglican troops always and everywhere had the right of an Anglican service, but Scots troops stationed outside Scotland had to settle for Anglican ministers or chaplains.

Therefore, the Treasury declined to remunerate Mitchell. They argued that such a payment would only destroy what rules the system had already. This answer also revealed a peevishness that Hodgson would forward this claim, since he had not fought to include Presbyterians as equals the previous year, and since including them now would re-create circumstances demanding new rules.[31] Hodgson therefore failed in this cursory effort to assist the Presbyterians, and seemed to interest himself no further in the matter.

Despite the setback and the merely passing interest of the chaplain general, this original failure did not deter additional Presbyterian efforts to achieve equality with the Church of England. Various ministers serving units stationed primarily in Ireland continued to apply for allowances of pay based upon the 1828 regulations. Finally, in March 1833, the Treasury conceded that since both the Church of England and the Church of Scotland were established by law in their respective kingdoms, and since the army already had recognized officially Presbyterian units, there could be no sound reason to insist upon the primacy of the Anglicans, at least in the army. By this time, Hodgson himself had been gone three years. His precedent disrupting the strict rule of establishment endured. If Anglican troops had the right of a paid minister of their faith at any station in the United Kingdom, the Presbyterians ought at least to enjoy the same liberty in Northern Ireland.[32]

Therefore, the Treasury and the War Office approved payment to a Church of Scotland minister who conducted worship services for troops stationed at Mullingar. A case-by-case approach lasted until October of 1835, when two different clergymen, one Anglican and one Presbyterian, each claimed pay for serving the nominally "Scotch" Seventy-eighth regiment then stationed at Galway. Lord Howick,[33] secretary of state at war, responded by instituting a majority principle. Henceforth, a unit's denomination[34] would be that of the majority of its troops, and only ministers of that faith could apply for government allowance to serve it. Furthermore, added the irritated Howick, because the "reasonable" rule of strict establishment had since been given up, the War Office now would accept the claims of Presbyterian ministers serving the troops, regardless of the location.[35] Presbyterians in Ireland between 1838 and 1841 then pushed for their own commissioned chaplains. This concession the government refused. Despite falling short of gaining actual commissions, Presbyterian successes put the two established churches on equal administrative footing within the army. Of the three major national churches, only the Catholics had yet to gain government allowances.

The pattern of Catholic "emancipation" in the army generally followed that of the Presbyterian, except that the Catholics had no inside allies and maintained no official hierarchy in Great Britain through which to petition the government.[36] However, by the 1830s the Catholics had some precedent on their side. During the Napoleonic Wars, the increased reliance upon Irish troops had led the government to relax official sanctions sufficiently to remunerate the services of Roman Catholic priests. Originally, these had mostly consisted of hospital visits to the sick and wounded at facilities in Plymouth and Jersey. This policy had been discontinued after the peace, as had payment to priests officiating for the Irish militia stationed in England.[37] In 1833 Sir John Hobhouse,[38] then secretary at war, sought payment for priests to visit military hospitals in Ireland as a concession to the large minority of Irish Roman Catholic troops. In the event, Hobhouse got only £40 each for priests at Chatham, Dublin, and

Cork to visit hospitals; he won this point only on the argument that sick soldiers had no ability to find a priest on their own.[39]

In 1835, based upon this history, upon the success of the Catholic emancipation of 1829, and upon the new allowance of money for Presbyterian clergy throughout the United Kingdom, some Catholic priests petitioned for regular government subsidies. In October, Father Welsh serving troops at Portsmouth requested pay. Howick at the War Office recoiled, and noted incorrectly on his rejection letter that the British government had never paid a Catholic priest to do anything but visit sick and injured soldiers. In December, Father Riley at Plymouth took his turn, and this time, now aware of former exceptions to the ban on paying Roman Catholic priests, Howick gave in, resigning himself to surrender rather than to face an endless string of petitions.[40] The following February, Treasury produced yet another regulation. Now the government would remunerate any military religious service performed by the three recognized churches.[41] In comments on the margins, Howick and the Treasury lords agreed to be cautious from now on. They also agreed that in order to preserve the nonestablished status of Catholicism in Britain, payment to priests would nominally support hospital duty only, although priests could include religious services at no extra charge to the government.[42]

Granting public money to Catholic priests made people nervous. Political emancipation of Catholics had passed Parliament only in 1829. Wellington had scuttled his conservative consensus in backing it. There remained plenty of Tories in and outside of the army who looked upon the increasing presence of Roman Catholics in British public life as a cause for alarm. It obviously irritated Howick that matters had developed this far. Writing to Treasury about Riley's claim he said, "In my letter of 6 October 1835, I pointed out that the admission of the right of Episcopal Clergymen in Scotland (who are dissenters there) to remuneration for their Services to English Regiments necessarily and unavoidably led to the recognition of a similar claim from Presbyterian Clergymen in Ireland for their attendance on Scotch Regiments in that part of the United Kingdom. But no sooner was it known that this claim had in some cases been admitted than the Catholic Clergy brought forward their own pretensions." In these circumstances, Treasury would have to sanction pay to all denominations of officiating clergy.[43]

Treasury at first tried to avoid the whole issue by arguing with Howick, and by ignoring the Catholics. They held that the 1828 regulations and amendments concerned Presbyterians in Ireland only. Current policy, they said, "makes no reference to Roman Catholic services. The claim for this latter duty at Plymouth was under consideration of this Office in 1833. No reply was made to the applicant on that occasion." Refuse Riley, they argued, on the grounds that the regulations do not consider Catholicism and that Riley applied for money without the sanction of the officer commanding the troops he served.[44] Howick thought it a little late for that kind of response.

While there had been no apparent worries from the military commanders when the government began to sponsor Presbyterian services for troops all over the United Kingdom, money to Catholics was a different matter altogether. Lord Hill,[45] general commander in chief in 1836, sent a letter to the War Office within weeks of the decision to grant pay to Catholic priests. Hill stated that he "had always viewed this subject [of religious services to the troops] as one of considerable delicacy and vast importance and would . . . have been glad had Lord Palmerston's simple and equitable principle [i.e., the strict establishment rule] been adhered to." He understood why allowances had been made to Episcopalians in Scotland and to Presbyterians in Ireland. But now the War Office was determined to allow for Roman Catholic priests as well. Hill asked for government help in warding off "priestly attempts at interference" in the regimental schools and other aspects of soldierly social life. After all, the schools educated both soldiers and their children, and would be "vulnerable targets" for infiltration. He wanted also to get restrictions on Catholic visitation of the sick in hospital, in order to protect hospitals from "insidious meddling and the discipline of the troops from the injurious consequences of such meddling." Hill closed by warning Howick that the new regulations had the added danger of allowing "the priesthood" to encourage marriages of Roman Catholic soldiers despite the wishes of their commanding officers.[46]

Howick found this sort of anti-Catholicism alarmist at best. He stood firm on the legal necessity of recognition. He reminded Hill that regimental commanding officers could eject any clergyman at will, so there would be little chance of successful Catholic "subversion" of the troops.[47] Even so, Howick was uncomfortable enough to note in his personal papers, "upon full consideration of this very embarrassing subject I am inclined to think that the best course that can be adopted will be to promulgate no new regulations whatever, but to deal with individual applications as they are brought forward."[48] He also noted that the present episode had brought to his attention that the War Office actually had no idea of the extent of Roman Catholic services currently conducted among British troops. He himself had no idea how much money he was discussing when he favored remuneration to all clergy. The best he could do was to guess based upon returned numbers of Catholic soldiers as of 1 January 1836.[49]

Conclusion for Chapters 1 and 2

Between 1796 and 1824, the office of chaplain general remained primarily a sinecure post. Its first two proprietors, John Gamble and John Owen, did little except to preside passively over a War Office system of regulations for military clergy. Neither man seemed concerned with non-Anglican soldiers, or their religious needs. Indeed, these chaplains general did not appear to worry much about soldier religion at all, since neither man conducted any inspections or reviews of the clergy who were under their guidance.

Robert Hodgson became the first chaplain general to pursue an active policy, but that hardly amounted to a vitalization of army religion. Hodgson's tenure disturbed the quiet among the army chaplains in legal and administrative terms. By attempting to be both an ecclesiastic and a military official, he managed merely to anger important people. As a churchman, he pressed to secure preferential rights for army Anglicanism. The logic of those efforts led not only to his original goal, but to the expansion of the government commitment to provide clergy of different denominations for the soldiers. As became apparent, the constant tinkering with regulations between 1828 and 1836, the necessity of Hodgson's legacy, evoked the frustration of army administrators.

Demonstrated in the case of the officers court-martialed at Malta, the attitude at the War Office favored calm and quiet over other concerns. The constitution provided for the established churches, each in its respective kingdom. The army, as a constitutional body, had only to operate within the purview of the church of each kingdom it entered. Nothing could be simpler. Hodgson's insistence upon issues of theology only proved this point. Meddle with the system, stir people up, and a cheap, simple system, whatever its efficacy, became confused and expensive.

As an official of the army himself, Hodgson attempted to protect and expand his own department, and to deepen its involvement in army life. Those designs brought clashes with Hardinge and Wellington. They resented Hodgson's efforts to build a cadre of chaplains of his own choosing, and to expand the budget of his department. Every shilling that Hodgson secured for his chaplains was another shilling out of the general army estimates. He was thus competing with the other needs of the army in an era when postwar governments were committed to retrenchment and to fulfilling promises of reduced taxes. Any officer, or in Hodgson's case quasi-officer, who opposed preferences of Hardinge or Wellington, let alone both, had to go. Thus Hodgson (and his department) went.

Despite Hodgson's fall, precedent from the period 1825 to 1836 later became the basis for an activist religious leadership in the British army. During these years, successive war secretaries admitted the proposition that government owed a financial responsibility to each of the three major denominations represented in the army. Anglicanism lost its de facto monopoly in the army. Certainly at this time the stakes were small. The religious liberties won by military Roman Catholics and Presbyterians affected only the limited society of the army. However, the pluralism established in the 1830s constituted a requisite for the army "revival" of the late 1850s.

3

A Conservative Hiatus: The Career of W. W. Dakins

In the long run, Robert Hodgson's tenure as chaplain general provided the basis for an army more representational of the different nationalities and religious expressions of Britain and Ireland. The immediate result of Hodgson's work was to stir conservative army leadership to halt the progress of chaplain "interference" with army discipline. This conservative (and army conservatives meant principally Wellington and his close allies) desire to minimize religious influence on the men was nowhere more evident than in the career of William W. Dakins, the man who replaced Hodgson. The Reverend William Dakins had been with the department since the reorganization in 1796 and through the 1810 appointment of John Owen as chaplain general. In June 1824, when the ailing (and apparently incapacitated) Owen finally died, Dakins began a shameless campaign for the office. Because Dakins was essentially a clerk and a painfully blunt self-promoter, no one took him seriously.

On 14 June, only ten days after learning of Owen's death, Palmerston wrote the archbishop of Canterbury. The secretary told His Excellency "that the Reverend Mr. Duffield, one of the Deans of St. John's College Cambridge has been very thoroughly recommended" to succeed Owen.[1] Palmerston sent similar letters to the archbishop of York and the bishop of London. He noted in each that he had encouraged Duffield to send along information about himself and his qualifications to be chaplain general.[2]

Dakins sent Palmerston his own application on 30 June. He was careful to note his thirty-one years experience in "Spiritual Duties to the Troops of the London District" and that for three years prior to Owen's death he, Dakins, had actually done all the work.[3] He went on to add that regardless of the actual appointment of a new chaplain general, he would appreciate a raise. In the event, neither Duffield nor Dakins got the job. The archbishop of Canterbury rejected Duffield as insufficient in church rank for the position. He decided instead upon the dean of Carlisle, the Reverend Robert Hodgson. Dakins got no consideration at all.[4] Palmerston peacefully dropped his own candidate and sent word along to Hodgson, who duly received official appointment 29 June 1824.

Both the church and the War Office completely ignored Dakins during this process (his own letter of application did not even arrive before Palmerston had accepted Hodgson). Hodgson's appointment prompted the spurned chaplain to begin a rather silly quarrel over prorated pay as chaplain general for the period between Owen's death and Hodgson's accession. Writing the War Office, Dakins decried his "blighted" hope to be the new chaplain general and pressed his claim for back pay as interim head of his department. An irritated Palmerston noted acidly that his clerk should "inform [Dakins] that the King has been pleased to appoint a new Chaplain General who will, I am confident, efficiently discharge the duties of his office, and that consequently Dr. Dakins will have to perform those duties only which belong to the situation he holds."[5] Palmerston awarded the extra pay to Dakins, who sulkily replied that in the future he "would confine [himself] only to the duties of the Assistant Chaplain General."[6]

The peevish and trivial nature of this administrative bickering revealed Dakins to be a petty man with a narrow conception of his office. He portrayed himself as the unappreciated and overworked engine of his department. His superiors in church and government seemed to see him as a troublesome minor official and a mediocre priest. In 1824, the army leadership still accepted the notion of a military department for army chaplains. Dakins, despite his thirty years as assistant, proved an undesirable choice to oversee the task of army religious instruction. By 1830, Wellington and Hardinge had decided to dispense with the trouble and cost of the Chaplains' Department. Hodgson's career there convinced them to reduce the influence of the military chaplaincy altogether. This time, Dakins was appointed the new "principal chaplain at headquarters," a reduced office created after Hodgson's ouster.

Apparently eager for even an illusory promotion, Dakins made no objections to the reduced pay and prestige associated with the humbled post of principal chaplain. His letter of acceptance reflected the recent humiliation of official army religion;

Wellington and Hardinge had converted an autonomous army department into a clerk's office. Dakins began by telling Wellington that the decision to gut the Chaplains' Department was "a measure highly consistent with the prevailing economy." He promised to run the office with the help of but one clerk (making an entire staff of two) and "begged leave" of Wellington to "offer my services on any terms consistent with your Grace's views of Reduction."[7] From the outset, Dakins adopted an attitude of surrender. Hodgson's clash with army authority had ended a brief phase of Establishment assertiveness in the army.

At any rate, Dakins's acceptance letter concluded with a brief summary of the duties of the office as he saw them: (1) to receive and pass on to the prelates the papers of candidates for chaplaincies, (2) to examine allowance claims from civilian clergy who performed worship services for army troops, (3) to order supplies of Bibles and Books of Common Prayer, as requested by officers, (4) to insure a supply of Society for the Propagation of Christian Knowledge tracts to military hospitals, and (5) to record baptisms solemnized by chaplains in the colonies.[8] The new principal chaplain made no mention of duties like bolstering the morale of the troops, assisting in discipline, encouraging religious practices among the men, or anything about the care of their souls. In fact, in all the pages of Dakins's correspondence, one is hard-pressed to find the word *God*. Such an attitude apparently fitted the spirit of the 1830 reorganization, which even the excessively cooperative Dakins came to regret. Ultimately, he had to fight for three years even to get his clerk. He lost his own offices and had to settle for a side room at the War Office.[9]

Dakins retired in 1844. True to form, his last official communications were blatantly self-serving letters, each of which sought to boost his pension to the highest possible level. In truth, he had performed well by the standards of his superiors. He had maintained a minute control on the certificates of payment submitted by civilian clergy serving the troops around the United Kingdom. He had operated the department on a tiny budget. Except for the case of the clerk, Dakins had not fought to expand his staff or the departmental estimates. His only positive accomplishment as principal chaplain was a royal military chapel built at Whitehall. On his own initiative, he did once try to assume the old title of chaplain general, even signing some letters as such. A terse War Office memo reminded him that the title was extinct and was not to be revived. Dakins meekly acquiesced and thereafter titled himself only "principal chaplain."

Dakins's career proved to be a trivial but instructive episode in the history of the British army. Between 1825 and 1830, Hodgson's politicking made the Chaplains' Department a wearying bother to his War Office superiors. Dakins's tenure was an antidote to Hodgson. However, Dakins was as much a symptom as a cause. The army in general and even the official church in the 1830s were exceedingly wary of reform measures. In that decade, British government made great progressive steps in the modernization of the regime: it reformed the law regulating parliamentary suffrage and representation; abolished slavery in the empire; attempted factory regulation; reorganized municipal government; and began to modernize Church of England administration. A government of this sort, a government susceptible to the moralizing pressure of Shaftesbury[10] or Wilberforce,[11] would have seemed interested in the progressive maintenance of its army and the humane maintenance of its troops. Indeed, the thirties and forties were years in which some reformers struggled to improve army practices, particularly in recruiting and discipline.[12] However, such activity was sporadic, of limited success, and reliant upon outside observers and philanthropists. Within the army itself, at least in the realm of personnel, quiet prevailed.

The duke of Wellington wanted things this way. After his disastrous brush with the Reform Bill and a more dignified stay in the House of Lords, Wellington returned to the army as commander in chief in 1842, where he remained until he died ten years later. In this final decade he distinguished himself both by becoming an invasion alarmist and by resisting reforms of all stripes within the army itself. He opposed experimentation in weaponry, change in uniform, and especially reforms concerning the condition of life in the other ranks.[13] His whole career Wellington remained convinced that the men of the other ranks were (and ought to be) the dangerous refuse of British society.[14] He believed that controlling such men required a strict, even brutal discipline.

To such a mind, service reforms implied destabilization. Wellington had clearly argued this general point when he opposed the Reform Bill in 1831. "I am convinced," he wrote during the debates, "that the system of government—or rather of no government—which the bill would establish will, by due course of law, destroy the country."[15] "It totally destroys every existing interest in the country from one end of it to the other, and establishes in lieu thereof one uniform interest—that of the little shopkeepers."[16] His government in 1828 authored the Catholic emancipation but only because the duke believed that security and the stability of Ireland hung in the balance.[17] In emergencies, he could be flexible. Every good general must know when to retreat and when to stand his ground. The situation in Ireland forced the government from its ground that it might avoid dangerous civil disturbance there. On the other hand, internal conditions of the army did not appear to compel reform. Quite the contrary, the duke believed that attempting army reform would demolish the harsh but precarious control of the rank and file.

Army leadership of the 1820s and 1830s did not accept the necessity of humanitarian military reform. The army had for many years been the main (it could be said only)[18] defense of the regime against anarchy. At least that is how insiders like Wellington, the duke of York, Lord Hill, most of the House of Lords, and George IV liked to put it. The Crown and the government therefore feared the slightest loss of control over the troops during the turbulent years from 1815 to 1848. The 1829 introduction of domestic professional police had not changed that fact. For some years, the police force existed only for London and some scattered locations in the provinces. The police were not always effective even where they existed. The traditional reliance on the magistrates and constabulary remained intact, and these officers would still have to call upon the militia or the army to enforce public order in times of riot. Ultimately, the army remained the enforcer of law in times of crisis throughout the nineteenth century.[19]

Indeed, the domestic safety of the regime rested upon the reliability of the army. And certainly the church was nothing if not of the regime.[20] What was the stance of the church at large regarding the spiritual needs of the soldiers? This era marked increased and justified fears among the respectable and ruling classes of lower-order insurrection. Did the church hierarchy assume any part in placating the anger of the distressed working classes? How did the Church of England perform in response to the popular pressures of the decades after Waterloo? Inside the army or out, how did the Church of England deal with the "other ranks" of British society?

In the 1820s and 1830s the Church of England did not aggressively confront the needs of the "lesser orders." Rather, the official church hierarchy of this era rallied itself to stave off secular government incursions into sensitive areas of ecclesiastic control: pluralism, absenteeism, diocesan boundaries, the ecclesiastic court system, and redistribution of church wealth to ensure more equal endowments among the clergy. At the same time, the Establishment faced grave social conflicts.[21] After all, two of the magistrates responsible for Peterloo were also clergymen. That murder of unarmed demonstrators went unpunished; the government of the day actually congratulated and thanked the Manchester authorities.[22]

To the public and even to some of the ruling classes and government, the Church of England in the 1820s and 1830s had become a nest of sinecures, corruption, cronyism, and spiritual desolation.[23] How could an Anglican priest of this era expect to win the hearts of soldiers? He would see them only once per week, if that. Most enlisted men would have come from the disfranchised and poorer working classes of city and country. Given the tone of the times and the lack of official army interest, Anglican clergy had little hope of affecting the soldiers at all.

Even more fundamentally, it is highly unlikely that many Anglican clergy would have had any interest in doing so. Among the church leadership of this era, opinions on state and order ranged from the very conservative to the reactionary. After the Reform battles of 1830–32 no bishop savored the idea of a Whig government attempting the reform of the church. Sir Robert Peel, in his "Hundred Days" government of December 1834 to April 1835, was able to launch the Ecclesiastic Revenues Commission to address reforms and control of church finance, preferments, and the tithes. He achieved this thanks to his conservative credentials, his alliance with the duke of Wellington, and his offer of commission seats only to the bishops.[24] The commission that thus evolved was semiindependent of the government and was much under the control of Bishops William Howley of Canterbury and Charles James Blomfield of London.

This church, fighting against political reform from the government, patronized (politically, at least) by arch opponents of parliamentary and army reforms, beholden for the majority of its parish appointments to secular nobility and gentry, would hardly be the church to seek out and evangelize the rank and file of the British army. To Wellington, the church could best serve the army as a political hammer with which to bash "seditious Methodism," which he believed would destroy military discipline.[25] In the 1820s and 1830s the Evangelicals and Protestants outside Anglicanism might pick up various issues of social justice and reform.[26] The official Church of England hierarchy was in no mood for or even capable of any such experiments.

Not by mistake then, the pliable rule of W. W. Dakins followed the troubled era of Hodgson. Dakins's time as principal chaplain became significant for its insignificance. Without any resistance from him, the department shriveled to a staff of two presiding over a body of only five commissioned chaplains. All other religious life in the army passed over to contracted civilian clergy, whom Dakins supervised only by reviewing their certificates of payment. By 1844, the year Dakins finally retired, the Royal Army Chaplains' Department existed mostly in the flow of paper between Dakins, his clerk, and civilian ministers applying for pay. To most respectable British subjects the army remained a sinkhole of dissolution, a necessary but thoroughly undesirable lot of pariahs.

Little more than a decade after Dakins retired, the British public seized upon the spectacular occasions of the Crimean War and the Indian Mutiny to criticize conditions in the army. Much of that clamor included calls to evangelize, and therefore civilize, the troops. However, for the fervor to attain to more than a passing fad required preconditions. The army had to be so organized as to be able to absorb and respond to the moral zeal. The legal environment had changed favorably, but the army in 1844 still lacked the most important precondition of all: leadership willing to effect real changes.

4
The Early Career of George Robert Gleig

George Robert Gleig[1] assumed the post of principal chaplain in 1844. Wellington must have assumed that Gleig would prove a vast improvement over Dakins. After all, Gleig was something of a protégé of Wellington, had some military experience, and would know better than to author the comically self-promoting epistles that had regularly slipped out from under Dakins's pen.

Gleig soon disappointed Wellington, but for entirely novel reasons. Between 1845 and Wellington's death in 1852, Gleig challenged the duke on a number of points. The new principal chaplain pressed for general education programs for enlisted men and their dependents. He backed reforms of weaponry, uniforms, and punishment codes.[2] Most importantly, he envisioned an army wherein Christian religion would become the foremost hope and means of elevating life in the ranks and of winning the support of the general population. Gleig's greatest rebellion against Wellington was his belief that enlisted personnel were essentially good and redeemable members of society. This alone constituted a fundamental break with Wellingtonian conservatism.

In earlier years, however, Gleig was much in the orbit of the great hero of Waterloo. As a young ensign, Gleig had served under Wellington's command in the peninsula, although they were not personally acquainted there. Gleig had gone on to serve in the 1812 war against the United States, participating in the sack of Washington, D.C., and the Battle of New Orleans. When he returned home and resigned his commission for half pay, he completed his master's at Oxford in 1821, having taken holy orders in 1820.[3] True enough, ecclesiastics did not form the inner circle of Wellington's friends.[4] But Gleig retained enough of the soldier in him to write his first, semiautobiographical novel, *The Subaltern,* which romanticized his service in Spain and spun some good military adventure tales.[5] The style and content apparently suited Wellington's tastes. Although he was commonly asked to read books of history, military science, or any topic that might relate to his glorious career, he made a point of commending the young author of *The Subaltern*. He even went so far as later to allow a dedication to himself.[6] That honor Wellington normally withheld from the many authors who sought his endorsement and the inevitable benefit to sales it would produce.

Moreover, in the 1830s Wellington patronized Gleig's church career in repayment of Gleig's services during the Reform agitation. The very conservative stamp of approval that the duke then applied to Gleig later allowed the chaplain to initiate army educational and religious reforms of the sort Wellington despised. Between 1829 and 1832, however, the two men had equally conservative opinions on the Reform Bill and its potential consequences.[7] During the height of the debates in Parliament, Gleig operated in Kent as the duke's informant on local politics. He also organized (or squashed, as Wellington preferred) political rallies and petitions among the local gentry and nobles. He was completely, even obsequiously, deferential to Wellington's anti-Reform views, as well as to his tactical advice.[8]

Thus acting as a publicist and mouthpiece for Wellington in the south, Gleig opposed Reform in terms as strong as ever the duke himself employed. In a lecturing letter to Lord Harrowby, who at the end of 1831 urged the House of Lords to compromise on a measure of Reform, Gleig wrote, "I apprehend, My Lord, that if the King's minister brings forward a measure which is, in your opinion, pregnant with mischief to the country, your simple duty is to reject it. Let the consequences of that rejection rest where they ought,—with him who proposed it. Your Business is to save your country from evils which you see."[9]

After the Reform fight, and throughout his career, Gleig maintained a passionate interest in conservative politics. He also nursed a lifelong commitment to the army, which he combined with his vocation as an Anglican clergyman.[10] He frequently contributed to *Blackwood's* and the *Quarterly Review*, dispensing a conservative wisdom and critique of various social ills on issues ranging from military operations to education to Parliament. His opinions during the 1830s pleased Wellington as well as had the "true grit" military adventure of *The Subaltern*, and perhaps worked to maintain the interest of the older man in Gleig's career.

While Gleig had a living in Ash between 1829 and 1834, Wellington often invited the young man to his country home at Walmer Castle, Devonshire. Despite Wellington's reputation for coldness and reserve, those who knew him in these years agreed that he was a congenial host. Gleig long remembered his first trip to Walmer in 1829. The occasion was a dinner and discussion of Sir Thomas Munro's correspondence with the duke. Gleig wanted permission to use it in a projected biography of Munro. Frightened to extend his stay for the night, and despite the long drive, Gleig insisted upon returning home that evening. After dinner and only a few hours of conversation with Wellington, he regretted his earlier fears. Gleig thereafter accepted many invitations from Wellington, riding, dining, and enjoying the hospitality of lodgings at Walmer.[11]

Hospitality was but one benefit of Gleig's place within the Wellington network. Early in their acquaintance, Wellington was quick to offer Gleig a Crown-living on his own estate in Devonshire. Gleig actually refused the offer, based upon the remoteness of the site and the insufficiency of the stipend. Wellington took the rebuff in stride and agreed to find Gleig something more suitable. Clearly, the younger man had designs on a career other than country parson. His friendship with the country's foremost military man and a powerful politician offered more to him than just a good hunt and a good table.[12]

Wellington made good on these expectations in 1834 when he helped secure Gleig's appointment as chaplain to the Royal Hospital at Chelsea. With the Reform fight over, Wellington set about rewarding the loyalists of the lost cause. Gleig originally received the offer of the post from Whig Reformer Lord John Russell.[13] He was so surprised by this tactic of political reconciliation that he immediately wrote Wellington to inquire what to do.[14] Wellington patiently explained the matter to Gleig and urged him to accept.

When parliamentary Whigs loudly rejected the appointment of such a Tory partisan as Gleig to any post, Wellington again intervened and reassured Russell that Gleig was no party man in the strict sense, and would confine himself to religious duties at Chelsea. The duke even sent Gleig a properly matching version of the explanation of the Kent days in 1830 and 1831 so that if asked, Gleig could answer in a way that corroborated Wellington's communications with Russell.[15] These machinations worked, and Gleig moved to London to assume his new post. His removal from the country near Wellington's estate at Walmer Castle also distanced the relationship between the two men. However, things remained cordial until 1844, when Gleig's Reform efforts as principal chaplain, a post later redesignated chaplain general, irritated the aging duke.

Despite his chummy times with Wellington, his reliance upon the goodwill of the older man, and his devotion to the army, Gleig remained what Wellington had never been, a strong churchman. Though he might have mourned his commission in the infantry, he had not taken holy orders carelessly. His literary output,[16] whatever its quality, revealed him to be an industrious man of some intellect. He combined that energy with a devotion to Christianity—his Christianity and that of the Church of England. That devotion ultimately put him at odds with his benefactor. Gleig himself realized that when, while still principal chaplain to the army, he began campaigns to revive the office of chaplain general and to institute schools for army noncommissioned officers; he finally destroyed what goodwill Wellington held for him.[17] Yet Wellington's health and capacities declined rapidly after 1845, so that the withdrawal of his favor did not substantially hurt Gleig.

The chaplain general's activist approach to his office put him in rather a unique class within the Church of England of the early 1840s.[18] Gleig combined a strict social and political conservatism with a reformist turn of mind. He could work with either Evangelicals or Tractarians, but both types bothered him. He did not make any voluntary gestures to include Nonconformists in army life, though he eventually accepted the institution of a large-scale Wesleyan ministry in the army. He worked well enough with Roman Catholics and Presbyterians because such cooperation reflected an equilibrium established under the constitution. Roman Catholicism he recognized as the de facto state religion of Ireland, and as the largest single non-Anglican minority in the army. Unlike Hodgson, he honored Presbyterian claims on his cooperation because he understood the constitutional equality of the established Church of Scotland with the Church of England. In general, he left alone the complexities of Scottish schisms.[19]

Moreover, Gleig's career in the army combined other anticonservative aspects. First, he sought to carry the Church of England to his soldiers in a manner more reminiscent of an Evangelical than of a conservative churchman with a military career. He did so for eminently conservative reasons: he did not want the men falling prey to the other influences—he might have said distractions—they faced. He could hardly sit by and watch his beloved army sink into the undisciplined immorality that he was sure resulted when the men lacked religious instruction altogether.[20]

Secondly, he essentially professionalized the chaplaincy, ahead even of the regular officer corps and in the face of a strongly antiprofessional tradition.[21] Thirdly, his professionalization of the chaplaincy had the effect of circumventing the constitutional authority of the church hierarchy, to the extent that his department eventually required a special act of Parliament to secure its existence against the lawsuits of civilian clerics seeking to corral army chaplains within the normal apostolic authority of the bishops.[22]

For a decade before the ignominy of Crimea pricked the conscience of the British public, Gleig devoted himself to reforming the system of spiritual care in the British army. He fought to eliminate graft and cronyism, to create a set of professional standards among the clergy under his control, and to apply the doctrines of his church so as to elevate the standards and expectations of life of British enlisted men and their dependents.

Given his activist approach and given the meager circumstances of his office in 1844, Gleig clearly stands out as the father of institutional religion in the modern British army. At his appointment to replace Dakins in 1844, the department was nearly nonexistent. As of July 1843, the entirety of the Chaplains' Department consisted of only five active staff chaplains.[23] At the start of Crimea, there were but seven. For the first decade of his chaplaincy leadership, Gleig had little to lead. After fourteen years of quiescence in army religion, Gleig had taken charge of a military religious establishment that was nominally plural but had virtually no staff (or status) of its own. During the lifetime of Wellington, and in the lack of any wartime test, Gleig had no choice but to get along with the system at hand. That he did not like doing so was eminently clear. Wellington's intransigence against expanding army religious services in part explained Gleig's emphasis on education between 1844 and 1852. Budget constraints explained the rest.[24] He made efforts to attack the system of hiring civilian clergy, but progress came slowly. He had to accept the general practice of farming out religious care of the troops to local civilian clergy, so he concentrated on getting better control of those ministers and the standards to which they performed.

Gleig set about this task with a two-pronged promotional campaign. One wing consisted of a long memo to Sidney Herbert;[25] the other appeared as an article reciting the same arguments in his beloved *Quarterly Review.*[26] In the War Office memo, Gleig objected to the entire current system of employing officiating clergy, which he saw as open to "grave objections." He wanted to review the rules for including troops at usual Sunday services at parish churches near their station. He questioned the wisdom of paying officiating clergy a piece rate for hospital visits and separate services for soldiers not accommodated in the parish church.[27] Such jobbing of the important duty of religious instruction could only hurt the army, both spiritually and in its capacity to fight. The article he intended as a sort of manifesto. He wrote,

> It is in its morale, much more than in its physique, that the value of an army consists; and the morale of an army, whether good or bad, is the result of so many and such constantly varying contingencies, that to reason about it in the abstract, much more to assume this or that concerning it, from the results which may have occurred a quarter of a century ago, would be nonsense.[28] One thing, however, is certain, that as the morale of all armies must, under every variety of circumstance, be to a great extent dependent on the sort of treatment which individual soldiers receive, so it becomes a point of the gravest importance for governments to weigh well and deeply the character, in every particular, of the training bestowed upon their troops, and especially upon their recruits . . . what we may call the Moral Discipline of the Army.[29]

Primarily, he feared that the present system failed to build any links between the clergy and the troops in their care, links he believed must be the basis for the "Moral Discipline." Here for the first time in a long time a military official argued that something more than perfunctory exposure of soldiers to religious ministrations might prove beneficial to individual men as well as to the army as a whole.

Gleig also argued that the present system demoralized the clergy involved because the manner of payment forced them to "job" their religious offices. Decent men might refrain from offering their services for fear of appearing to pad their government allowances. In such a case, the care of the men suffered because of clerical scruples aroused by a crass system. On the other hand, less than decent clergy did avail themselves of easy government money. The system of officiating clergy left the ministers powerless to promote services for the troops without running the risk of appearing to grub fees, or of succumbing to just that temptation.[30]

Gleig saw the system remunerating visits to the sick and

wounded as equally flawed. The army paid for hospital visits on a per instance basis, scaled to the distance the clergyman had to travel to the facility. This method "of doling out . . . shillings . . . in compensation for the shoe leather which [parsons] expend[ed] in walking to and from the regimental hospitals"[31] did not adjust pay for the number or types of cases in a given hospital. The army took no recognition of the fact that "five terminal cases require more attention than fifty of such maladies as young soldiers are too apt to contract."[32] "There is something so revolting," wrote Gleig in the *Quarterly Review*, "in the whole of these arrangements, they so completely lower the dignity of the ministerial office and the tone of feeling among all parties, that we cannot be surprised to find that the general effect is bad."[33] The entire pay system had to go.

Gleig proposed to regularize pay. Give fixed salaries for general parochial care of troops at their given stations, he argued. Then the government will promote a regularity of habit among the officiating clergy, which will produce more regular care of a superior quality. He also argued that in order to make mandatory religious services a reality, the War Office should withdraw the "rainy day" option. At the time, commanding officers could cancel church parade if the weather appeared "threatening." Many used that excuse to dispense with the trouble altogether. Services should be regular, mandatory, and regulated not by commanders, but by the Chaplains' Department.[34]

Aside from affecting the spiritual tenor of the forces, these simple adjustments would have altered greatly the nature and function of Gleig's office. Under Dakins the office of principal chaplain had become one of reviewing and responding to civilian clergy pay vouchers. That duty made the principal chaplain little more than a glorified clerk. In the first instance, Gleig's new suggestions would allow him to transform his job. Regular salary disbursements would obviate the necessity of officiating clergy filing the pay certificates with the chaplain general's office. Gleig's role of reviewing the authenticity and paying off the certificates would be at an end, leaving him free to perform other tasks.

Additionally, Gleig's proposed system of pay would eliminate the interference of local commanding officers. Under the old system, the commanding officer requested the services of an officiating chaplain and was the conduit for relaying pay certificates to the War Office and the chaplain general. Salaried pay would place the chaplains directly under Gleig, who would thus get a defined budget and some direct control over personnel. They would not be his personnel yet (as would commissioned chaplains), but they would answer to him.

Lastly, regularization of officiating civilian clergy might just make religion a positive force among the troops. Gleig wrote, "The soldier is the state's servant, in a more absolute sense of the term than any private gentleman's butler is his servant. And his state cannot grudge, does not grudge, a little outlay of money in order to better his chances of becoming a good man—as well as a good soldier."[35]

Hodgson had defined his role in the army as that of preventing "error" and promoting the organizational interests of Anglicanism. Dakins had assumed a chastised office and had operated like a chastised man. Gleig differed from his predecessors in that he experimented with reforms as a matter of course. In this way he benefited from the changing status and environment of the Church of England in the 1840s.

At the height of Dakins's era as principal chaplain, the church itself had struggled with serious flaws in its establishment, and with general unpopularity. In the ensuing ten years, things had changed. Sir Robert Peel's 1834–35 reforms of church finances had matured, equalizing a bit the extremes in remuneration between poor country parsons and landed prelates. Following Peel's Hundred Days, Whig governments built upon his foundation by passing acts to reform the tithe system and to regulate clerical pluralism and absenteeism. These relieved the church its stigma as a nest of sinecures.[36]

At a more popular, perhaps sensational level, by 1845 John Henry Newman had withdrawn from the church to convert to Roman Catholicism. A body of Anglican clergy, younger in years and spirit than it had been for generations, was eager to liquidate his legacy.[37] Newman's departure deflated the Tractarian controversy, and allowed a serious rift to heal. Yet his era too had not been without benefit, for after him the Anglo-Catholic movement "found new standards and motives for the [Anglican] clergy as such. They became more distinctively professional. They ceased to hunt, to shoot, to sit on the magistrates' bench, and to behave, as they had for the last hundred years, as a rather more learned branch of the squirearchy."[38] Meanwhile, various missionary societies brought the church to "the masses" at home and abroad through urban and colonial missions.[39]

Gleig, who by now viewed himself as a protégé of Peel, deliberately maneuvered to take advantage of the opportunities for reform. He envisioned for himself a role in the army beyond that of caretaker or champion of the status quo. Contrary to popular thinking in the 1840s, Gleig believed the British soldier to be a worthy object of paternal, but genuine, religious concern. Certainly the farming out system had not improved the moral life of the troops. Gleig believed that religion, more than the strictures of traditional military discipline, would form the basis of an organic bond between the officers and men. Religion was also the link by which the army and its mission could become meaningfully connected to Britons at large. Arguments about enticing the lower classes into supporting and joining the army because it meant guaranteed employment and steady food supplies did not suffice. Such compensations did not build real loyalty or commitment. Gleig was convinced that a believable and real military spirituality would.[40]

In the *Quarterly Review* article and in his memo to Herbert, Gleig had argued primarily from the standpoint of creating a better army, in terms both of efficiency and moral standing. Yet in the article, he added another dimension fundamental to his vision for the army. Not content merely with schemes to increase troop discipline through religious indoctrination, Gleig wanted to build an army spiritually integrated into the entire population. He believed that this was an "Anglican" army, drawn primarily from the small communities and countryside of England.[41] He argued that the popular disaffection from the army rested not on fears of servitude, nor upon fears of government repressions, but upon the "godlessness" of army life. "It is not because their son has bartered personal freedom for a shilling, that the father and mother of the recruit refuse to be comforted. . . . [A] deeper seated and more praiseworthy apprehension [is theirs]; they look upon soldiers, of all ranks, as a godless and dissolute race; and therefore they weep that their [boy] should have cast in his lot among them."[42]

Yet despite this seemingly fanciful interpretation, Gleig had hit upon a basic key to army/civilian relations. Because the British army was a volunteer force, and because in the 1840s it took its recruits for a "lifetime" enlistment, it was an entity set aside from general society. Gleig pointed to the continental strategies to integrate their military establishments into their general societies: maintaining large establishments; relying upon regular troops for civil order more readily and forcefully than did Britain; resorting to conscription. To incorporate the general will into the mission and accomplishments of the army, British leaders needed to create a basic, organic link between the troops and the populace. Gleig believed he had found that link in an activist Anglican ministry within the military.[43] Therefore, from the first of his administration, he set about building that ministry and forging that link. His efforts anticipated and prepared the way for the popular embrace of the army that occurred in conjunction with Crimea and the Mutiny.

In this first effort to reform his office, Gleig enjoyed only limited success. To his memo, Secretary at War Sidney Herbert responded that the "Wet Sunday" rule should go, but that the other suggestions were unnecessary alterations. Herbert simply denied that pay for hospital visits and separate services was too low. Salaried pay was out of the question on the grounds of expense. However, it seemed reasonable to "consolidate fees for Clergy where large numbers of troops regularly quartered." In the end, he lectured Gleig, "zeal should not depend upon pay."[44] As for facilities, the secretary agreed that in the future barracks should not be constructed without some provision for a school room and a chapel. Upon that conclusion, official concession from Herbert ended.

5

Professionalization at the Royal Army Chaplains' Department

In the course of events, not Gleig's logic but the debacle of the Crimean War convinced the War Office to give Gleig his regularized, professional body of chaplains. When the war began in 1854, the army could muster only four regular chaplains to accompany the entire force sent to the peninsula. Even before the troops saw combat, all the allied armies suffered casualties from heat and disease, leaving the British chaplains with enormous duties of sick and burial details. Soon after arrival in Varna, one of the chaplains died of fever. The three remaining men were obviously overwhelmed.[1] By early fall, the expedition had landed on Russian soil and fought the battles of the Alma, Balaclava, and Inkerman; all of these, combined with the winter onset of nasty weather and equally nasty supply problems, plunged the British army into perhaps its most notorious period of suffering prior to the Great War.[2] In the *Times* and in parliamentary inquiries, the public learned of disastrous supply deficiencies, administrative incompetence, and the high price in suffering that the troops paid for such inadequacies. Gleig had few resources with which to make his department an effective part of the war effort. Only the intervention of the Society for the Propagation of the Gospel (SPG) saved the government from yet one more humiliation emanating from the expedition.

On 24 October 1854, the society began a voluntary subscription to fund a detachment of chaplains for Crimea service. This drive so succeeded that by the end of November the War Office had accepted twelve such volunteers, along with trunks full of Bibles and religious tracts, for transport out to the eastern army.[3] The War Office considered the problem solved, but by March 1855, the SPG had additional funds and supplies to equip another twelve volunteer chaplains for Crimea. Eventually, the society's wartime contribution comprised a total of twenty-five sponsored chaplains, four of whom died in the line of duty.[4] Gleig kept up a publicly proper appreciation for SPG efforts on behalf of the army. Being serious about the positive role of religious instruction, which he thought was an essential supply for men in combat, the chaplain general attended SPG fund-raisers and spoke of army gratitude.[5] On the other hand, the War Office had little choice but to accept the embarrassing charity of this civilian organization. Ten years before, Gleig had attempted to obtain basic reform, but had suffered rebuff on the grounds of economy and Herbert's specious argument that religious ministrations depended more upon the zeal of the pastors than upon the mundane necessities of salary and rank. Herbert's refusal to let Gleig reorganize his department left the army open to later criticisms that it was indifferent to its own soldiers and, along with the War Office, was incompetent at its own administration.

After the war in Crimea, the Chaplains' Department, like other departments in the army, underwent a review and reform. Public outcry, like that which surrounded the issue of combat nursing and military hospitals, was muted by the aid the SPG had rendered. The Roebuck Commission on the Army before Sebastopol made no negative comments about the department, but instead generally used chaplains who had been to the front as credible witnesses to other events.[6] Therefore, Gleig and his office remained secure. The largest part of the reform consisted in making the chaplains' corps regular, full-time commissioned officers. This process had actually begun before combat.

On one last occasion at the outset of war, Gleig attempted to regularize the rules of the preprofessional system along the lines of his 1845 proposals. In the spring and summer of 1854, Gleig sponsored a rewriting of the regulations concerning officiating clergy and their scales of pay. After some confusion, the finalized version of these new rules established fixed, and unequal, rates of pay for Anglican, Presbyterian, and Roman Catholic clergy serving the troops. Gleig had succeeded only in rationalizing and codifying the use of civilian clergy, a practice he hoped one day to abolish or curtail extensively. He achieved nothing toward establishing a new internal system of army religion, or providing ministers and materials to travel with the army on campaign. Additionally, his new system in 1854 had some glitches. Most of the difficulty with the new regulations centered upon the problem of keeping proper track of services and pay in the wartime situation of mass and rapid troop movements across the country.

The institutionalization of plural denominational recognition did not pose the worries it had fifteen or so years before, although the changes did not pass without some resistance.

When the War Office published the 1854 regulations, minor protests arose among the general public that a fixed pay scale for officiating Catholic clergy amounted to state establishment of that church. In Maynooth College and in some of the particular instances of government subsidies to Catholic priests during and immediately after the Napoleonic Wars, the British government already had by 1854 a long-established policy of recognizing the services of Catholic clergy. However, the new chaplains' regulations nevertheless prompted Wilbraham Taylor, secretary of the Church Protestant Defense Society, to write in protest to Sidney Herbert.[7] Taylor argued that paying Catholic priests encouraged them to build more chapels. Next, he said, they would seek separate services for Catholic soldiers (which the army already allowed if a Protestant officer were present). Taylor feared Catholic autonomy would lay open the possibility of subversion and, in any event, ran counter to the Protestant constitution.[8] Herbert circulated the letter to Gleig. Both agreed to ignore the protest, Gleig recommending, "We should merely acknowledge receipt of this bigoted and mischievous letter."[9] In the 1830s deliberations concerning army religious services, military officers, including the commander in chief Lord Hill, had voiced similar complaints against the involvement of Catholic clergy. By now, more than twenty years after emancipation, the pluralism extended to the three major denominations was secure and beyond antipapal cant.

Only the Irish Presbyterians raised a serious protest, not over issues of denominationalism per se, but over preferential pay awarded to Anglican chaplains. In May 1855, the General Assembly of the Presbyterian Church in Ireland sent a public letter to Panmure,[10] secretary for war since the Palmerston cabinet had replaced Aberdeen's government that February. Indeed, under the new plan, Presbyterian ministers received only 70 percent of the pay given to Anglican chaplains for similar duties performed.[11] Such disparity, protested the assembly, was "invidious, and thus calculated to create a spirit both among Ministers and Members of the Episcopalian and the Presbyterian Churches which it is most desirable should not exist." Educating Presbyterian ministers, it was claimed, required more time and more expense than went into making Church of England clergy, and therefore, concluded the assembly, Presbyterian ministers ought at least to receive equal, if not greater, pay for services to the army.[12]

Gleig, looking over the letter, agreed that the principle of equal pay was unobjectionable, but he thought Anglicans actually had more duties to perform in volume, if by no other standard. He was not inclined to honor such a complaint emanating from Ireland. Ministers of the church in Scotland, where after all Presbyterianism was established, had raised no objections to the payment scheme, so why should the War Office initiate more changes without some "official" request? Finally, he asked Panmure if the War Office should indulge any more tinkering, seeing that the department was just getting regularized at all.[13] Panmure agreed with these sentiments and sent a rejection to the Irish Assembly. Formerly, he wrote, Presbyterian ministers had only received pay for services performed to officially Scottish regiments. The new regulations paid Presbyterian ministers for serving any group of twenty-five or more men. This, concluded the secretary, constituted a liberality that "the General Assembly has not presented sufficient reason to change."[14]

Gleig's efforts in early 1854 did not challenge the assumption that army religion ought to rely primarily upon the offices of cooperating civilian clergy. Though he wished the contrary, he had no authority to change the basic system. These new rules merely regularized the relationships between these clergy and the army. Actual creation of a permanent corps of officer chaplains took a little longer and eventually required parliamentary action. Talk in Parliament about making commissioned chaplains centered on the ambiguous status of the SPG men sent to Crimea. Though they remained officially civilian, they received the title "assistant chaplains" and they operated under army control and in harm's way.

During the fighting, some critics of the war raised questions in Parliament concerning the benefits such assistant chaplains could hope to receive. Palmerston's government was forced to admit that no benefits would accrue to the men if they survived or to their families and relatives should they be killed. Unlike, for example, assistant surgeons, assistant chaplains were ineligible for pensions because the government considered them only on temporary assignment to the army. While the work of the chaplains and the conditions they served under were not a contentious issue, critics and army supporters alike used this example to expose army irregularities or to urge on Palmerston's government the general program of army reforms.

General Sir De Lacy Evans, the radical member for Westminster and a divisional commander during the mobile part of the war in the fall of 1854, was typical of reform proponents. An unusual man, he combined a military career with political radicalism. He generally defended the performance of the army in Crimea, not the least because of his own participation in the fall campaign.[15] He was a leader in efforts to blunt the criticisms in the "Report on the Army before Sebastopol." Therefore, unlike Roebuck and his commissioners, De Lacy Evans cited successes of army performance in Crimea to support increased interest in the army and nonpunitive reform.

On the occasion of one of his many parliamentary speeches during debates over the Roebuck report, he recounted chaplain heroics without giving credit to the SPG assistant chaplains. The army chaplains were, he said, a bright example of the best efforts of the army in Crimea. They had "had more arduous duty to perform than the chaplains in any other war of the same duration."[16] He hardly exaggerated, for as he spoke in early April 1856, the army still had only eleven chaplains for its entire establishment of 200,000 men and officers.[17] The assistant chaplains from the SPG increased that number to over thirty. However, taking into account the four permanent garrisons in the British Isles, the army itself could send only seven chaplains into the field. Moreover, the few chaplains available faced difficult terms of service. An assistant might have to serve in his unsecured position ten years or more before receiving a commission. Even then, the retirement benefits for commissioned chaplains were substantially less than those for other officers. Echoing Gleig's discontent with the overall situation, De Lacy Evans condemned the current system of contracting out the religious services to the troops stationed at home. The practice overtaxed the civilian clergy and did no justice to the special needs of soldiers. Given all these problems, the radical general demanded that Palmerston sanction awards to Crimean chaplains and designate funds to expand and professionalize the regular army chaplains' corps.[18]

In response Palmerston agreed that the chaplains in Crimea had done noble service and that the public expectation of reward for those sacrifices should not be disappointed; but he defended the use of civilian clergy.[19] His response was hardly surprising since he was a principal founder of the civilian contract system. For the twenty years from 1809 to 1828, as secretary for war, he had never shown much enthusiasm for army religion. Rather, he had sought to minimize administration and cost in that area by adhering to the use of civilian clergy. He restricted paid services to those of the established churches and only within their own kingdoms.[20] Now he repeated his confidence in that system, although the administrative changes of the last twenty-five years had made it a confusion.

Palmerston's answer did not satisfy his questioners. Sidney Herbert, who as Peel's secretary for war had refused Gleig's request for reform, now seconded De Lacy Evans. He urged Palmerston to secure more commissioned chaplains.[21] Based upon the harsh criticisms of the Roebuck Report, public opinion was ripe for a kinder, gentler British army, but Palmerston refused to act during the parliamentary session and under the pressure of debate. After dissolution, on 1 October 1856, the government gave in. Horse Guards and Lord Panmure, secretary of state for war, announced the ministerial decision to expand the Chaplains' Department to include twenty chaplains and thirty-five full-time assistants. This new force was to be ready at all times for active field service as well as garrison duty, with emphasis on the ability to move to remote theaters of war whenever necessary.[22]

Formal sanction of this professional body of officer-chaplains came by way of royal warrant in November 1858. According to the reorganization, the Royal Army Chaplains' Department would exist under the direct control of the secretary of state for war, with daily oversight by the chaplain general. All active chaplains would be assigned one of four classes, which would also correspond to a military rank. Pay and pension were according to scale of class and length of service. Final discretion for increased salary or promotion without regard to length of time in grade lay with the chaplain general and the secretary for war. Chaplains of the fourth class equated to captains; the third class were majors; the second class ranked as lieutenant colonels; the first were full colonels. Gleig, after an unseemly squabble concerning his relative rank and the official housing he thereby rated, settled for major general.[23]

This order specifically gave rank even to Roman Catholic chaplains, whose services as officiating civilian clergy had been recognized since 1836. The army acknowledged the reinstituted Roman Catholic hierarchy in Britain by allowing that official nominations of priests as chaplains fell to the bishop of Southwark. However, the de facto power of appointment remained with the secretary of state for war, as that officer retained the right to reject any nominee for any reason, and without explanation.[24]

The following year, Gleig instituted the wearing of uniforms and the adoption of all military courtesies between the chaplains, other officers, and enlisted men. Thus, by the end of 1860, Gleig finally had a professionalized, regular corps of chaplains integrated, on paper at least, into the greater body of officers.

This professionalization posed a problem for both the administration of the chaplains and for the Church of England at large. For decades previously the army had relied upon the local civilian clergy in the area where various military detachments camped or were stationed. It had never considered the relationship between roving military chaplains and the hierarchy of the state church. Gleig in 1845 had tried to abolish the reliance upon civilian officiating clergy, and had failed. Sixteen years later he had his professional chaplains. Now he discovered that having won the battle of army recognition he had to fight against the monopoly of the very civilian clergy he had wished to dump.

The problem centered upon the legal position of ministers of the Church of England, and therefore did not involve either the Presbyterian or the Roman Catholic chaplains. Contention did arise, however, as soon as the mobile Anglican chaplains began to perform church services for the their troops without regard for the parish of the station, or the incumbents of these. According to the law, every ordained minister in the Church of England held his parish appointment through the authority and license of the Anglican episcopate. Every Anglican bishop who exercised this authority was supposedly vested in a see, the territory of which was an inseparable component of his total authority. No minister of the church could officiate church offices without license from his bishop; no bishop could issue such a license outside of the territory of his see.

By nature, army chaplains in the new system moved about the country with the changes in station of the units. Each time a unit moved, there existed two basic possibilities for its spiritual care. As under the old system, the soldiers could attempt to use existing civilian facilities, attending the local parish church or inviting the local minister to come to them. Otherwise they relied upon army clergy. After the reform, units even away from the major stations and garrisons had their own army clergy to come to them. If these clergy practiced the liturgy or church rites, however, they began to assume the licensed prerogatives of the local incumbents. Moreover, they undermined the claim of local civilian clergy to fees associated with those practices. For example, if during the stay of a military unit in a particular spot the military chaplain performed a marriage for a soldier, baptized his baby, perhaps also buried anyone who died in that period, he usurped the right of the parish priest to perform those offices. He also usurped the claim to the fees that went with each service. Such fees often constituted an important part of the income of a country parson, who would not forego them lightly.

For obvious reasons, then, civilian clergy often resented the intrusion of military personnel into their parishes. Local clergy did not want noisy, disreputable soldiers in their churches and chapels. They often did not want the extra burden of bringing religious services to the troops at some other site. They certainly did not want some clerical interloper barging in, assuming authority in their parishes, and siphoning off income in the process. Within five years, the War Office faced a lawsuit stemming directly from such conflicts, and threatening the legal existence of army chaplains altogether.

The War Office preparations to regularize the chaplain corps in 1858 had included producing a legal opinion about the relation of the new chaplains to the episcopate. At that time, War Office advisers found no basic contradiction in the new arrangement. In his report legal officer Sir John Harding wrote

> We are of opinion that a Chaplain in the Forces, commissioned by the Queen, can exercise in England, towards Her Majesty's troops exclusively, those spiritual functions for which he is appointed, without the license of the Bishop, or the assent of the Incumbent. We believe that such license or assent has not hitherto been required in any case, and that the want of either has never been supposed to render either the functions of the Chaplain invalid, or the Chaplain himself liable to punishment in any of the Ecclesiastical Courts. . . . We think, however, that such a Chaplain can only exercise his functions . . . on behalf of those persons who actually form part of or belong to the forces or regiments for which he is appointed and within the limits or precincts . . . where those forces or regiments are stationed.[25]

On the basis of this opinion, the army made no further effort to validate its new chaplains with the state church. However, as the last clause explained, it could carry on business as usual only if army chaplains were careful to stick to soldiers alone, and did not minister to their wives, children, or any camp followers.

This obviously posed a significant restriction on the utility of army chaplains, so in 1860 Sidney Herbert, now secretary for war, pressed for a further clarification. Again Harding maintained that army chaplains might perform offices of marriage, baptism, and burial for soldiers and their families. But now he doubted that such events could legally be registered. He argued that despite this deficiency, local incumbents could not make claim to fees for services performed in their parishes, even if the local priest alone could legally register all such events.[26]

A similar anomaly existed in the case of all church and chapel buildings erected for religious services to the troops under the direction of the War Office. In 1863 the rector at Woolwich protested the performance of burial rites in the garrison chapel there, contending that the consecrated ground must be parochial and under the jurisdiction of the episcopate. When the War Office investigated the validity of those charges, the results raised some serious doubts as to the legality of army practice. Contrary to earlier opinions, legal officer Sir Roundell Palmer concluded that while military church buildings "were not parochial churches and were free from parochial authority," it was by no means clear that burials or weddings performed in these churches were legal. In fact, he was convinced that there existed no way to license these churches "under any of these existing statutes for the solemnization of marriages."[27] The only way to solve the problem was to secure legislation making explicit allowances and guarantees for army church services.

The army did indeed set about creating a bill to secure the rights and privileges of military chaplains. With the advice of the law officers, the War Office completed the bill in the spring of 1865. To all appearances it settled the issue. To grant proper authority to army chaplains exempted from the normal controls of episcopal discipline, legal advisers Harding and Palmer recommended putting them under a new, specially created bishop or archbishop. The War Office could request one of two options: The Church of England could place a civilian bishop over the whole department, chaplain general and all; it could make the office of chaplain general itself a bishopric with its see constituted not in geographical territory, but by the body of army chaplains. The army could not accept the first option; the church rejected the second. A roving military bishop might attempt to assert himself in any area where military personnel were stationed. He would destroy the administrative authority and independence of the local bishops. Upon a private preview, the bishop of London[28] rejected the bill outright, so strongly that the War Office gave up the idea of further consulting the archbishop of Canterbury.[29]

Gleig himself did not respond to the growing number of complaints against his chaplains until 1867. By June of that year, he was finally persuaded that both the Anglican hierarchy and the duke of Cambridge, the commander in chief, had become irritated with the irregular status of the Royal Army Chaplains' Department and the friction that it caused. Gleig therefore called together a meeting of all his active chaplains in the British Isles. Personal communications to Gleig from the Horse Guards had warned him that both army and church leadership believed the Chaplains' Department was trying to expand its special status in the military at the expense of the state church. One goal of the general meeting was to make a public denial of this charge. Under this pressure, Gleig tactlessly chided his chaplains that any deviation from the guidelines he would set forth in his talk would result in immediate dismissal from the service.[30]

Gleig planned to placate his critics by preaching the total subordination of the army chaplain to his secular commanding officer. "I must remind you," said the chaplain general, "that a clergyman who accepts a commission as a Chaplain to the Forces becomes, by that act, an officer as well as a minister of religion. . . . As an officer, he is subject to the very same rules of military discipline which extend to other officers. It is idle in him, after taking this latter obligation upon him, to plead conscience as authorizing disobedience to the orders of his superior, whatever these may be."[31]

Chaplains must remember that, contrary to civilian usage, the Church of England in the army shared equal footing with the Presbyterians and the Roman Catholic Church.[32] This being so, Anglican chaplains were to do nothing in practice or to the chapels of military stations that would tend to offend or alienate the sensibilities of the other chaplains. "The feelings of these minor congregations and of their ministers must be respected equally with ours, and any attempt to disregard them would be on our part not less unwise than unjust. Wherefore the Government has with perfect propriety arranged that while we have our chancel, our Communion table, our prayer desk and pulpit, the Roman Catholics are allowed at their time of service to set up their own altar, and the Presbyterians to occupy, when their turn comes, the same pulpit which we occupied when preaching to our people."[33] To maintain this balance, Gleig ordered his men to abstain from any alteration of the worship space. "Even the customary and graceful practice of hanging flowers and evergreens at Easter and Christmas must either not be adopted at all, or adopted only with the entire concurrence of the officer commanding on the spot—on whom devolves the responsibility of seeing that nothing is done calculated to offend the religious prejudices of any portion of the Garrison which worships in these common chapels."[34]

Likewise, continued Gleig, Anglican chaplains must do nothing to attract the attention or disapproval of their civilian brethren in whose parishes the military stations might lie. Chaplains must not collect any of the usual fees for services; neither must they enter in any practice which might provoke theological contention with other Anglicans. Gleig forbade, on pain of dismissal, any bowing, facing to the east, elevation of the Host, or other High Church practice that might lead to complaints against the liturgy within the army.[35] He concluded with a final admonition that whenever any issue might arise threatening conflict with either military superiors or civilian clergy, chaplains should appeal to the authority of the commanding officer on the spot. Only after full consultation with him ought the chaplains even consider appealing to the chaplain general. In no instance should they decide potentially controversial questions on their own.[36]

By this new set of orders, Gleig intended to quash rumblings within and outside of his department. He hoped by resorting to this rather extreme stance that he could make his chaplains somewhat invisible behind military authority. If the chaplains cooperated fully with military superiors, he reasoned, the army would take care of its own, and would prevent the complaints of parish clergy from endangering the existence of the Chaplains' Department. Unfortunately, Gleig's authoritarian approach alienated his own men and did little to satisfy his critics. Shortly after he published his controversial address there appeared an anonymous pamphlet entitled "The Church in the Army." The pamphlet author rejected Gleig's address point by point, accusing Gleig of undue authoritarian pretensions within the Chaplains' Department and of submitting the sacred obligations of the clergy to the whims of secular officers. Publication of the pamphlet stirred even more controversy in the army and the church. Rather than cowing his men into submission and out of harm's way, Gleig had managed to exacerbate the problem.[37]

Meanwhile, during all the internal wrangling, the Reverend Thomas Mills, incumbent of the parish containing the Richmond Barracks near Dublin, decided he could no longer stand the intrusions of his military counterpart. He sued the Reverend H. Craig, the local army chaplain, for infringing on his rights as incumbent. In May of 1867, the Dublin Consistorial Court found in favor of Mills and ordered Craig to "abstain from performing divine service or administering the sacraments, or preaching in the chapel or barracks, or buildings in or attached to the Richmond Barracks . . . or elsewhere in the parish of St. Jude's without the permission of the Rev. Thomas Mills." Just for good measure, Craig had to pay court costs. The main effect of the judgment was, as War Office memorialists later put it, "to render all the ministrations of Military Chaplains, being members of the Established Church, illegal."[38] Now either the army would have to come up with legislation acceptable to the Anglican episcopate, or the Chaplains' Department would have to cease operations.

As a result of this case, the army became immediately concerned to correct the situation and to secure the autonomy of its chaplains. Despite the fact that a first version of a bill to do just that had met with stern ecclesiastical disapproval, the War Office introduced an Army Chaplains Bill in Lords in June 1868.[39] The plan would give the Crown the power, upon the consent of the bishop whose diocese might be involved, to set aside land connected with a military station to be a "royal peculiar," no longer under normal parochial jurisdiction. The secretary of state for war could then appoint chaplains to perform church duties within the boundaries of the peculiar, and could also build and have consecrated chapels that likewise would remain independent of normal ecclesiastical control. The Crown could, at its pleasure, appoint any bishop to be dean of these peculiars and to be the ecclesiastical authority in them.

This proposal by no means pleased the bishops present in the House that day. As had the bishop of London three years before, they resented the erosion of episcopal authority and the intervention of state secular officials in the consecration of churches and the designation of bishoprics. The ecclesiastic opponents agreed that the army ought to have a secure and well-defined provision for the spiritual needs of the troops, and regretted that some clergy had interfered in that work. They could not admit the need to accept the suspension of apostolic authority or the dismemberment of various sees. They also objected on the grounds that the government had not made clear whether it wished to create a new bishop to be the dean of the extraparochial districts called for in the bill. There were "too many unattached bishops already." Why not make each bishop superintendent over the peculiars in his diocese?[40]

At this point, the bishop of London[41] rose to say that while the concerns of the bishops were worthy of note, the problem at hand was to insure the role of the established church in the army. The best way to secure the Chaplains' Department was to appoint one bishop to head all the Anglican chaplains. Proponents agreed. They pointed out that the present bill had the preliminary approval of the two archbishops, mostly because the court decision at Dublin had created an emergency situation. The government had no intention of creating a new bishop, and furthermore believed the bill so watertight as to prevent the necessity of the chaplain bishop from ever having to face court battles like the one in Dublin. These assurances led the bishops to acquiesce. The House agreed to the second reading and scheduled the third two days later.[42]

As things developed, it seemed the government had been less than forthright with their lordships. When the Chaplains' Bill came up for its third reading, both the archbishops of York[43] and Canterbury[44] attended upon the House. The archbishop of York indeed agreed to the measure and to the government's explanations of its various provisions, but Canterbury was not so sure. He argued that the authority over the proposed peculiars would by no means be clear, and that such ambiguity might cause all sorts of legal mayhem. Others pointed out that even ecclesiastical lawyers were not sure what a "peculiar" was or who might administer one. This general objection resonated, and the government then decided to request a suspension of debate.[45]

When the debate resumed the following day, it became clear that some horse trading had been done. Sitting as a Committee of the Whole, the Lords commenced debate on the final government offer to the worried bishops. The government admitted that it could not justify the creation of "royal peculiars," due to the nebulous legal status of such an entity. Yet special areas for army chaplains might still be set aside under the rubric of "extraparochial districts." Normally this term would indicate only the suspension of the authority of the parish priest, but the retention of supervision by the bishop wherein the "district" lay. The government could hardly place the military chaplains' corps under the direction of a body of nonmilitary bishops whose composition would change as the chaplains moved from station to station. The solution lay in allowing the Crown to appoint or revoke, as conditions warranted, a bishop or archbishop to oversee the "districts."

This flexibility meant that at certain times, such as when a body of chaplains remained stationed at a big camp like Aldershot, they might indeed operate under the superintendence of the bishop of Winchester, in whose diocese the camp lay. In other cases, such as stations with only periodic military presence, the Crown could place chaplains there under the special control of a bishop appointed for the duration of the anomaly caused by the military presence. Given that such a system would institute no permanent changes in episcopal structure and that the episcopate could petition the Crown to invoke or revoke various appointments to meet specific conditions, the Ecclesiastical Lords withdrew their objections and the bill passed its third reading.[46] It cleared the House of Commons without debate, and became law 8 July 1868.

Gleig, who did not play a role in the parliamentary decision making, resented the act. He had desired the government to create a new bishop—namely, himself—to preside over the army chaplains. He argued the point in a memo sent to undersecretary Sir Edward Lugard.

> You might with equal propriety and legality send a civilian to command a Company or a Regiment not giving him a commission from the Crown, as you can appoint a clergyman nominally of the English Church to officiate to the Queen's troops in England, he getting no license, so to do, from the Bishop. . . . Neither the Secretary of State nor the Commander-in-Chief has ever interfered, or is likely to interfere, with the directions which I have, from time to time, given to the chaplains in the matter of the dress and in the performance of their proper duties. The same unanimity would prevail were I in Episcopal orders; the only difference would be that in the latter case the laws of the Church and of the State which enacts them would be observed, whereas the whole of our proceedings are and have been, since 1796, illegal.[47]

This was the plan originally proposed under the abortive bill of 1865. The prelates then had flatly refused to grant allowance for this interference by the army in the episcopate. The 1868 debates made clear that the bishops still rejected the idea of creating a bishopric out of the chaplain general's post. In the end, the War Office forestalled any further risk of confrontation by getting passed the Army Chaplains' Act of 1868 as a part of Cardwell's general army reform package. Gleig never was made a bishop. However, when he retired in 1875, the War Office appointed the Reverend Piers C. Claughton, a lifelong civilian, bishop of Colombo, 1862–70, and archdeacon of London, to be chaplain general.[48] He proved ineffective as a military leader, but his presence appeased the bishops in Lords and thereby stifled any further conflict between parochial clergy and the Chaplains' Department. On the basis of this modus vivendi, the act itself was never implemented.

Conclusion for Chapters 4 and 5

Gleig's career as chaplain general dominated the nineteenth-century development of the Royal Army Chaplains' Department. When he arrived in 1844, the department existed practically in name only. For nearly the first ten years of his administration, Gleig had to accept the nominal staff of army chaplains and work instead through the system of contracting military religious services to civilian clergy. He detested that system both for its ineffectiveness and because he believed it blocked the development of a sense of community, based upon shared religious practices, within the army. He hoped to create an army with an autonomous religious and moral life; with an ethic that extolled not only the brute skills of the warrior but the elevated conduct of the hero. In this way, by creating an army with a moral-religious as well as a strategic mission, Gleig believed he could generate an organic connection between the army and the public at large. The war in Crimea provided Gleig with the opportunity, and the resources, to expand his vision of a moral, and morally disciplined army.

Previous histories of reform in the British army have missed the slow development within army administration that proved to be the foundation for the reforms after Crimea. The usual approach has been to start the story of the modern British army in 1856, or in 1868 with the advent of Lord Cardwell as war secretary under Gladstone. Indeed, the changes emanating from the aftermath of the Crimean experience and from the Cardwell reform movements fundamentally reshaped the British army. However, these changes did not appear from thin air. All of the major military reforms had long prehistories, some of progression, some of stagnation.

At the level of general society, the most visible change after Crimea was the burgeoning tendency to see the army not as social pariah but as an honored, patriotic institution. This transformation was not instantaneous, but between 1860 and 1899 the army shed a 150-year-old reputation for debauchery and oppression, and took on the twofold mantle of patriotic and Christian defender of Home and Empire. The development of the office of chaplain general after 1796, and especially after it reached its nadir by 1844, is a key component to that greater story.

In the 1860s missionaries and reformers turned to the army with an eye to enlarging the role of Christian religion in the definition and aims of the military establishment. They did not find a ready-made army of saintly warriors. What they did find was an army with a strong tradition of denominational pluralism, with a precedent for activist religious leadership among the ranks, and with the basic facilities at its home stations for the religious education of the men. All of this was due to the fifty-year history preceding Crimea, and especially to the efforts of George Robert Gleig. Hodgson had by accident created a denominationally plural army. Gleig made it his purpose to bring dignity to military religious practice, and thereby make a better army. In the event, different groups and individuals took advantage of the generally favorable official environment to bring new ministries to the army, and to expand the scope of their practice.

6

A Kinder, Gentler British Army

Some of the first practical fruits of what Gleig had once called instilling the "moral discipline"[1] of the army took shape in experiments with the men stationed at Aldershot. These experiments, made in the context of Crimea-era reforms, explored the application of a *secular* ethics of the "home" and "respectability" to problems of army discipline; while religious reform had changed the official denominational composition and religious practice of the army, the Horse Guards and much of the officer corps remained dubious of the value of military religion.

Nonetheless, the reform movement and the Crimean war experience had changed the rules of the game of army discipline. Now, even the hardest and most secular officers had to work with the intangibles of "character building" rather than with the older methods of jail and lash. There also emerged a civilian parallel in a missionary drive among the army. That effort later enjoyed great success by relying upon tenets of "home" and "motherhood" in the context of vital Christianity. First military efforts at social reform concentrated on controlling the power of the "home."

Practical problems of military public morality grew out of Aldershot from the inception of the camp. Founded in 1855, Aldershot was designed to meet the contingencies of the Crimean War by providing the army with large, open ground of varied terrain for the training of large combat units and their officers. The army of course had other permanent garrisons around the British Isles;[2] these were notorious for rowdy soldiers and distasteful public displays of drunkenness and lewdness.

Civilian populations in these areas had long had to adjust themselves to the presence of the troops around them. For some residents, the saloon owners, dance-hall proprietors, moonshiners, gamblers, and prostitutes, the opportunity to hustle up money by pandering to the soldier's base desires was too good, or too essential, to let pass.[3] These people, through force of want and poverty, and in some instances through choice or in hopes of easy money, clustered around the smaller garrisons to convert soldier pay into pleasure and income. For others, the respectable citizens of garrison towns, the people not connected with the military presence or who dealt with it only in the mainstream economy, the proliferation of "vice" was the curse of a military station.[4] Aldershot (town and camp) quickly developed these sorts of problems, but was remarkable among military posts for several reasons.

Aldershot was an entirely artificial development, a town and camp created by command. It was brought into existence by the army, and was totally dominated by the army presence. Moral or behavioral problems among the men stationed there clearly would be army problems; no one could claim preexisting trouble emanating from civilians. Second, Aldershot was the pet project of Prince Albert and Queen Victoria, whose reputations as supremely clean-living monarchs served only to increase the public scrutiny of the camp.[5] Third, Aldershot grew into a very large garrison, commanding between five thousand and fifteen thousand men, with additions every year at autumn maneuvers. In sum, Aldershot in its early years was highly visible, solely reflective on the army, increasingly notorious, and considered a prime target for moral reform.

Public concerns for Aldershot circulated in the press. Charles Dickens visited the camp in 1859 and publicized the squalor there. For Dickens, the camp resembled the increasingly familiar urban slums growing in industrial towns.[6] Enlisted quarters stretched out in monotonous rows of rudely built, dirty little hut-houses. Barefooted children, playing with the refuse of the army, wandered about unpaved or gravel roads, which were often filthy from improper sewage disposal. Many soldiers lived and worked in temporary shelters as basic as tents. Soldiers were slaves to the military clock, and rushed to duty every dawn with the reveille. Rank alone could not shield a man from insanitary conditions. Dickens mourned as much for the young officers at Aldershot as for enlisted personnel. Subalterns lived in similarly rugged conditions, ate equally poor food and, between noon and mess at seven, had no settled occupation other than relieving boredom and avoiding superior officers.[7]

To combat these conditions and to fight the men's off-duty resort to alcohol and prostitutes, Parliament in the 1860s commissioned studies of the camp and the town that had grown around it.[8] The results were not encouraging. The huts in which enlisted men and their families lived were crowded and dirty. Unmarried men were crammed twenty-two to each forty by twenty-one foot hut, rendering thirty-four square feet per man. Married men and their families crowded into similar huts, often ten families per building. Death from disease was two and a half times more frequent in Aldershot than in the surrounding countryside and villages. Camp sewage and waste from privies in the town backed up into the local Blackwater River, which sometimes overflowed into the streets of the town. Groundwater ran black and putrid. The army and the civilians squabbled over whom to blame, but the filth remained.[9]

Investigators also documented a moral life at Aldershot wholly in contradiction with official public standards. In 1861, army captain Pilkington Jackson, following an initiative of the late Sidney Herbert, began his inquiry into the moral and physical environment of Aldershot. Between 1856 and 1861, average troop strength in camp was approximately 13,350 noncommissioned officers and enlisted men. To serve this population, the village at Aldershot in 1861 could boast of eighteen canteens, twenty-five pubs, and forty-seven beer houses, making a total of ninety drinking establishments—one for every 150 men.[10] Given that only a fraction of the soldiers could be on liberty at any one time, the ratio was actually much higher. In his visit to the camp in the summer of 1859, Charles Dickens surmised that no more than 3,000 men could be on liberty at once.[11] Assuming like numbers of bars in 1859 as in 1861, these 3,000 men would then have had one watering hole for every 34 of them.

To the army leadership, such a situation had several disturbing implications. In such an environment, the men were likely to be habitually drunk. That in turn meant problems with order and discipline, and vice. One-third of all court-martial offenses at Aldershot between August 1860 and July 1861 resulted directly from drunkenness.[12] As Jackson took pains to illustrate, drunkenness made for more than just belligerent troopers. The number of drinking establishments open to the troops at Aldershot, he argued, correlated with the high incidence of venereal disease there. The drinking halls often doubled as brothels, with owners passing off the prostitutes as barmaids and servants. Into the 1860s, Aldershot remained about the least healthy place to serve in the British army, and soldierly recourse to commercial sex constituted a major reason why.

Hospital admissions there, both in absolute and proportional terms, outnumbered those of any other station due to the exceedingly high rates (even by army standards) of venereal disease. Of all hospital admissions, venereal disease, or "diseases incident to lust," accounted for an average 34 percent, ranging between 24 percent and 43 percent for the years 1856 to 1860.[13] In a garrison where the total number of hospital admissions each year exceeded actual troop strength (meaning that individual men were hospitalized two or more times per year), such figures represented a crisis. The plethora of bars, the atmosphere of heavy drinking and commercial sex literally killed troops, and certainly wreaked untold devastation upon the lives of others. As Jackson wrote of the situation, "No system could be better imagined or more successfully carried out, if the object were to sap gradually the health of the soldiers, to induce early debility, and to hasten premature death."[14]

Jackson's presentation of the moral issues of Aldershot had a distinctly functionalist, or utilitarian, tone[15] and an almost total patriarchal bias. His concerns were troop strength, order, discipline, and efficiency. Such should not be surprising coming from a military officer. While some observers decried the inhumanity and degradation of vice, the official army view of "morality" did not and perhaps could not divorce itself from the function of the army—that is, to maintain a male force of maximum efficiency and strength.[16] Jackson's recommendations at Aldershot would reflect his emphasis on environment and function. Other reformers would rely upon increasing opportunities to build the moral character of the individual soldier through religious instruction.

At any rate, Jackson (and the army) in 1862 had to decide what to do about his startling discoveries at the camp. He expected little or no help from the civilians living near Aldershot. From his point of view, they were at the root of the problem. He described the village as "inhabited principally by publicans, brothel keepers, prostitutes, thieves, and receivers of stolen property." The parish had a dismal record in prosecuting any of these offenses, Jackson concluded, because such prosecutions went against "the wishes of the ratepayers, a large number of whom, and the most influential, derive[d] pecuniary benefit from the evils in question." In fact, in the six years since the camp had been formed, Aldershot had not seen any such prosecution, either against the brothel keepers or the prostitutes.[17] Jackson recommended that the army itself would have to provide alternative recreations to the men if the plague at Aldershot were to be stopped.

Indeed, the authorities viewed prostitution and the spread of venereal disease as nothing short of a plague. The Contagious Diseases Acts of 1864, 1866, and 1869, which emerged from investigations similar to Jackson's, were unambiguous on that point. Designed to confront the venereal disease crisis in garrison towns, the acts enabled police to detain suspected prostitutes, administer genital examinations, and quarantine diseased women. At the time of Jackson's original report, however, army authorities could not yet detain or deport the women who "plagued" the soldiers. Soldiers had to be persuaded to stay away from commercial sex.[18]

Sexual wisdom of the day held only the woman to be a mutable sexual character. Therefore, the argument over morality at Aldershot focused upon the supposed influences of femininity, in its negative and positive potential. In 1860s Britain, army sexual ethics, indeed all official sexual ethics, cast the prostitute in the villain's role.[19] Some voices might decry the depravity, or at least the poor judgment, of men who frequented prostitutes, but the women bore the onus of guilt and perversity. Writing of a research junket to Aldershot, William Acton popularized the rhetoric of condemnation. He described the brothels of Aldershot as ample "hunting grounds" for women "content to surrender their persons" for a shilling.[20]

In Victorian sexual ideology, a "fallen woman" became the seat of sexual evil, the agent of disease, and an instigator of base male passions.[21] On the other hand, a "virtuous" woman was believed to be free of the strong sexual drives, which males supposedly experienced as an appetite and fallen women as an addiction or perversity. Males had a relatively static sexual character (as sexually desiring agents), which could be harnessed for good or left to run amok, depending upon the chastening influences (or lack thereof) of feminine piety in the male development.[22]

Females, even ones formerly "pure," who once descended into sexual license faced the perils of eventual abject degradation. Describing a class of "gentle" prostitutes he believed to have identified in the world of London commercial sex, Acton wrote,

> The woman, the castle of whose modesty offered stoutest resistance to the storm of the seducer, often becomes in time the most abiding stronghold of vice. Saturated with misery and drink, perhaps then crime and disease, dead long in heart, and barely willing to live on in the flesh—ceasing to look upward, ceasing to strike outward, she will passively drift down the stream into that listless state of moral

insensibility in which so many pass from this world into the presence of their Judge.[23]

As a being above all this, the virtuous woman could perform the socially vital task of elevating the thoughts and behavior of men, and of providing an example to women who had strayed into fields of "perversity." At Aldershot, the army focused on the "fallen woman." To combat her, Jackson sought to introduce "virtuous femininity" through the appropriation of the physical environment in which the "virtuous woman" operated: the home. Without relying on actual females, the army turned to the home model in its attempts to reduce and restrain vice.

The logic ran as follows. The domestic scene is the preeminent sphere of activity for the virtuous woman. In this space she exhibits and perpetuates socially elevating behaviors such as sexual restraint, courtesy, sentimentality, and piety. To promote those virtues among the troops requires the proper venue for their dissemination. Therefore, the soldiers must have access to "homelike" environments in order that the men absorb these desirable values and behaviors. The army placed emphasis on the home environment with less willingness to accede authority to any women. Other civilian reformers hit upon the same model. Fully using the role of the woman, the civilians believed that given such an alternative, and maybe just a little prodding, most of the enlisted men in the army would gladly respond to the presence of such "women in homes" by attending them in preference to bars during off hours and by adopting the values found within.[24]

It is a resounding confirmation of the power of "domestic ideology" in mid-Victorian Britain that diverse observers of the army vice problem came to the same conclusion: that a "home," both meaning a particular emotional environment and a particular physical arrangement of space, could combat vice.[25] Such thinking resembled the notions of equating religion with the physical building of a church, or democratic-republican governmental styles with a particular version of Greek revival architecture. It is likewise notable, since in the case of vice the army had "a problem with women," that feminine virtue, administered in a feminized space but in a nearly all-male population, appeared to be the "natural" antidote to feminine perversity: the army diagnosis of prostitution.[26] The explicit role of Christian religion as the medium of virtue remained contentious. Jackson, who was the parliamentary voice of Horse Guards on this issue, wanted the home experiment. However, he wanted it free from the possible competition of a specific religious creed.

In his reports to Parliament, Jackson revealed himself to be a hearty supporter of the "utilitarian" (as opposed to "sentimental" or religious) home ideology as a weapon against vice. By the time of his 1862 report on the situation at Aldershot, he had already for several years been expert on the issues of camp discipline. In 1859, after having become disgusted with conditions of life at Gibraltar, Jackson himself had sponsored a "soldiers' institute" in the fortress. With his own money and on his own initiative, he rented a house. He preferred that to creating a lecture hall or coffee room because of the ties the private-dwelling environment would promote among the men.

Jackson used his home to promote civility and personal improvement, as well as to build a "clubby" cooperative spirit among the soldiers. He established rules of subscription and hired a former sergeant to manage the club. He charged a subscription fee and sold refreshments at cost, arguing that bearing some financial responsibility would increase the members' sense of common endeavor and belonging. He forbade any alcoholic beverages or games of chance, substituting games requiring skill, singing, magazine reading, and educational lectures.[27] Within six months, the success of the institute in attracting soldiers away from the Gibraltar bars and brothels won official notice and approval. Gibraltar governor Lieutenant General Sir William Codrington petitioned the government to take over the lease on the institute property and thereby to insure the permanence of the club.

Jackson claimed that his Gibraltar Institute had reduced fighting among the rankers by giving them a common stake in the availability of quiet and relaxation, and by bringing them together in a homelike setting. The alcohol-free environment naturally eliminated drunkenness and the violence that had resulted from it. Jackson proudly asserted that with these results he had won over not only the governor, but "the colonels of regiments, the chaplains of all denominations, the officers of the garrison, the medical staff, and indeed every respectable resident at Gibraltar."[28]

Significantly, the philosophy behind the institute stood at odds with recent military religious reforms. Jackson abstained from introducing an explicit religious character into his institute. He argued that such a presence might induce division among the men along lines of denomination or, worse, convince them that the home was merely a ruse for increasing discipline. Partly, it was. The quiescence of the troops was the goal, and preserving the "neutral" character of the home served this end. Jackson himself said as much in a letter to Major General Eyre, commander at Chatham.

> Bearing in mind the great variety of opinions on the subject of religion, I deemed it necessary, in order to prevent discord and dissatisfaction, and to avoid wounding deeply rooted convictions and unreasoning prejudices, to make the 'home' thoroughly and honestly a neutral ground, so far as religion was concerned.[29]

Armed with this experience, Jackson in 1862 recommended and got a similar experiment at Aldershot. He called for the creation of four separate facilities for the camp, and recommended they all follow his Gibraltar pattern. He even listed all the games to be played, the fees to be collected (because "soldiers, like other men, . . . set a higher value upon what they exercise self-denial to acquire"), and the items for the refreshment menu.[30] He justified this micromanagement by citing the failures of other institutes that had deviated from his principles.[31]

The campaign against vice at Aldershot was an important turning point in the history of the British army; formerly, the bulwarks of discipline had been the lash, the jail, and the gallows.[32] From Crimea onward the army sought to develop good behavior via socialization and education.[33] Army leadership was learning to bring up instead of beat up obedient soldiers. To do so they turned to the institutions that they believed defined and shaped respectable life outside of the military: school, church, and home.

Yet home and church in particular could be subversive institutions from the army point of view. They were, after all, archcivilian and archfeminine. Jackson had tried to cull the apparent benefits of "home" from what he viewed as the undesirable dross of religious influence and actual feminine control. By the 1860s, his view of the necessary neutrality of military religion was already compromised by the activism of the Chaplains' Department and by evangelical influence in British society. Wary of undue civilian influence though he might have been, Jackson betrayed himself with his very choice of strategy against army vice. His efforts to appropriate the home constituted a blatant admission that army life was indeed uncivilized and could not reform itself within its own traditions.

7
Winning the Troops

Clearly the efforts to establish discipline among the soldiers based at Aldershot camp included familiar elements of "Victorian" sexual mores as well as not so familiar experiments in the meaning of *home, woman, virtue,* and *religion* among lower-class Britons. For the army, the stakes were efficiency, sobriety, command, and control. The army tinged its schemes of moral behavior with a heavy dose of utilitarianism. Significantly, it was not this approach that attracted the most soldierly cooperation.

The working alternative to Captain Jackson's views eventually arose from the missionary efforts of women evangelical Christians.[1] In every category, these women bucked the propriety of the regular army. Women, being little regarded in the public sphere of nineteenth-century British society, were perhaps least well regarded by the army. Military officers viewed women as potential sexual and hygienic threats to the men. Even in the 1850s and 1860s, evangelical piety and moral reform were contentious and controversial among political and military leaders of Britain.[2] However, the success of the women reformers in gaining acceptance among the army's rank and file defied convential wisdom. Apparently, official opinion and moral theory did not jibe with the internalized notions of right and wrong and with the family or domestic ideology held true by the men. Instead, the story of the Aldershot missionaries seemed to validate the basic theories of George Robert Gleig. The missionary reformers called the men to change from within, relying on an ethic derived explicitly from evangelical Protestant Christianity. They transmitted this call by appealing not to efficiency, or even to "manliness," but to cultural norms of femininity they believed the men would understand, and to which even soldiers might be expected to be open: mother, home, domesticity, and female purity.

Traditional accounts of army reform in this era have emphasized factors like the foundation and growth of Aldershot as a training center, technological innovation, war experience in Crimea, and the 1857 Mutiny in India. Most historians have ignored the sweeping influence of the evangelical revival of 1859 and the long-term increased receptivity within the army toward soldier religiosity that began with Gleig's early career.[3] So too have many scholars missed the general importance of traditional religious expression, often publicly championed by women, in the reform of British society at large. Yet the careers of women evangelical missionaries to the army demonstrate the centrality of religious experience in reforming the army and subsequently winning for it general public approval. British nineteenth-century popular military nationalism had its roots not only in new forms of political organization and participation, but also in a successful effort to redeem the institutions of the state in terms of traditional categories of moral thought.

Louisa Daniell was the widow of a British army officer. Never in good health for the last decades of her life, she nevertheless, after the death of her husband, took interest in philanthropic work. She was an evangelical Christian, a member of the Wesleyan Connection who actively pursued not only her personal religious life but work in the Wesleyan Conference, especially as a home missionary.[4] She and her daughter labored from the mid-1850s onward in order to fight (her list) godlessness, Mormonism, the "Roman perversion," and drink.

Louisa Daniell made her first mission to the "less fortunate" in 1857.[5] She was that year taking a recuperative rest in the countryside around Rugby. While lodged in a particular hamlet (her daughter referred to it only as "P——") she began to pass her time by taking stock of the moral condition of her neighbors. This she found wanting. She set to work creating and guiding a local Bible study group, a sewing and industrial school for young girls, and a savings bank for young men. Additionally, as the village population included several Mormons, she sought to correct their errors with specialized attention and gifts of New Testaments.[6] From these beginnings, she expanded her work to five missions in the area, including one in Rugby that sported a permanent lecture hall and a full-time staff missionary.

By the summer of 1862 her efforts had reached a large enough scale that she had attracted the attention of other Methodist lay missionaries. They suggested she consider expansion to Aldershot. By her own inquiries, Daniell found that for the summer of 1862 Aldershot would have a military population varying between 12,000 and 24,000. The government planned to provide four army chaplains, one Presbyterian minister, two Roman Catholic priests, plus four scripture readers from the Soldiers' Friend Society. Since at best that meant one spiritual worker per 1,000 troops (assuming the lowest number of soldiers), she agreed that her help was needed there.[7]

Daniell and her daughter paid a first visit to the camp in August of 1862. Aided there by some converted officers and soldiers, they began holding Bible classes and recruiting new members. They assured the commander of their desire to remain "undenominational and neutral," although as Methodists she and her daughter frequently referred to Catholics as "perverts."[8] An early declaration of "nondenominationalism," despite implicit criticism of the state church and explicit insult to Catholicism, served Daniell well in her efforts to gain official acceptance of her presence at Aldershot. As a woman, she could not be an official representative of the Wesleyan Conference, and therefore escaped the stigma of "sectarianism." Moreover, she made no demands for official money. Army leadership was eager to clean up the camp. With the help of her confederate officers and with the tolerance of the camp command, she opened a mission hall on a piece of land near the cavalry barracks.[9] By the next February, after only five months' work in Aldershot, Daniell was ready to open a full-scale home. On the second of that month, 1863, she held a dedication ceremony at which the ubiquitous seventh earl of Shaftesbury,[10] an evangelical activist, laid the cornerstone to the new building. Construction on the building was completed later that year, and the Daniells welcomed their first soldiers on 11 October 1863.[11]

The very layout of the new building declared its intended purpose. Despite the fact that "the institute," as Daniell called it, was to serve as many of the thousands of soldiers at Aldershot as possible, the Daniells forsook the meeting-hall or coffee-shop format. Instead, they promoted the image of a home, which meant a single-family abode of the gentility and refinement one associated with the upper-middle class and the gentry.[12]

Over the course of time, nineteenth-century homes in Great Britain and the United States increasingly displayed particular conventions in style and organization: the entrance hall, which separated the visitor coming through the door from immediate access to the actual living space; the parlor, a room devoid of common function and designed for the purpose of socializing in conformity with special rules of civility; an open staircase in the hallway, as opposed to a closeted stair in the kitchen or along a chimney; bedrooms and kitchen separated from the living and receiving space and hidden from casual view; where possible a garden or some other closed, controlled space around the house to set it apart from its surroundings.[13]

The use of a hallway meant that the actual living space was a sanctuary, without direct egress to the outside world. The parlor, an otherwise functionless room, also simply protected a space. Within it, refined people did nothing but be genteel with one another, whether receiving company or gathering for family reading or polite conversation.[14] Open, broad stairs implied the open reception of visitors and guests to finer apartments above the ground floor. The garden set the whole structure apart from the everyday world and divided the "in here" from the "out there." Ideally, the domestic space of the home nourished qualities and values not for ready mixing with public life, just as Daniell argued that evangelical Christianity separated a soldier from common soldierly vice. This notion, coupled with the cult of female domesticity that grew up in middle classes of England and America in the first decades of the nineteenth century, projected the home as the repository of refinement.[15] It rejected public values of competition, confrontation, and contact with the unwashed masses. It promoted or protected, in association with the figure of the "woman of the house," nurturance, cooperation, quiet, and personal civility.

The Daniell "home" at Aldershot adhered to this very scheme, and for similar reasons. Miss Daniell wrote that the whole was patterned after a southern English country home. It had a garden, and gables from which the founders eventually grew clinging ivy. Inside, the house centered upon a reception hall attached to the front door. Actual sitting space was contained in rooms just off this hall. These rooms were for the most part dedicated to the service of nonalcoholic drinks, smoking, reading, and game playing. However, the home also boasted a parlor wherein soldiers could sit by the fire and enjoy pleasant conversation or devotional talk with home staff, all of whom were to be women. In the entrance hall, a broad, open staircase led to the finer drawing room upstairs, where officers came to read the Bible or to discuss the progress of the home and mission. The kitchen, bath, and bedrooms for full-time staff were separate and apart from the common rooms.[16]

This creation of a particular kind of private space for missionary work with the soldiers at Aldershot set those efforts apart from tent meetings and revivals. Mrs. Daniell was explicit that her project should win the hearts and minds of soldiers by "recalling" to them the love of mother and the values of home. She intended to gain at least their friendship, even where she could not get conversions, although the latter remained her great hope. Her belief in the potency of these chosen tactics was absolute. Neither she nor her daughter appeared to consider the possibility that the vast majority of enlisted personnel might never have seen the inside of such a building and called it home.[17] However, the missionaries were wiser in their belief that the soldiers, at some time in their lives, would have all had a female figure who represented stability and support to them. Women of the working and poor classes constituted the center of family life.[18] These experiences of "home" and "mother" seemed universal to the Daniells, and they enlisted the meaning of these symbols in their campaign to save soldiers' souls. Therefore, instead of the meeting hall or the coffee shop, they chose an actual home as the setting from which to promulgate Christianity and Christian personal ethics among the soldiers.

Moreover, while they recognized male authority, both women intended to lead the mission themselves with the aid of other women.[19] Who else embodied the values they sought? Upon her first arrival at Aldershot, Louisa Daniell met and spoke with several authorities, "the vicar, chaplain, etc. to whom we said that from our hearts we desired to work *with,* and not against, those who were engaged in the same Master's service in the place, although we could not put ourselves *under their control.*"[20]

Louisa Daniell died in the summer of 1871, but her daughter continued the work, assisted by numerous women reformers and missionaries who had joined the project since 1862. Soon after her mother's death, the younger Daniell began to cast about for means of expanding the mission to other military posts. Officers of the Engineers who transferred frequently between Aldershot and Chatham requested a home for the latter base, but Daniell instead took up a different strategy. She decided to use her money to follow entire units as they transferred away from Aldershot. She first tried this plan in the fall of 1872 when she purchased a small house in Weedon, in order to continue her ministry to two batteries of artillery transferred there. She kept that house open until the artillery transferred again in 1874, after which she too pulled out of Weedon.[21]

Following established connections instead of creating new

ones at new stations remained the preference for the Daniell home mission at least in part because personal acquaintance with officers was key to gaining access to the troops. Over the next few years, Daniell took over existing homes at Colchester, followed some transfers to Manchester, and in November 1874 began work to revive a "languishing home" at Plymouth. The problem at Plymouth, as she diagnosed it, was men. For the previous several years the home had had only male leadership, owing to the withdrawal of its "energetic honorary secretary," a woman who had been "the mainspring" of its former success.[22] Males apparently could not maintain a sufficiently domestic atmosphere to win the hearts of soldiers. After the return of female control, Daniell was happy to report Plymouth back to normal and the soldiers returning in great numbers.

Despite the success and apparent permanent monopoly of the Daniells at Aldershot, they were not the only workers in that field.[23] Aldershot and subsidiary English bases formed the core of the home garrison experience of the nineteenth-century British army, but Ireland also demanded a large commitment of troops. The army had several important bases in the country. Curiously, the Daniells had an independent Irish counterpart, who began her own ministry to soldiers about the same time, under similar circumstances, but without any prior knowledge of the work at Aldershot. Her career focused on Ireland, later India, and only during World War I included the great English camp. Elise Sandes was the daughter of Anglo-Irish gentry, born in Tralee in 1849. She dated her own conversion to an evangelical faith to the summer of 1861, when she and her father attended a revival meeting and both received the Spirit. From that day forward, she claimed for herself a calling to evangelize.[24]

Like the Daniells, Sandes began her particular mission to soldiers through her desire to do general missionary work. After her father died in 1866, she often spent school holidays at the Dublin home of her friend, Marie Fry. Fry had also had a conversion experience. When she was seventeen she began inviting drummer boys from the Royal Irish Constabulary and from military units stationed nearby to attend teas and hymn sing-alongs in her garden. After thus gaining the acquaintance of the young soldiers, Fry would pursue them with personal entreaty and letter writing in an effort to convert them.[25] It was through this informal and self-created network that Sandes entered upon her work with soldiers.

After six years of this sort of personal ministry, Sandes, again like the Daniells, decided to expand her work by following transfers from Tralee to Cork. As were Aldershot or Plymouth in England, Cork was a major military depot in nineteenth-century Ireland. It was a notorious site of heavy drinking, gambling, and prostitution. Over the winter of 1876–77, when some of her converted soldiers at Tralee received orders for Cork, Sandes decided to follow them there to help in the fight against "backsliding." Like the Daniells at Aldershot, Elise Sandes decided that when she opened her mission at Cork, a home atmosphere would provide the best setting for her efforts. Like them, though her lack of money for a well-built house kept her from gentry aspirations, she relied upon a building that mimicked the layout of a respectable, middling home. The converts she had made at Tralee had enjoyed the surroundings of her own home there. What better way to strengthen the men than to provide the same surroundings as when they first accepted conversion?

As she described it, the basic idea came to her while standing in the sinful streets of the Cork military district during her first visit there in 1877. She wrote, "It seemed unutterably sad and awful to think that the devil should have it all his own way the moment these men stepped outside the [Cork] Barrack-gate. . . . What could I hope for those who were wavering and easily influenced? Could I expect them, alone, unaided, and strangers to the power of God, to stand against the flood-tide of sin surging all around them? There I stood . . . and as, with a bleeding heart, I watched and prayed, my ideal of a Soldiers' Home came to me." A house made a home would be her fortress against sin.[26]

Her explanation of this choice is worth quoting in detail. It is a manifesto of female purity and of domesticity as the strength of the army home mission:

> My experience has been that, under God, the secret of success in Soldiers' Homes is to make them true substitutes for the homes these men have left, and to have those in them who can really take the places of their mothers and sisters. . . . To keep thoughts of "home" ever present with our soldiers is one of my endeavours, and "Now, just think it is your own mother who is talking to you," is often an unfailing plea when I want some lad to listen to my advice.
>
> I believe no human influences move the heart so powerfully for good as memories of a good home and pure women's love, and that such memories put the right kind of grit into our men when they are called upon to fight for their country. . . . What a soldier values is not a fine building or a well-regulated reading room, but a HOMELY HOME, with a warm, motherly heart in it that cares for him. There-

> fore I try to make my Homes not merely institutes or clubs, or mission halls, but in the truest sense of the word "homes."[27]

This strategy contradicted much of official army philosophy about "soldiers' institutes." The army had also had its experiments, but relied upon the form of "home" to induce behavior that would surpass the standards of the saloon. Sandes and the Daniells rejected the utilitarian approach of the army and its sterile attempts at co-opting "home" to make institutes simply more fun or pleasant than bars. The women insisted instead that emotion, an explicit and interventionist evangelical missionizing, and fundamentally, a woman's control of a home environment were the ingredients that made for better and happier soldiers. To a point, the goals were the same. Sandes was explicit that "her boys" would need grit and perseverance to fight when called. She was frank about the necessity to defend Great Britain and the mortal perils of the battlefield. Like army leaders, she believed her efforts would make for better soldiers. Unlike army leadership, she did not stop there.

For her and the Daniells, a better soldier was only an avenue to a saved soul. Immorality in the army was not just a problem of efficiency, but a question of choices and alternative ways of life. "Sometimes," Sandes wrote, "I am told that our Homes would be more popular, more successful, if the religious element were excluded. I believe they would, even from a human standpoint, be dead failures. The power of God in this work is the real secret of success. If God were excluded, what could we say to the poor, helpless victims of sin, and drink, and vice, who come to us continually and ask, 'Is there any power that can save and keep me pure?'"[28] Apparently she understood her audience. The first efforts of Sandes and the Daniells spawned a whole generation of women army missionaries and homes. Prior to 1914, the homes remained central to army post social life at home and in the empire.[29]

In addition to this rejection of a utilitarian approach to vice, the work of the Daniells and of Sandes contained an implicit (sometimes barely so) critique of the male-dominated military establishment. Louisa Daniells refused to submit her work to the oversight of male authorities at Aldershot. Her daughter had to rescue a Plymouth home from the bungling control of male curators. Elise Sandes hired primarily single young women to help her with her Cork home, and instructed them all to accentuate a close, "womanly influence" in their time with the soldiers.

They were all to be "sisters and mothers." For Sandes especially, only the mother figure could repair the ravages of sin to which, through the carelessness of male army leadership, the young soldier was exposed.[30]

The women, who proclaimed their femininity without proclaiming any feminism, manifested this critique of male domination in several ways.[31] In pursuit of their ministries and reforms, they regularly broke the rules of female decorum. They spoke at public meetings, often to mixed or all male audiences. Under normal circumstances among respectable European or American society in the nineteenth century, female public speaking was considered to be in very poor taste, or worse. In the 1870s for example the English reformer and anti–Contagious Diseases Acts campaigner Josephine Butler worked under the same burden. The frequency with which publicly active women suffered under the prohibition of public speech, even while preaching, testifies to the significance of the missionaries' use of public address.[32]

The women traveled independently and approached men and politicians for support and patronage. In 1878 as she began her home in Cork, Elise Sandes found herself in desperate need of cash. Armed only with some letters of introduction for potential English patrons, she traveled alone from Cork to London, took her own hotel room, and began to solicit appointments with businessmen and nobles who might be willing to contribute. Though she met with sympathetic London Evangelicals, they were skeptical of a single woman doing such work, and at first she struggled to win any support.[33] Young Miss Daniell, daughter of the missionary pioneer, was less intrepid in confronting this barrier. In 1872 and 1873 when she began to expand her ministry, at first to Weedon and then to Colchester, she too traveled alone and independently petitioned for support. However, when she secured houses for her use or had to negotiate with businessmen, she availed herself of a male spokesman.[34]

The missionaries also challenged male social standards by rejecting marriage in order to pursue careers of their own choosing. Louisa Daniell did so by beginning her work only after the death of her husband. Her daughter opted to pursue missioning the soldiers instead of raising a family. Young Marie Fry, the inspiration to Elise Sandes, died too young to have to make the choice between domesticity and the drummer boys. But in doing so she gave Sandes a vision of virginal self-sacrifice. Her example, and the experience of the soldiers' needs, convinced Elise Sandes to forsake marriage in order to be "mother" to all the men who entered her homes.

Most importantly, the female missionaries through their work self-consciously posed a feminized program of Christian morals and ethics against male and secular standards of military conduct. Against bar and canteen, they pitted the Bible, "the home," and the female space it encompassed. Against roughness and austere stoicism they championed emotion. The autobiographies of Daniell and of Sandes are replete with instances of copious tears falling down the cheeks of repentant sinners, male and female. Such a device was a commonplace among specimens of evangelical literature in the nineteenth century, but was definitely not a commonplace among descriptions of soldiers. In Great Britain the prevailing pre-Crimea image of the soldier, even emanating from the army itself, was of an animalistic brute, barely under control and good only for killing and plundering. Soldiers were supposed to be hard, ferocious men, not the broken, suffering, and striving fellows depicted by Sandes and the Daniells.

The development of the army camp and the work of the missionaries at Aldershot are important for a number of reasons. First, the community of soldiers that evolved there, unsavory as it could be, nonetheless became the first such army endeavor to enter into the mainstream of public consciousness and concern. Previously, a military post in one's neighborhood constituted an imposition, a sanitary and moral hazard, sometimes political oppression. The war in Crimea and the sufferings of the troops there, and the Indian Mutiny with its explicit reception in Britain as a conflict between Christian civilization and heathen barbarism, both did much to awaken public sentiments of empathy with common British soldiers.

Additionally, by the late 1850s the army had a two-decade-old successful process of integrating the three major religious denominations of the kingdom into its ranks. That integration made possible a serious implementation of religious life among the soldiers in an effort to improve their condition and their quality. The Revival of 1859, the Cromwellian renaissance sponsored by Thomas Carlyle, and the removal from the scene of the misanthropic (at least where enlisted personnel were concerned) duke of Wellington combined in the 1850s to ripen the army both for missionary attention and for public consideration as something other than the worst collection of British social scum.

Aldershot was unique in this transformation in that it was the first army community to be perceived not as a penal colony, but in a similar light with the troubled working-class neighborhoods of Britain's major cities. Charles Dickens and army reformer Captain Jackson both made explicit use of the worker community comparison: Dickens in a critique of the rugged conditions of the camp, and Jackson to remind his superiors of the need to create wholesome alternatives to the presumed usual recreations of the lower classes. The women missionaries who eventually devoted their lives to preaching the evangelical gospel to army troops all saw the soldiers as wayward lads, even disadvantaged youth. They, as well as Jackson, sought to integrate these army strays into morally mainstream Britain through the channel of the home, itself a collection of symbols representing civilization and right behavior. The missionaries' charitable images of soldiers were a far cry from the common aspersions cast on soldiers during the first half of the century by such diverse observers as the duke of Wellington, William Cobbett, Shelley, Chaplain General Robert Hodgson, as well as in the disdain of most of the Nonconformist churches and their press, and of most of the working class.[35]

Because Aldershot was so big, it offered the first opportunity to would-be reformers outside the military to gain access to a large number of soldiers all at once. This fact in turn made the camp the first entrepôt by which reform sentiments could attract a mass following among the troops. Figures are hard to come by, but the testimony both of the missionary women and of concerned officers indicates that literally thousands of men, in preference to the local nightlife, regularly passed through the soldiers' homes at Aldershot. Once inside, whether they heeded the spiritual call or not, they complied with the missionary code of behavior.[36] Before the 1850s, the British army at home occupied a number of stations, with garrisons or units in transit rarely numbering more than a few thousand at any one time. During the summer months, and culminating in autumn maneuvers, Aldershot could be home to as many as twenty-five thousand men and officers. The Daniells and, later, Elise Sandes and the Wesleyan Methodists led by William Harris Rule[37] all came to view Aldershot as the foundation of any ministry to the army.

Conversely, Aldershot became the proving ground upon which these missionaries demonstrated to the military authorities that a religious influence upon the troops from outside the official command structure could be the agent of much good, including enhanced discipline and military efficiency. Mrs. and Miss Daniell, and especially Elise Sandes, all won testimonial praises from military officers who verified the efficacy of their ministries. Eventually, Sandes gained even Sir Garnet Wolseley as a patron when he and his wife sponsored the opening of a Sandes' Soldiers' Home at Dublin.[38]

Finally, Aldershot demands attention because it became a venue for activist Christian women to make a working critique on male and secular standards of behavior and morality in the most male-dominated of British institutions, save possibly the navy. The conversion of supposedly weak feminine traits into the basis of reform and criticism of male preserves was a pattern common to women reformers in much of the nineteenth-century west. On the continent, such a strategy appeared in both feminism and antifeminism. It dominated the practice of nonexplicitly political female community building among the middle classes in both France and Germany. In Britain, the gender ideology of femininity grounded the fight against the Contagious Diseases Acts, sections of the suffrage movement, and later even the separatist radicalism of the Women's Social and Political Union. The women army missionaries did not interest themselves in political reform or in head-on collisions with male authority. Nonetheless, they relied upon social doctrines of superior feminine piety to gain access to the army, to mold the forms (home and motherhood) that their Christian ministries would take, and to pose a religious alternative to ancient army systems of discipline and control.

8

Havelock and the Birth of the Christian Hero

In the previous chapters, the investigation has centered on the effects of quiet, internal, and long-term changes in the religious administration and environment of the army. Well before the notorious publicity associated with the Crimea and the imperial self-congratulation following the suppression of the Mutiny, government ministers, church officials, and even army officers created, through hard experience, what they believed to be an equitable system for the real working of religion among the troops. Beginning around the time of the Crimean War, missionaries such as Louise Daniell or Elise Sandes made the first civilian forays into the new administrative landscape. In the 1830s or early 1840s, their efforts likely would not have succeeded. But by the 1850s, twenty years of precedent and ten years of George Robert Gleig's activist leadership at the Chaplains' Department had created a military ready to receive and to accept the ardent attentions of civilian missionaries.

By that decade, such interest actually played into the long, albeit slowly, developing trend of religious life in the army. Rather than constituting a watershed for the evolution of the army, the successes of the missionaries and the explosion of public moral concern for the army at the time of Crimea and the Mutiny represent the fortuitous element of unforeseen events that catalyzed a popular recognition of the need for army reforms. This recognition accelerated the pace of change within the army, but was not the source of that change.

Entirely new after 1856 was a popular fascination with a new type of military figure, the embodiment of the "moral" army, the Christian military hero.[1] In the next thirty years after the Crimean War, the Christian hero evolved, primarily through the careers of two men, into an archetype of popular meaning for what the army had become since 1809. The army produced two great Christian heroes policing the nineteenth-century British empire: Henry Havelock and Charles George Gordon. The public willingness to accept notions of the pious soldier, to see martyrdom in a combat death, to exchange *raison d'état* for *raison de Dieu* all illustrate a significant change in the popular myth surrounding the army.

Around the time of Waterloo the British soldier was a social pariah. Enlisted men carried with them a stigma, and officers at least a public suspicion, based upon assumptions of the brutality, drunkenness, criminality, and godlessness of the army. Forty years after Wellington's victory, Henry Havelock personified a break with that tradition. His life and spectacular final campaign proved to be the point of contact between the quiet, internal development of the army community and the public credibility of that change. When Charles Gordon achieved his martyrdom, the ease with which partisans cloaked him with that mantle demonstrated new public assumptions about military men.[2] Very real and difficult labors built the solid foundations upon which the heroic Gordon, much more than Havelock, came to rest. By 1885, popular notions about the meanings of a military career already included notions of the respectability and the moral discipline of the soldier. If it had not been so, perhaps Gordon's heroic reputation could not have survived the frenzied public obsession that it did.[3] Something had changed drastically in military-civil relations since 1815.

Therefore, these stories of Havelock and Gordon function as a conclusion to this study. They of course provide specific information about the phenomenon of the Christian hero. More broadly, however, comparing the two men reveals how far public expectations and assumptions about Christian heroes outstripped the real lives of the men themselves. This progressive advance of opinion and myth was sustained not by the individual men alone, but by the successful conversion in the public mind of the entire army. That success was based upon decades of internal change in the army, and upon the accretion of public recognition of that change through civilian-military encounters like those of the female missionaries at Aldershot. Through all of this experience, George Robert Gleig's vision of a popular army linked to the masses and classes of Great Britain through the generation and sustenance of a publicly credible military morality came true. The sanctification of Gordon attests to the fact.

By 1885, the year Charles George Gordon finally succeeded in getting himself killed at Khartoum, he was a man thrice famous. Moreover, he was a commodity, his fame a product of a particular discussion in British society that encompassed the interrelated concepts of empire, conquest, and Christian mission. This specifically British dialogue of self-explanation had relatively recent origins. Not quite thirty years before, the fortunes of war and empire had provided the British public with another Christian military martyr in the person of General Sir Henry Havelock, a lifetime soldier who spent his entire career in India. He died while suppressing the Mutiny of 1857, at the siege of Lucknow. Without his precedent, Gordon might not have achieved his own martyrdom in the form he did.[4]

Twenty-five years ago, Olive Anderson made pioneering observations about the social transformation of the British army, which by the turn of the twentieth century the home public perceived as a band of white Christian crusaders.[5] For her the explanation of that change lay in drawing connections between the "advent of adulatory attitudes towards Britain's professional soldiers, [and] . . . civilian imitation of military organization, discipline, paraphernalia, and certain features of British religious life."[6] Anderson concluded that positive attitudes toward the military became possible after the public debate about the Crimea experience and about the performance of British soldiers in the Indian Mutiny. The process of public acceptance of the army accelerated also with the coincidental increase in attention paid to domestic missions as religious groups in the 1860s began to target populations in the home islands for care and conversion.

According to Anderson, army leadership acquiesced to the religious revival of the army because of manpower problems after Crimea. This thesis does not seem sufficient. Certainly the British army that went to Crimea was undersize and short of reserves. The wartime effort to raise the Foreign Legion demonstrates the fact. But Britain had faced military manpower shortages before. Most notably during the wars of the French Revolution and Napoleon (also earlier in the Seven Years' War and the American Revolution, wars notable for British resort to mercenaries), British armies suffered chronic shortages of troops. Yet during these crises, army leaders never turned to religion to increase the attractiveness of service. The era of the 1830s witnessed evangelical victories (and noble "lost causes") such as the abolition of the slave trade, the abolition of slavery in the empire, the first efforts at factory legislation, assaults upon corporal punishment in the military, as well as nonreligiously motivated reforms such as the parliamentary and municipality reform. At that time though, military leadership rejected the idea of moral reform among the ranks or officer corps. Even after the religious reforms within the army, manpower problems did not disappear, nor did they after the extensive works of Lord Cardwell. The manpower thesis appears inadequate.[7] The timing and the content of the army decision to accept religious changes and new religious practices among the troops stemmed from changing expectations about the army that grew up inside and outside of it.

Thus enters the concept of Christian heroism. Along with (and on the basis of) administrative and institutional changes in the army there occurred growth and metamorphosis in the public conversation about the army and about the Christianity it confronted at home and represented abroad. Even as Gordon bounced along on camelback toward his death at Khartoum, what already had resulted from nearly thirty years of public moral scrutiny of the troops and leaders of the army was the expectation, even the demand, for a morally good army.

The belief in a morally good army in turn explained something of the empire to the British people, and of the practical value of Christianity to those who would justify its dominating public presence. It will become evident that what the public (and authorities) were evaluating when they spoke (or wrote) of Havelock or Gordon was far less the men themselves but a created understanding of the "Christian Soldier"; of a "white" empire over the "nonwhites"; of the "out there" in which each man died; and finally of a "British Christianity" itself.

Of these ingredients, Christianity poses a particularly difficult problem. One need not accuse nineteenth-century Britons of having politicized Christianity to serve their own imperial ends. Citing instances of cynicism would hardly constitute a discovery. It is better simply to note that Christianity among nineteenth-century Britons was a many-faceted phenomenon. As Anderson showed, British Protestantism encompassed a political and military imperial component in the 1880s. This study links that development to internal army reforms even prior to Crimea. This politicized synthesis created a complex environment wherein sincere Christians who also represented the British government or state could easily conflate their spiritual and secular allegiances. Motives for action could be mixed to a bewildering degree, which is to say that a simple model of cynical cultural imperialism will not help us here.

Nonetheless, this highly politicized state Christianity does account for some important effects. The confrontation between a Christian nation and non-Christians, the very distinction between them being a common means of British imperial self-definition, demanded that the distinction be clear. British soldiers had to be "Christians," and they had to be so in a way that collapsed the very real differences among them and exaggerated their "differentness" from the "subject races."[8] This notion augments Anderson's explanation of the emergence between 1856 and 1900 of a "Christian" as opposed to an "Anglican" army in a country with an established church.[9]

The political tendency to see a "British Protestantism"[10] allowed for a particular version of Crusade ethic that put to rest difficulties concerning the legitimacy of the paradoxical notions of "Christian army" or "Christian warrior." This was not a paradox unnoticed at the time. The Peace Society, for example, kept in publication during the Crimean War years pamphlets that sought to dissuade on Christian moral grounds young men from wanting to fight in the Crimea.[11] Perhaps the successful notion of Christian warrior is but an exchange of nomenclature with the concepts of "manly Christianity" or "muscular Christianity." Nonetheless, this Crusade ethic linked the general population to its imperial agents, its army.

At the turn of the nineteenth century the British soldier was an object of public scorn. Only the worst of society was believed to inhabit its ranks. For the army later to go forth as a national representative, as it did in part at Crimea, and as it did wholly in the acquisition and maintenance of colonies, something had to change. If having an empire was a success or a good thing, it did not easily follow that the worst people in British society would have won it and protected it. Should not they rather have been good, or at least have had a healthy presence of good in them? Or, failing that, would observers in British society have then had to acknowledge the possibility that the empire was not a good thing?

Christianity as a policy rationale justified an aggressive stance and vocabulary in the press and popular discussion about the empire. It became unto itself one *raison d'être* of empire. "We're here because we're here because . . . ," to quote a later group of British soldiers. This is very clear in the case of Gordon. When once he was trapped in Khartoum, regardless of why he had gone there, or whether he could extricate himself, or even whether he represented the British government at all or instead was a private functionary in the pay of a foreign government, rhetoric about Gordon's piety became interchangeable with the inherent value of British presence. That presence, in turn, became the reason expressed in the papers why the government should undertake difficult, protracted, and expensive military operations to extricate Gordon. This is not to equate imperialism with politicized Christianity. But as a review of the public speech on Havelock and Gordon will show, this "Christianity of empire" became a means at home to explain and understand the British imperial presence overseas.

Return then to the heroes.[12] Born at Monk Wearmouth in 1795, Henry Havelock was the son of a shipbuilder and financial speculator. His mother was an Evangelical Anglican, and took great pains to instill her faith in her children. In Henry she was successful, and throughout his youth, early education, and first years in the army, he appears to have remained a loyal Anglican of the Evangelical bent.[13] His older brother was an army staff officer in the peninsular campaigns and at Waterloo, and used his good record to get Henry a spot in the infantry. Henry accepted a commission in the Ninety-fifth Regiment of Foot but, having no family fortune, had thereafter to rely upon means other than purchase for promotion. He remained with this unit in England for eight years, then transferred to the Thirteenth Foot bound for India in 1823. Since he could not purchase, assuming a vacancy in a unit bound for long-term foreign service was a logical career move.[14]

Later, as a part of the mystique of Havelock's hero image his glacially slow rise in rank was attributed to his religious belief.[15] When he arrived in India in 1823, he met and fell in love with Hannah Shepherd Marshman, whose father was a well-known Baptist missionary in Serampore. Hannah and Henry finally married in 1829, one of the first results of the union being his conversion from Anglicanism to the Baptist faith. From this personal choice evolved the promotion story; historians have relied upon it since. Anderson noted that Havelock "had apparently been the victim of the prejudices of the governing class, particularly the officer class" and that "it was on account of his religious zeal that he had suffered."[16] This conclusion reads too much twentieth-century secular assumption back into the actual record.[17]

Before 1867, the British army relied heavily upon the system of purchase for the promotion of its officers. More than fossilized tradition, this system remained a conscious choice and the favorite of the duke of Wellington. It was designed to secure highest rank only for aristocrats and gentlemen of means, and supposedly as a safeguard against cronyism.[18] Nonpurchase officers had to rely upon either the attrition of warfare and disease or the retirement of superiors (who did not sell their slots first) to open paths of advancement. Commonly, men of merit and long service in the Crown's Line Forces suffered the indignity of being superseded by younger, less experienced officers who nonetheless had the cash to purchase ahead in rank.[19] One critic of the system in Havelock's era complained that he had watched a senior major passed over for command of a regiment by a younger purchase officer. The older man was a veteran of Waterloo, "had fought in Spain under Wellington, in India under Gough, and at the Cape under Smith. He had thirty years experience and had more than once led the regiment into action. The junior had but ten years in the army, and being twenty-six years of age, must have been born four years after his senior had entered the service. But he had the requisite fourteen hundred pounds [to purchase promotion]."[20] Under such a system, personal opinions alone could hardly have accounted for all difficulties associated with achieving rank.

Other slips of conduct beyond the realm of one's religious convictions could be important, too. Indeed, Havelock's Evangelicalism was unfashionable and did earn him disapproval of some brother officers.[21] But so did the unwise decision, made not once but twice in his career, to publish accounts of army operations: in Burma and later in Afghanistan. In both works Havelock criticized his superior officers and the conduct of the campaigns. These books did little to earn him the esteem or confidence of the officer corps. It is in spite of these two literary efforts that he enjoyed what career successes he did.[22]

During the time Havelock was fighting his last campaign in India, the story of religious repression began to gain credence in the English press. In October 1857, there appeared in the *Times* coverage of a meeting of the Hibernian Bible Society at Belfast. At the meeting, one Reverend Mr. Graham rose to speak in praise of the Christian hero and related the following story. He had it on good authority, he said, that whether in the field or in bivouac, Havelock, as a regimental commander, had long been in the practice of raising what Graham called "the Bethel Flag"[23] over a tent of a Sunday morning and inviting the men in for Scripture reading and preaching. Apparently Havelock even baptized converts who experienced a change of heart at these meetings. Soon however, "complaint was made" (by whom Graham did not say) that Havelock's behavior was disruptive and ungentlemanly. The issue came before Gough, Indian commander in chief. Before acting, he reviewed the crime and discipline records of Havelock's regiment. Finding that the statistics for drunkenness, flogging, and imprisonment for Havelock's unit were by far the lowest in the army, Gough supposedly said, "Go tell Colonel Havelock, with my compliments, to baptize the whole army."[24]

The story is interesting for a number of reasons. For one, it contains all the elements of what would become the pattern for the English Christian hero. Havelock appears much more the missionary or the preacher than the soldier. His presence in India combines saving souls and administering baptism with the military maintenance of empire. There is the "resistance" from nameless complainers who try to stop Havelock's ministry. By blatant implication—the reference to "gentlemanliness" and the fact that the complaints go to Gough—some other officers in Havelock's regiment are the opposition. This notion fit well with the evangelical diagnosis of the Mutiny: official compromise with the heathen and the slothful attitudes of officials who refused to rule India with an explicitly Christian government.[25]

Havelock's own assessment of the Mutiny varied from this theme. He generally agreed with the idea that "morally lax" government in Bengal contributed to the rising, but his overall perspective, as one might imagine, was military. He wrote, "The fact stated in a few words is, that this vast body of mercenary soldiery [the mutineers] felt its power, and formed the guilty determination of using it. It was met with words when it should have found bayonets and grape-shot, and the peril of its temporary success has been and is great." Yet he added, speaking of the necessary campaign of repression, "It has to me, at sixty-three, all the charm of a romance. I am as happy as a duck in thunder."[26]

The story concludes with the vindication (and a mainstay of evangelical literature was the vindication of tested believers) when Gough's review of the matter convinces him of Havelock's worth. The power of evangelical religion to run the empire shines in the low crime statistics among the men under Havelock. Therefore, the story closes with Gough's prescription of a dose of Havelock for the whole army.

Four days after the preaching story ran, the *Times* printed a letter to the editors in partial refutation. This letter, signed "Amicus," was apparently written by none other than Havelock's wife, for it portrays the author as an "intimate" confident of the

General for over thirty years, and relates conversations that occurred privately between Mrs. Havelock and Lord William Bentinck. Amicus admitted that Havelock had led prayers among the troops, but denied he had ever preached and, even more emphatically, that he had ever baptized anyone. She pointed out that the General was of the opinion that "independently of the religious benefit of these [prayer meetings], it was a most desirable object to keep the men from licentious indulgences in a conquered town by the strength of Christian principle."[27]

She also felt compelled to make more detailed corrections to the version originally published. The issue of Havelock's religiosity did not come up when he was a regimental commander (relatively late in his career) but much sooner, after his conversion to the Baptists in 1830. In 1835 Colonel Robert Sale, commander of the Thirteenth Foot, offered Lieutenant Havelock the adjutancy of the regiment. Some junior officers of the Thirteenth attempted to block the appointment on the grounds that as a religious "fanatic," Havelock was no gentleman. The case went before Lord William Bentinck, who was then commander in chief in Bengal. Mrs. Havelock visited him in support of her husband's claim, a bold move based upon her former work for Lady Bentinck as an interpreter. In a meeting that followed, Bentinck did indeed make reference to the low crime rate in Havelock's half company (a significantly smaller unit than a regiment); but he also was annoyed by the backbiting complaints against Havelock. He approved Havelock's appointment, and in jest at the close of the interview said, "Tell Lieutenant Havelock, with my compliments, I wish he could make Baptists of all the army."[28]

The differences in the two versions offer some food for thought. In the second, ostensibly from Mrs. Havelock herself, the resistance to Havelock's appointment seems as much a class issue as a theological one. Brother officers complained not only against Havelock's theology per se, but that a gentleman would never appear the enthusiast of any stripe, nor would he fraternize with the lesser classes in the other ranks.[29] Moreover, Amicus emphasized military discipline and control in order to explain Havelock's religious instruction of his troops. Finally, there is the lighthearted manner in which she accepts Bentinck's comment about Baptists in the army. These differences in the story, versions of which began to circulate in the British press within a month of Havelock achieving any fame at all, demonstrated how quickly and in what manner the politically Christian public appropriated Havelock to their purposes.

Contrary to the story of religious sacrifice, Havelock's military efficiency during his career earned him several staff appointments: regimental adjutant, divisional aide-de-camp, deputy adjutant general to the Queen's Troops in Bombay, and finally adjutant general for the Queen's Troops in India. Some of these positions involved brevet promotions[30] and offered bonuses in prestige and pay to supplement the deficiencies of each in Havelock's substantive rank. Moreover, each of the several such appointments through which Havelock sustained himself, his family, and his military career involved the approval and support of a patron. Authorities granting Havelock such appointments included Lord Hardinge, the duke of Wellington, Sir Hugh Gough (famous for his bloody battles in the Sikh Wars), and Lord Bentinck, commander in chief of the Queen's Forces in India. These men, hardly a pack of evangelical cronies, preferred Havelock for his efficiency, language skills (both he and his wife could translate Bengali), and knowledge of operational procedures.

So, while Havelock achieved substantive promotion slowly, and while he did occasionally run into expressions of antireligious prejudice, there is little reason to conclude that his career suffered solely from the antireligious notions of his military superiors. Indeed, any officer with as little money as Havelock had would have struggled desperately to maintain himself and a family, let alone progress up the ladder of promotion. Only later, when Havelock's special status as Christian warrior and conqueror of heathen hordes evolved out of his Mutiny campaign, did the prejudice story gain widespread credence and importance.

After all, a common evangelical interpretation of the Mutiny concluded that God had allowed Christian rule in India to falter because it had made compromises with pagan idolatry. Subsequent historians adopted the promotion story because it figured largely in an 1860 biography of Havelock by his brother-in-law, J. C. Marshman, himself of perhaps the second most important Baptist missionary family in India.[31] This biography, discussed below, was precisely the sort of text which created the domestic public knowledge of the army abroad.

There are other facets of Havelock's personality that do not correspond to his public persona or to the character historians have attributed to him since his death. For one thing, he had a rather worldly interest in education and the classics, idolizing the Latin of Livy and Caesar.[32] "Middle class" by virtue of being the son of a shipbuilder/owner, he himself was educated first by a private tutor, then at public school at Charterhouse. He very much enjoyed his early education, and even approved of the hazing and stern discipline at the school. For the rest of his life he looked back upon his school years with affection. There is no mention of his having suffered in any real way for his beliefs or from any corruption at the school.[33]

As an officer, Havelock became a gentleman. As such he enjoyed a good dinner, good conversation, and even a good glass of wine. Indeed, he did promote temperance among the troops, but anyone familiar with the drinking habits of the mid-nineteenth-century British soldiery would understand that policy without reference to religious motivations. Eventually he did follow a regimen of drinking only water himself, but he believed it good for his ailing liver as much or more than for his soul.[34] His views on alcohol had much to do with class prejudice, strongly reinforced with the unpleasant experiences of watching British troops drink themselves stuporous and/or mutinous in Burma, Bengal, and Afghanistan and during his own glorified campaign against the 1857 Mutiny. He never separated the issues of clean living and social (and military) discipline, so it is inaccurate to portray him as a doctrinaire teetotaler. At any rate, abstinence as a strict article of general evangelical Protestant Christianity became common only later in the nineteenth century.[35]

Havelock died at Lucknow on 24 November 1857, after having suffered four days from a bout of dysentery. On 25 September, he had successfully completed at least part of his task by forcing passage to the British population besieged there. Unfortunately for him, he had done so with a force insufficient to fight a withdrawal from the city. He and his command settled in with the British already at Lucknow, a surrounded garrison. They remained so until a further military force under Sir Colin Campbell relieved Lucknow for a second time on 17 November.[36]

This unsatisfactory half achievement stemmed from a military blunder Havelock made the night he reached the Residency at Lucknow. Instead of consolidating his forces and reconnoitering his ground, he decided, when within a mile of his goal, to force a direct march to the compound by way of a heavily defended street. The resulting carnage weakened his already understrength column, and did nothing for the garrison that could not have been done the following day, by a safer route. Back in England his reputation remained immune from this mistake.[37]

So Havelock the person differed significantly from Havelock the persona. As often happens to people who become famous, what others said about him became more important than the man himself. The geographic distance between Havelock and his public only exacerbated the tendency. Communications from India to Great Britain in 1857 could take weeks, even with the use of telegraph.[38] In the absence of timely information, organs of public opinion suffered great pressure to create a knowledge of Havelock. During the time of the actual fighting in India, reports filtered back to London via telegraph, personal letters, military dispatches, and diplomatic courier. These sources supported the *Times* coverage of the Mutiny between May 1857 and January 1858. Despite the time lag in communications, the campaign, and particularly the reported massacres of British women and children, was followed with hysterical interest at home.[39]

In most of the reports in the *Times*, Havelock's actual combat exploits received thoroughly military consideration, without much reference to his person, character, or mission. Yet the the tone of the national conversation concerning the Mutiny was highly charged with issues of religion, morality, and divine will. The *Times* reflected this in its extensive coverage of the National Day of Humiliation and Prayer, the reporting of which included lengthy transcriptions of sermons and prayers of penitence regarding the British failure to Christianize India.[40] Additionally, in letters to the editor, and in anecdotal coverage such as the story from the Hibernian Bible Society meeting, the paper helped to create the broad public understanding of the man who embodied the best Christian efforts to break the usurping heathen. With knowledge of his death in England, various commentators outside the daily press began to expand upon the meaning of Havelock, creating of him a Christian avenger against the heathen masses of darkness.

Immediately that it became known in England, Havelock's death excited a great public lamentation. Beginning in January 1858,[41] the *Times* carried almost daily coverage of public subscriptions to erect monuments to the General or to make gifts to Mrs. Havelock. In February, these reports still appeared with weekly regularity, biweekly in March and April. The last of these to make the *Times* appeared in June, a full six months after public knowledge of Havelock's death.[42] Significantly, in death and while Havelock yet lived, his greatest supporters were not officials of the government or the court. Instead, he was a "people's man," especially the darling of critics of aristocratic control of the armed forces.

In a letter to the editor dated 25 September 1857, one reader of the *Times* complained of the government's failure to reward Havelock's services in India. England ought never forgive her governors should Havelock be allowed to die without an appropriate display of gratitude to him. After all, the French would never leave such a hero without official national honors. The editors concurred, using the opportunity to poke at the government. In a long note at the close of the letter, the editors remarked, "Our Correspondent should make allowance for the fact that there is scarcely a Minister in London, that Lord Panmure is more intent on the destruction of grouse than of Mutineers, and the 'fountain of honour itself' is far away in the Highlands, out of reach even of telegraph."[43]

The government of course had to respond to such criticisms. On the twenty-first Havelock had been awarded a Good Service pension of £100 a year for his campaign before Cawnpore. A week later, after an outcry at the paucity of the award, he received a Knight Commandership of the Bath.[44] He died unaware of these honors. With his death, responsibility to laud him passed from his superiors and the government to a public who needed and wanted him more.

9

The Hero Becomes an Icon

During the first months after Havelock's death, and with the fading interest of the daily press, biographies began to appear that built in the public mind a union of Havelock's piety and his martial skill. Several of these were tremendously popular.[1] J. C. Marshman produced the authoritative text. His biography of Havelock was characteristic Victorian fare: praising, admiring, and based upon the stringing together of one letter or diary entry after another. Marshman's value stemmed from his thoroughness, and from his preservation of many Havelock letters. Additionally, Marshman spoke authoritatively as a veteran of India mission work, and as the General's brother-in-law. This ponderous and very respectable book, which did not appear until 1860, enjoyed an enduring popularity, supporting a reprint in 1867 and a second edition in 1878.[2]

In contrast, one of the earliest tributes, *A Biographical Sketch of Sir Henry Havelock*, by the Reverend William Brock, entered its fifth edition before the close of 1858.[3] It is a curious fact that historians of the Havelock phenomenon have missed the significance of Brock and his little book. Like Marshman, Brock too had been a personal friend of Havelock. But in 1858, he had also been the prominent first pastor of the Baptist Bloomsbury Chapel for ten years.[4] He was an experienced debater and apologist. In 1834 he made extensive speaking tours of Norfolk and Suffolk decrying West Indian slavery, unmasking the planters' attempts to use "apprenticeship" to stave off the impact of real emancipation.[5] The talents Brock thus developed appeared in full force in his polemical defense of Christian empire. In 1859, after his Havelock biography was out, he was one of the first pastors in London to take advantage of the theater format for his preaching, a means by which he continued to reach large numbers of people.[6] He was, for all these reasons, a man of some public celebrity, and his Havelock book enjoyed all the more popularity for that fact.

The career and reputation of Brock are of some importance and make him worthy of a pause. Was it so natural for a Baptist minister in the 1850s to champion a military man and the cause of empire? For most of the nineteenth century, Nonconformity as a block remained critical of empire and imperialism.[7] This was true perhaps for reasons of class, as Nonconformity rested squarely on the shoulders of the middle and lower-middle classes, who had much to pay for and little to gain from empire; perhaps for reasons of politics, as by the 1860s the Liberal party successfully ensnared these same constituencies; and perhaps for reasons of philosophy and religion, as in the 1850s Nonconformist ideas on foreign affairs traced origins to spokesmen like Richard Cobden and John Bright.[8]

Moreover, in the mid-1850s, Nonconformity and Dissent still had battles to win at home. Non-Anglicans did not have full and equal participation in the state, despite the landmark 1828 repeal of the Test and Corporation Acts. In 1857, a non-Anglican still bore with several social disadvantages because of his religious identity. Until 1868, the Church of England benefited from the imposition of church rates upon all residents of a parish, regardless of actual religious affiliation. This caused much disgruntlement; cases of "rate resisters" forfeiting their property were common. Until 1871, the ancient universities maintained a ban on anyone but an Anglican obtaining a fellowship or tutor's post. Even the rite of burial was an official Anglican monopoly until 1880.[9] Many Nonconformists in the 1850s still experienced a certain alienation from the state and monarchy; they were willing to agitate for reforms like disestablishment of the state church, willing to resist the state and its taxes if such supported the unjust establishment. Axiomatically, Nonconformity as it existed among the solid middle classes, as it existed among the Baptists of Bloomsbury Chapel, kept its sons out of the army.[10]

The historical consensus on political Nonconformity holds that as late as 1870, that section of British society remained ardently antiimperial.[11] By 1900, however, the situation had changed, and the majority of Nonconformists, like Britons at large, had converted to the imperial banner.[12] Historians usually explain that fact by referring to a number of new circumstances: the passing of Gladstone (and his failure on Home Rule); the subsequent emergence of the Liberal Imperialists; the particular circumstances of the Boer War, including the race oppression attributed to Boer rule in South Africa; the economic integration of the middle classes into imperial and general overseas trade; and the political integration of Nonconformity into society and state. Brock and his apologia for Havelock give pause to these generalizations. Obviously, his campaign predates the general Nonconformist conversion by some thirty years. His position at Bloomsbury Chapel made him a leader among the numerous lower-middle-class and artisan London Baptists, the very sort of Nonconformists who supposedly marched lockstep with Gladstonian antiimperialism.

For Brock, then, Havelock presented several opportunities. Foremost, Brock knew the general and wanted to memorialize a good man. Secondly, Havelock illustrated Brock's favorite evangelical strategy. In contradiction to antiimperial wisdom, Brock believed the empire was precisely the field for zealous Christian piety. For some time there had raged a fierce debate among the British as to whether or not India would best be governed by an explicitly Christian imperial regime. According to Brock, Havelock's career was the "irrefutable refutation" of the establishment knock on "enthusiasm." Thirdly, this argument constituted a potential bridge between Nonconformity and Anglicanism.[13] Critics of the East India Company (EIC) ban on missionaries and its refusal to organize its political power in India along Christian lines existed in practically all the Christian denominations of Britain. The Mutiny, if cast as a failure of the EIC secular policy and a triumph for the religious champion Havelock, could give birth to a great ecumenical consensus on good rule in India and, consequently, on political decisions at home. As Brock explicitly argued in his book, Havelock's story was a prophecy for the Christian party in Britain to seize direction of the empire. It offered the chance for the "outsider" Brock to lead mainstream opinion, and to do so validated by the very religious background that had made him an "outsider" in the first place. These were Brock's arguments, and his book sold very well indeed.

There are other reasons as well to take Brock's book as the model of Havelock hagiography. More than having an author famous in Nonconformist circles, Brock's biography was the first such publication to benefit from a reliance on some of Havelock's actual papers. It had the approval and cooperation of J. C. Marshman, who later produced that comprehensive volume acclaimed to be the fullest portrayal of the "authentic" Havelock. Finally, in his book, especially the first third, dealing with Havelock's early life and military days, Brock was at pains to define the imperial Christian hero through Havelock. Therefore, and especially because the book was such an instant success, Brock's biography goes a long way toward establishing the details of the Christian hero, and the ways in which episodes of Havelock's life became public explications of the ideal.

From the outset, Brock argued that the true value of Havelock's story was the hope and direction it offered for Britain's future hold on India.[14] For Brock, British rule was unambiguously identified with the Christianization of India. That indeed ought to be the ultimate reason for the imperial presence in the subcontinent. In his opening apologia, Brock pleaded with even pacifist Christians to pray for the soldiers in India. "Under God, more than we can imagine depends upon them, and will depend on them, in the transition which India is preparing to undergo," the first step of which would be the thorough Christianization of the colonial government itself. "Of all patronage of idolatry they [Christian soldiers like Havelock] will be ashamed, and against all official attendance on its services they will protest. The European community in India will gradually get to be as much ashamed of it as themselves, whilst the native communities will be made to feel that the Christian religion is a reality, and not a sham; a religion too which, for its practical benignity and power, deserves to be examined by them, and personally received."[15]

Brock next set out to defeat the notion that Christianity had to be weak, or passive in the face of resistance; or that otherworldliness might make the Christian an underachiever in this life. This he did by creating out of Havelock's childhood and schooling an image of a young boy at once fearless, thoughtful, and disdainful of peer pressures, yet appreciative of worldly achievements. In a section titled "Incipient Godliness," Brock described Havelock's first efforts at pious living while enrolled at Charterhouse. There, we are told, most boys rejected vital religion and slandered the believers with the epithets of "Methodist" and "canting hypocrite." Heedless of their slurs, Havelock and a few stalwarts held their own Scripture readings, discussed and debated printed sermons, and helped each other to develop faith.

But the key here is Brock's urgency to assure the reader that Havelock was every inch a "true boy." While the young student strengthened his resolve to be godly, he nonetheless longed for the pleasures his classmates pursued. "The lovers of pleasure might seem to have the best of it. [Havelock] did not pretend to any sort of stoicism whatever. He did not deny for a moment that what they said was true about fun and frolic. Old heads were not to be looked for on young shoulders."[16]

But Havelock, despite the call of fleeting earthly pleasures, grew vitally through his faith in God.

> In his esteem the fear of God was neither doleful nor dismal in the least degree. He could cultivate that, and read Greek and Latin with any of them. He could search the Scriptures and pray to God, and yet do anything that it was manly or virtuous to do, either in the playground or elsewhere. And there was nothing manly or virtuous that he was not all the more ready to do because in simplicity and godly sincerity he walked with God. . . . His Christianity increased rather than diminished his enjoyment. His godliness felt that it had the promise of the life that now is, as well as of that which is to come.[17]

From this premise, Brock then proceeded to translate "manliness" to power. It was not enough for Havelock merely to dodge emasculation by his Christian faith. Brock would have him exert the manhood that Christianity actually enhanced. In other words, Havelock's Christianity did more than stay out of the way; it was the actual reason behind his power and heroism. An essay on manliness, though a handy tool, was far from Brock's purpose. He wished to gather up all of Havelock's admirable traits within his Chrisitianity, because Christianity had far more social power than other categories of achievement. Marshman made the same point in the last pages of his *Memoirs*. For him, Havelock's Christianity was the source of the general's strength and the inspiration of his military prowess. With refined but fervent Baptist beliefs, the General tapped into the heritage of the English soldier-saint. Marshman wrote, "More than any other chief did he appear to combine the great military talents of the generals of the Commonwealth with the fervour—though not the fanaticism—of their religious feelings."[18]

Brock concerned himself first with intellectual power. A Christian conversion of the evangelical sort, which Havelock finally experienced in transit to India in 1823, did not require the believer to compromise his intellectual powers; it focused them. Christian faith, in part, was an intellectual achievement. "Accustomed as [Havelock] was to the exercise of his intellectual faculties, and somewhat competent by his educational training to investigate and decide upon the merits of a case, he examined the claims of the so-called glad tidings [of Christ] upon his attention, and he decided that they were by all means to be received.

It was not fanatical, . . . it was philosophical to accept the mission of Jesus Christ as Divine."[19]

Havelock convinced himself, then the power of his intellect began to sway the religious beliefs of others.

> To those . . . who were willing to converse on the subject, [Havelock] showed that never were men more mistaken if they imagined they must sacrifice their mental manhood in order to have faith in the Redeemer, or if they supposed that they must cease to exercise their minds the moment they exercised faith in the Son of God. No pains did the Lord's freeman spare in the attempt to convince [others] that the exercise of faith in well-attested evidence is one of the noblest exercises of mind, and that the employment of mental manhood in conforming oneself to Christ is the sublimest employment to which any manhood can attain.[20]

This spiritually charged power also heightened Havelock's proficiency as a military officer. Here Brock relied upon an anecdote, which by the time of Havelock's death had become household currency in Britain. Early in his career, Havelock participated in the subjugation of Burma. One night during the campaign, runs the story, a British encampment that included Havelock's Thirteenth Infantry Regiment was attacked by surprise. When Sir Archibald Campbell ordered a "particular corps" to the defense, the men of that unit were too drunk to fight or take commands. With the situation deteriorating and the camp in danger, Campbell is supposed to have bellowed, "Call out Havelock's saints; they are never drunk, and Havelock is always ready." Immediately this was done, the Thirteenth repulsed the Burmese attack.[21]

Having established Havelock's intellectual and martial prowess, Brock needed only to link the increase of personal power, grounded in Christianity, to an increase in national or imperial power. Again describing Havelock's first foreign campaigns in the Burmese War of 1824–26, Brock portrayed the young officer as self-consciously integrating his Christian experience into his military efforts. "Havelock was practically anxious about the heathen and their salvation. With the men whose especial object it was to preach the Gospel to the natives, and to translate the sacred Scriptures into the vernaculars of India, he had great sympathy. [No matter who] would despise them, and counsel their dismissal, at any risk he would take their part. It was, after all, not by the sword that India could be retained. Unless a moral and religious influence could be propagated, well was he assured that our dominion there must ultimately lick the dust."[22]

Thus developed the picture of the Christian hero and the role of Christian religion in his life of adventure. It is important to note that by the time Brock and Marshman wrote, they did not feel it necessary or desirable to defend Havelock as a Baptist hero. Discussing possible obstacles posed by Havelock's religion to his promotion, Brock relied not upon Anglican versus Dissenter but instead upon the image of Believer versus Unbeliever. Marshman did the same, claiming, "There was more moral courage in [Havelock] assembling his men to read the Bible and to sing psalms, amidst the jeers of his brother officers [who did not worship at all], than in leading them to storm a battery, amidst the bullets of the enemy."[23]

As he sought to link the notions of evangelical Christianity to the successful maintenance of power in India, Brock carefully cultivated a sense of an ecumenical confrontation between a band of believing Christians and their pagan subjects. Just as Havelock belonged to the Thirteenth Foot but thereby served within an entire army, Brock argued that Havelock belonged to the Baptists, but thereby served the greater cause of Christianity in India. He quoted a speech made by Havelock to the Evangelical Alliance (which Havelock helped to found) at Bombay in 1849: "[Havelock] conceived that all [members of the Alliance] brought with them their faith in all its strength and vitality. They left . . . at the door of the place of assembly the husks and shell of their creed, but brought into the midst of their brethren the precious kernel."[24]

There is in Brock and in Marshman an effort to play down the specific idea of "Dissenting martyr" while replacing it with a more nebulous image of "struggling Christian." Commenting on Havelock's practice of Bible services with his men, Brock wrote, "No proof was necessary of a man's being 'a Baptist soldier' before he could be allowed to join in the praise and prayer and instruction of [Havelock's] assembly. Every man in the regiment was welcome. But the design not being to sectarianize, the Lieutenant left their coming or their staying away entirely free."[25]

Marshman heartily agreed. He emphasized a particular letter from Havelock to the elder Marshman in which Havelock, far from conspiring to make Baptists of all the men, worried that his efforts with the Baptist troops might be a transgression. After all, Havelock had no recognized ministry within the Baptist church. "I have . . . on three occasions read them a sermon, but as often as seven times preached to them, that is read to them a discourse composed by myself. I would gladly know from you what is your opinion. Is this an [*sic*] heresy? Is it contrary to Scripture, since I have not been 'separated' to the work, but belong to a secular and active calling? . . . We have no minister, or I should not dream of intruding in the sacred office."[26]

Far then from the sectarian troublemaker, this Christian hero is the imperialist *par excellence*, for he offers a great unity of purpose and solves many of the logical and ethical problems of imperial enterprise. Firstly, his real mission is religious, the spread of Christianity; not the fractious Christianity of contending sects and denominations, but a unified (Protestant) Christianity held almost synonymous with Western civilization, in line with authority and national purpose. This Christianity itself is a creation for the hero, as it ignores the infinite varieties within the Western churches, and assumes the precedence of the social-political role of religion over the personal-spiritual. The very question of the morality of the imperial presence is begged by the immediate reference to the good of spreading this harmonious Christian religion.

Some could argue that this mission might necessarily entail the spread of "good government." In some vocabularies the two were synonymous. Havelock's hero image illustrates the point magnificently. He is a religious leader, not an infantry commander. He ministers to and teaches discipline to his troops. He does not order them or expend their lives in combat. He rallies them. His military successes, in Burma, in Afghanistan, or during the Mutiny, are by the grace of God. Although the hero faces some obstacles from ungodly coimperialists, his only real enemies are the godless heathen whom he will subjugate; it is made clear not only that the subjugation is just, but that the indigenous people need it.

All of this was a particular myth for domestic consumption, not a reality of empire on the ground. There is little historical record to support the crude notion of British imperialism assaulting a target population with Bible in one hand and sword in the other. Instead missionaries and military/imperial authorities were often themselves at odds. The problem of a general division between missionaries and imperialists in the nineteenth century relates to a division of motives. The commissioner, army officer, or governor looked upon an imperial charge with an eye to quiet administration, stable control over native populations, or even profitability of enterprise in his region. The missionary arrived in a colony with expressly different goals.

After all, the missionary impulse was one to spread Christianity. This necessarily entailed a cultural and spiritual confrontation between the missionary and the "missionized." Such conflict hardly conduced quiet administration or easy control. But the missionary operated from personal motives like a self-defined humanitarianism, a personal asceticism, a sense of religious debt, romanticism, apocalypticism/millenarianism, and finally Christ's own admonition to go forth to all the nations.[27] These had little to do with a quiet presence.

Moreover, whereas colonial authorities represented but one government within boundaries set by conquest, international arbitration, or *de facto* military presence, missionaries roamed where their calling took them. Representatives from the different denominations of one country frequently competed for converts out of the same native population. It also meant that whereas administrators and soldiers faced serious political and martial restraints upon unlimited expansion, especially in areas with other colonizers close by, missionaries could dare to the extent of personal courage. There is little here to suggest a complicitous relationship between missionaries and imperial agents.[28]

Various incidents of clashes between the missionary and the imperial official occurred throughout the British Empire and at home in the nineteenth century. Havelock in India would have been familiar with them. Between 1793 and 1813, in the years shortly before his arrival, factions within the British East Indian Company fought a bitter battle over whether or not to reverse the company ban on missionaries in Bengal. The Evangelicals in favor of lifting the ban eventually won, but the consequences of that argument reverberated until the Great Mutiny of 1857.[29] In 1806 Sepoy troops mutinied at Vellore, and reports in England that fear of religious coercion had motivated the mutineers set off a furious debate. Both during and after the 1857 fighting, British observers and officials squabbled over the religious culpability, or lack of it, of the company administration in Bengal.[30]

Havelock was a paradox. As a military officer in India, he was an enforcer of the British presence there. As an evangelical Christian, he belonged to a group of people who throughout the nineteenth century were suspicious of British imperial authority and critical of official religious complacency. The Havelock phenomenon defies explanation in terms of imperialist theory; it should be recognized as an image that emerged out of his career was for domestic consumption. It was not a recipe for imperial authority. It instructed the home public (or at least a part of it) in how to understand the existence of an empire, not at its inception or in its administration, but as a given reality of everyday life.

It is difficult to imagine another moment since the era of Cromwell and the New Model Army when there could have been a credible union between soldiery and religion. Certainly, such an ideology did not emerge during the wars of the French Revolution and Napoleon. Nobody in 1820 would have believed a word about pious British soldiers securing Christian rule anywhere. A disreputable army, like the one of 1819–20, or a disreputable military establishment such as supported the yeoman cavalry at Peterloo, simply could not withstand the burden of a popular Christian-soldier. If the army had not itself undergone change previous to the 1850s, there would have been no vessel to receive the contents of Christian militarism.

Other Cultural Factors: The Cromwell Renaissance

In addition to the politics of empire, cultural changes in Britain reflected upon the place of the army. Two currents, perhaps interrelated, contributed to a renaissance of a military-religious ethic. The first was the revival of the reputation of Oliver Cromwell. Since the days immediately following the death of the lord protector and the scattering of Puritan bones in the courtyard of St. Margaret's, Cromwell had haunted popular British mythology. He was the archetype of tyrant, regicide, defamer, and destroyer of the constitution, and religious fanatic. His combination of religious zeal and martial skill remained a bogeyman to the Anglican establishment of the eighteenth century. Brock, in praising Havelock, had called him a Cromwell in a Wellington, but cautiously insisted that Havelock was free of all "enthusiasm."

In the early 1840s, the traditional anti-Cromwellian opinion began to change, thanks in part to the works of Thomas Carlyle. In these years, Carlyle was just emerging into a general fame in England and Scotland. He had begun his public intellectual rise with admirable translations of Goethe, and a biography of Schiller in the 1820s. For more than a decade after these moderate successes, his career proceeded only fitfully, energized in the late 1830s by his history of the French Revolution. After that success, he developed a series of lectures, of which perhaps the most popular was his collection on heroes and hero-worship. These he presented to the London literary circles. The *French Revolution* established Carlyle as an eminent historian. From this secure base he launched into his controversial sympathetic reading of the seventeenth-century Puritan movement and a subsequent defense of Oliver Cromwell.

For Carlyle, the case was simple enough. His own readings of seventeenth- and eighteenth-century Cromwell biographies had convinced him of their scholarly inadequacies. The authors were primarily defenders of the Restoration or, a little later, the Glorious Revolution. Either allegiance in Carlyle's eyes condemned them as political hacks. They were not historians. His experiences with German Romanticism primed him to see something different in the life of Cromwell. Carlyle saw a Hero, a Great Man, in the grandest sense of the term. He saw a man utterly convinced of God's real presence and overwhelming interest in all aspects of human life. Carlyle's Cromwell was above all things sincere, never motivated by anything other than a zeal to promote Protestant religion.[31]

According to Carlyle, Englishmen of the eighteenth and nineteenth centuries dared not insult Cromwell, no matter what his sins. At least he had sinned boldly and in pursuit of God's will. Later men, sons of flabby peace and compromise, wrote Carlyle, had contented themselves with only quiet, lukewarm religious platitudes. In the 1840s, the English ought earnestly to seek Cromwell and his spirit, before all the heroism of that time became simply unrecognizable to modern men. Carlyle warned, "The Age of the Puritans is not extinct only and gone away from us, but it is as if fallen beyond the capabilities of Memory herself; it is grown inintelligible [*sic*], what we may call incredible. Its earnest Purport awakens now no resonance in our frivolous hearts. We understand not even in imagination, one of a thousand of us, what it ever could have meant."[32]

Carlyle's portrait of Cromwell generated controversy and much popular attention. In 1840, the lecture series "Heroes and Hero-Worship," in which he unveiled his Cromwell, earned him over £200. A book, which would elaborate the thesis and present the collected writings of Cromwell, took nearly five years more. Finally, in 1845, Carlyle released *Oliver Cromwell's Letters and Speeches*, which, despite the lapse of time, rekindled the debates stirred by the lecture series. The four-volume work was a market success, bringing Carlyle's income to nearly £800 in the first years after its publication and remaining a moneymaker thereafter.[33]

Other Cultural Factors: Protestant Revivalism in 1859

The advent of pluralism, professionalism, and efficiency in the religious administration of the army stemmed mostly from administrative and ministerial decisions. Credit was due also to the efforts of George Robert Gleig to change army standards respecting the competence and duties of chaplains. Yet, while Thomas Carlyle prepared the mind for a combination of soldier and saint, and while Robert Hodgson and George Robert Gleig prepared army leadership to accept a plurality of active religious voices in the army, it remained to some other force to raise up individuals prepared to exploit the potential of an army revival. These people eventually did come, but neither by way of intellectual daring nor bureaucratic restructuring. They were not internal reformers of the army, nor for the most part soldiers at all. They instead emerged out of a tradition of Evangelical revivals, culminating in that of 1859. Certainly Evangelicals made long before 1859 interested themselves in the army. But the ranks of the "Fifty-niners" produced those successful women missionaries who worked the Irish camps and Aldershot. It was also the fervor of the 1859 revival following so closely upon the experience of the Indian Mutiny and its overtly crusading ethos that created a permanent public demand for Christian soldiers.

Because Britain was a distinctly class and multinational society, we must look at evangelical influence from more than one perspective. A movement a century old by the decade of the 1850s, evangelicalism existed across many denominations. With utmost respectability among the Anglicans, it had become a powerful yet still controversial force in the British mind and had penetrated into the centers of British social and political power.[34] Boyd Hilton has suggested that the economic policies and ideologies of Victorian governments were in fact much more based upon theology and eschatology than on secular economic theory. It was not utilitarianism or its counterarguments; it was certainly not any theoretical commitment to laissez-faire that drove British business and trade policy for much of the nineteenth century. Hilton sees nineteenth-century British intellectual culture as awash in theology, debates over "natural philosophy," and the moral implications of economy. Moreover, this predilection expressed itself not only among academics or the clergy, but most vocally among "an assertive upper middle class. This class, which looked to Robert Peel as an ideal of statesmanship, depended largely on rentier wealth and comprised not only capitalist-minded agrarians and City business men, but also provincial élites with metropolitan and Oxbridge aspirations."[35] Such a man was, for instance, George Robert Gleig, though no Evangelical himself. In his conservatism and his vision of good order in the army, he eventually rejected the older, aristopaternalist ideas of the duke of Wellington.

Among the popular classes too, evangelical fervor gained not only the dominant heights of public conformity, it received a renewed burst of energy in the 1850s. This energy peaked in the revival of 1859, which came to the British Isles by way of America and through the Ulster-Irish Presbyterian connection across the Atlantic. First reports were sent home by a delegation of representatives of the General Assembly of the Presbyterian Church in Ireland. The revival then took off in Ulster. It grew so rapidly that by the summer of 1859, Ulster churches and meeting halls regularly overflowed with masses of joyous, repentant, sometimes hysterical seekers of God. For the most part, the full impact of the revival was limited to the Protestant northern counties, but it did reach Protestant communities to the south. Among its products would be army evangelists Elise Sandes and Mary Fry of Dublin. After southern Ireland, it spread to the other kingdoms.[36]

The exact origins of the revival in 1858–59 in England, Scotland, and Wales are debatable. The Scottish experience was no doubt tied to what happened in Ulster. The Church of Scotland maintained a steady interaction with its colleagues in Northern Ireland.[37] By 1861, some church officials distanced themselves from the spontaneous and enthusiastic outbreaks of emotion and prayer associated with the Awakening. The General Assembly nevertheless recognized that the movement was of some duration, not simply a flashpoint of religious expression; that in Scotland it was geographically and in terms of social class diverse and broad; that the apparent leadership was dispersed among lay and clerical members; and that, no matter what possible improprieties of enthusiasm might have occurred, the Awakening produced 15,000 new members in 477 parishes by the close of 1859 alone.[38]

The revival also appeared in Wales, particularly among the great numbers of Wesleyan Methodists in that country. The origins of the Welsh revival were distinct from those of Ulster and Scotland. Some activity seemed to predate the excitement in the other two lands. Additionally, there was no close network of communication and cooperation between Welsh and Scottish churches such as existed between the Ulster Presbyterians and the General Assembly in Scotland. The obstacle of the Welsh vernacular only broadened that gap.[39] The Welsh movement also had American ties in the person of the Welsh-born American revival preacher Humphrey Rowland Jones. After a brief career in the American revival of 1857–58, this Methodist Episcopal minister, who once had been rejected by the Wesleyans, returned to his home to preach and convert on the American model. This activity spurred also the Calvinistic Methodists, under the leadership of preacher David Morgan. By 1860, Welsh Congregationalists and Baptists reported similar waves of revival and a rise in attending members, as finally did the Church of England in Wales. As had been the case in Scotland, the revival experience in Wales appeared geographically and socially broad, and the various churches there all reported converts by the thousands.[40]

The English phase of the revival began, logically enough considering the Scottish influence, in the north of the country. Methodists of various stripes around Newcastle and Durham reported great successes in organizing prayer meetings and filling lecture halls for devotional speakers. Within the year, Gateshead and Carlisle also had flocks of converts, primarily among Methodist sects. Another American-trained preacher, E. Payson Hammond, opened a series of sermons in Liverpool in the summer of 1861. Charles Finney, the great American abolitionist and Evangelical, was already in England by Christmas 1859, preaching primarily to Methodist and Congregational churches in Bolton. Finney's 1861 efforts around Manchester produced disappointing returns, but even there converts numbered in the hundreds.[41]

In London by 1859 theater preaching had become the solution to housing the great crowds eager for evangelical preaching. Havelock's biographer, the Reverend William Brock, was among the first to exploit this idea. Sadler's Wells and the Garrick specialized in accommodating the respectable masses. St. James's and Exeter Halls were patronized by the middle and upper classes. St. Paul's Cathedral and Westminster Abbey also sponsored large-scale preaching services. Exact numbers of attendance for these mass sermons are sketchy, but all the evidence indicates large crowds. For example, the combined "free church" efforts of the Baptists, Congregationalists, Methodists, and Presbyterians using St. James's Hall in Picadilly "attracted an aggregate of 250,000 each winter" between 1859 and 1864, a sizable claim. Whatever the actual number of people attending, theater preaching attracted tens of thousands to its audiences, and spread to the Soho, Surrey, Marlybone, and City of London theaters.[42]

In his metamorphosis, then, Havelock had ample assistance, or at least few obstacles. His character as "hero" personified an unprecedented confluence of the soldier and military virtue with deep and varied forces of religious fervor throughout Britain and Ireland. Never before, though the tides of revival had swept British and Irish populations, had a military figure ridden the wave so successfully. As of Havelock's time, the army had penetrated popular British religious consciousness.

10

Gordon and the Image of the Christian Hero

Despite of the particular combination of ideas, personalities and events that went into making Havelock a national Christian hero, that phenomenon did not remain uniquely attached to him, or even to soldiers of his era. Instead, it became an institutionalized expression, a tradition, of the good that the army and imperial representatives of Britain carried forth to subject people. By the day of Charles George Gordon, a veritable public machinery of Christian heroism could hew an idol from the roughest stone. The public saw in both men pious, courageous, and self-sacrificing soldiers. Both men advanced not only the British Empire, but the work of God. To both were attributed characteristics of Christ himself. That comparison was especially popular in Gordon's case, and appeared not only in pulp biographies but in the newspapers. At the commemoration of his death, deans and archdeacons in Anglican churches and cathedrals across the country proclaimed the supposed likeness. The praises of Havelock had some basis in truth, though hardly such as to justify the hyperbole. The worship accorded Gordon was so extravagant it had to emanate from some source beyond the man: a public predisposition, based upon the tradition of Havelock and new realities within the army, to see a saint in the soldier. Even allowing for the vagaries of celebrity, the man Gordon simply did not fit the legend.

Gordon was born in Woolwich in 1833. His father, Henry William, was an officer of the Royal Artillery. His mother, Elizabeth, was daughter of a London merchant. By all accounts, Gordon in his childhood did not display the serious introspection attributed to Havelock.[1] For several years, the family moved about from station to station in Great Britain, Ireland, and the colonies, during which time young Gordon developed a reputation as an unruly child and a bully.[2] Apparently, his character did not improve with his enrollment at the Royal Military Academy in 1849; in the next three years he was involved in two fights and was demoted by six months' seniority. Ultimately because of his conduct he was directed away from the Royal Artillery to a career in the Royal Engineers.[3]

That particular branch of the British army merits some consideration. Havelock held a commission in the queen's infantry, the same branch as Wellington. His was an officer corps dominated by aristocrats and gentlemen, bound by a particular code of martial ethics and held together by a particular *ésprit de corps* relying upon a nobility of spirit if not always blood. By "army" most Victorians understood "infantry" or "infantry and cavalry." Gordon served in the Engineers, the preeminently middle class, and inglorious, branch of the military. His father was an officer in the artillery, a corps likewise beneath the level of gallantry and nobility of the infantry and cavalry officers. The Engineers did not rely upon purchase. They did not face anything like the social demands made upon line officers. They were expected to be not gallant or chivalrous, but technical, businesslike, practical, entrepreneurial. Even the enlisted men, known as Sappers and Miners (only officers were actually Engineers), were considered a breed apart: less rough and tumble, more educated and civilized, less debauched than Other Ranks of the Line—in other words, a pedestrian lot. The Engineers were the sort of corps ready-made for contrast with the traditional aristocratic hegemony in the miliary as well as the associated vices of nepotism, purchase, debauchery, and irreligion. They were not the branch, however, to fuel the stuff of romantic heroism.[4]

At any rate, Gordon's childhood and education hardly provided any prefabricated materials for the usual evangelical hero. Although one of his first biographers would later claim that he demonstrated a marked Christian piety in early life,[5] later works have not substantiated that assertion. When Gordon finally did begin to experiment with vital religion, shortly before his tour of duty in Crimea, he explained the change in letters to his sister. He wished to share his experiences with their parents, so that they would see the light.[6] However, just which faith and doctrines he had discovered remained very unclear.

Not even in his first combat assignment in Crimea, coming after his turn to "religion," did Gordon offer much in the way of Christian hero material. He served well, was a good combat officer, and was courageous to the point of a personal disregard for danger and death.[7] Yet, unlike Havelock, he did not seem to reach out to other Christian soldiers or to suffer any scruples of religious faith. Unlike Havelock, whom brother officers considered "a bit of a dull dog," Gordon continued to be a "lively fellow" at mess while in Crimea. He was self-consciously pleased because he had plenty of clothes and food during the hard Russian winter of 1854–55. He even wrote to his mother not to believe the horror stories about the Crimean army that were appearing in the *Times*. The officers were fine. "The men are the sufferers, and that is partly their own fault, as they are like children thinking everything is to be done for them."[8]

Gordon's first exposure to public acclaim resulted from his improbable command of the proimperial, mercenary "Ever Victorious Army" (EVA) during the latter stages of the Tai-Ping Rebellion in China. He had remained in eastern Europe for two and a half years after the end of fighting in Crimea. During this time he worked on the survey commission to establish the boundaries of the Peace of Paris. With the end of this work, and after what was for him a difficult tour at home, he requested transfer to China in order to participate in the Anglo-French War of 1860. He missed most of the fighting between the Chinese and the Anglo-French army sent against them, but worked for the occupation of Peking, building barracks for the troops and making personal efforts at charity for Chinese paupers.[9]

He first saw combat in China only after the European forces holding Peking agreed to operations against the Tai Ping Rebels operating in Kiangsi and Anhwei. His performance in these campaigns of 1862 convinced the British general Sir Charles Stavely of Gordon's fitness for command. When the Europeans moved to take control of the mercenary EVA, Stavely looked to Gordon. In an effort to maintain the power of this private merchant's army, yet to control its looting and terror against civilians, the British convinced Shanghai Chinese officials to accept a joint British-Chinese command of the force. Despite not being an infantry commander and having only limited combat experience, Gordon got the job.[10] For almost two years, March 1863 to November 1864, he led this motley force in a series of successful fortress reductions and field battles, culminating in the capture of "Soochow." All the while, reports of the exotic campaigns and of the benefit to the Chinese from exposure to British law, order, advice and administration filtered back to admiring newspaper audiences in Britain. Gordon became "Chinese Gordon," a public, but not yet Christian, hero.

Times coverage of his efforts in China began in May of 1863, when England first learned of his command of the Ever Victorious Army. Between that month and December 1864, the newspaper produced periodic reports on Gordon's defense of Shanghai and his overall progress against the Tai Ping. Reports of his first victory at "Tait-shan" came in June; a notice of EVA capture of five rebel cities all in the month of October reached London in December.[11] The image of Gordon presented in the *Times* increasingly became that of "can-do" man, the expert on the "native mind," teaching efficiency to the backward Chinese.

In July 1864, Gordon had a hot dispute with Chinese imperial authorities over the executions of some rebel leaders whose safety he had guaranteed. For a time it appeared he would resign and wash his hands of the EVA altogether. Reporting this story, the *Times* correspondent watched Gordon train the units that would become the post-EVA imperial force. To the newsman's thinking, Gordon's special talent lay in imparting efficiency and organization to his Chinese students. Once Gordon had left, the report stated, the kernel of a European-style army he bequeathed to China would go far in protecting imperial rule, if only Chinese officers would remember to lead the troops in a European fashion.[12] Moreover, Gordon's withdrawal during part of this dispute, the *China Mail* noted, had severe effects on the EVA. "Had Colonel Gordon chosen to remain in the field . . . both Woochow and Nankin would have fallen in two months; as it is, the siege in both places may be prolonged indefinitely."[13] Apparently only the British Gordon could whip the Chinese into an adequate defense of their own empire.

As he prepared to return to Britain, the *Times* made the announcement in the same column as the court news. They published an extract of a letter from Gordon to his father, presenting the old man with a captured sword and a rebel battle flag stained with the blood of a slain Tai Ping leader. There was no date given for Gordon's own arrival home.[14] He himself desired to avoid too much direct personal celebrity, despite the fact that he liked newspaper coverage of his deeds. He wanted distance. That the *Times* concerned itself at all with the doings and travels of a solitary major of the Engineers is remarkable. Staveley himself, commander of the British expedition in China and the man who had arranged Gordon's command of the EVA, received little coverage.

Gordon earned his second brush with fame thanks to his employment by the khedive of Egypt as governor general of Equatoria and the Sudan colonies. From 1872 to 1879 he personally supervised the establishment of governmental outposts, the creation of rudimentary bureaucracy, and (albeit feeble) attempts at the suppression of the slave trade. During this phase of his career, more than any other, he developed (through his own agency and through the assumptions of various groups in Britain) the identification of his military and religious careers. Particularly, the naive hopes pinned upon him (with very mixed results) by the Anti-Slavery Society in Britain nonetheless created of him a Christian hero dedicated to the civilization and the redemption of the "Dark Continent."[15] His life thus far was vastly different than Havelock's. Gordon seemingly had paid no dues on behalf of his religious convictions, or anything else. He was famous, admired, and promoted.[16]

His last and most glorious campaign was his most incompetent and disastrous. Since a failed attempt to establish himself in the colonial government of South Africa in the early 1880s, Gordon had maintained a sort of retirement. However, in 1884 he accepted a reluctant offer by the British government to return him to Sudan to oversee the evacuation of the collapsing Egyptian presence there. The cabinet did not want him. Evelyn Baring, British consul in Cairo, feared his instability. Gordon himself originally favored his own schemes to travel to the Belgian Congo to perform undetermined duties for King Leopold of the Belgians. Instead, Gordon returned to Sudan, purportedly to conduct the withdrawal. In actuality he attempted to hold the territory against the Mahdist rising of the Sudanese Muslims. The story of Gordon's last trip to Sudan is just that complex. Debates persist over why he went, who actually sent him, what he was supposed to do there, and why, after he became trapped in a siege at Khartoum, nobody in government appeared in a hurry to extricate him. He died in combat when the city fell to the Mahdi in January 1885, after a siege of nearly a year.[17]

During the siege of Khartoum, British public opinion increasingly focused upon Gordon's presence on the scene, and the national interest and spirit he embodied. The *Times* published frequent reports, such as were available, on his efforts and trials in the Sudanese city. Early in the summer there was no hint that Gordon might fail. While by July it became apparent he was trapped, *Times* coverage still portrayed him as a military commander with the field situation well in hand. Rumors even circulated in July that Gordon had crafted an Egyptian force at

Khartoum strong enough to sally against the Mahdist besiegers, and that he had thus won some field victories.[18]

After the truly dire nature of Gordon's situation became clear at home, the rhetoric concerning his plight took a curious turn. Gladstone's governments had always to deal with strong imperialist sentiments among the constituents.[19] As Gordon's peril deepened, and as Gladstone balked at a further imperial commitment in Egypt, the argument of the Christian hero began to emerge as an irrefutable argument with which proimperialists hoped to coerce antiimperialist Liberals into action.[20] Although the public had already accepted him as a soldier of unusual piety,[21] the image of the sainted Gordon was now hammered in the forge of political debate about his danger at Khartoum.

On 22 September 1884, the *Times* ran a feature article on the trouble in the Sudan. Gordon, said the editors, was a military success at Khartoum. Wolseley's lately begun rescue ought instead be dedicated to securing the territory and authority Gordon had been defending all the previous months. A successful evacuation, Gordon's original mission, was no longer even the question. The *Times* argued that a British commitment to a permanent presence in Egypt and the Sudan was already made in the person of Gordon himself. The same was true of success there. "General Gordon has rendered its [Khartoum] retention easy and safe. His indomitable courage in circumstances of the greatest discouragement has in any case conferred inestimable benefits upon his country, and also upon the Government which turned to him in its need and turned its back upon him in his."[22]

One week later, the *Times* repeated the tactic. In its regular, full-length coverage of the Egyptian situation, the paper again lionized Gordon and his work at Khartoum. This time, the editors went one step further and identified him with British and Christian spirit and ideals. Gordon had so far shown "unflinching courage," "unwavering fortitude," "inexhaustible energy and resource," and a "splendid devotion to duty." The article claimed that the risk of English ideals at Khartoum, in the person of Gordon, was sufficient reason for Wolseley to relieve, but never to evacuate, the town. With Britishness at stake, Khartoum must be held. "But when Lord Wolseley and General Gordon have joined hands, what is to happen? Is this country prepared to allow the carrying out of the half-hearted policy of rescue and retirement, which Lord Wolseley was sent to pursue, or will it insist that a town ever memorable in English annals and unquestionably essential to any thorough management of Egypt shall remain the outpost of civilization in the Soudan [*sic*]?"[23]

In any event, Gordon and Wolseley were destined never again to join hands. By the time advance elements of the British relief column arrived near Khartoum, the Sudanese Muslims had taken the city and killed Gordon. For a few days at the end of January 1885, British imperialists held a silent, suspenseful vigil. On 12 February, the *Times* proclaimed the awful truth: Gordon was dead. That day the paper ran a full-page obituary in which the editors made the explicit connection between Gordon's religious nature, his military profession, and his exploits and achievements for his country. While he had been of "mild or indifferent" religious opinion in his youth, the General later established a reputation for personal piety. "In Gordon, whose mind was tinged with a strong religious feeling of the Puritan type from the earliest period, [self-confidence] became the intensified and increasing belief that he was a selected emissary and chosen agent of God." This opinion the author seriously accepted, given the "greater Good" Gordon had served as leader of the EVA, in local philanthropy at Gravesend, in attacking the slave trade in the Sudan in the 1870s, and in his general example.[24] This obituary incited a spate of eulogizing over Gordon, the likes of which put to shame even the hyperbolic praises expended on Havelock.

In the days following the public announcement of Gordon's demise, letters to the editors of the *Times* flowed in, all lauding the General as a military and spiritual hero. Twice, he was compared to Old Testament prophets who, while admonishing the Jews with the truth, earned for themselves ignominy and death, only later to be celebrated by the repentant people who had rejected and killed them.[25] Perhaps in the Conservative-leaning *Times*, these praises of Gordon and aspersions on the government ought not to have been surprising.

Indeed, the Liberal press tried to play down the martyrdom.[26] However, popular feeling apparently ran in much the same channels as that expressed in the *Times*, for the rhapsodizing climaxed in the very successful national day of commemoration for Gordon. On 14 March 1885, in the major Anglican cathedrals as well as in churches around the nation, thousands of people from all classes flocked to memorial services and funeral orations honoring the dead hero. From the sermons preached to the crowds that day arose, in its fullest glory, the image of the British Christian hero.

At the service held at St. Paul's in London, for example, the sermon pressed the very limits of absurdity. It was said that, by his military activities in China, Gordon had saved no fewer than 80,000 to 100,000 lives. Moreover, in "saving" people, Gordon in his career had rescued them from more than mortal danger. He had offered himself sacrificially to free them from themselves. The Christ analogy is painfully blunt: "[Gordon] wanted to die for the Sudan, and he prayed God that the 'weight of their sins be on me and crush me instead of those poor sheep.'" Once, continued the deacon whose name the paper did not record, Sudan had been a Christian land, but it was long since flooded over by fanaticism. "There might God give an abundant harvest to that glorious crop whose seed had come from English homes and English hearts. . . . In His own time and way might He ordain that one result shall be a fuller and truer life for the dwellers in that country where those precious lives [Gordon's and those of the soldiers of the column sent to relieve him] were yielded; that peace and freedom may flourish in all those borders; and that the love of Jesus and the sanctifying power of the Holy Spirit may water and enrich the regions that are thirsting for a God but imperfectly known as yet."[27]

At Westminster, the Christological analysis continued. In the sermon there, Gordon was proclaimed a loss for "all Christendom," a man mourned by "millions of Chinese" and "countless Africans." He had not died in vain, but rather had laid the dear foundation upon which masses of others would be lifted up to civilization.

> The time will come when law and order, peace and justice, shall displace slavery and corruption, cruelty and anarchy; when the cry of the oppressed and downtrodden . . . shall have an answer; when the work of a Gordon here, and a Livingstone there, an adventurous traveller, of a beneficent Monarch, and of young Englishmen who are even now hazarding and laying down their lives in Central Africa shall bear fruit. . . . [Gordon] will not have died in vain if we, soldiers and men and women far removed from the soldier's life, can catch something of his simple, self-sacrificing spirit; if his example can aid us to enter that spiritual life, that entire trust in an unseen God, that power of living in communion with Him and with a world above.[28]

The service at Canterbury repeated the refrain. Gordon "had showed that a soldier as a soldier might be a true servant of God; and . . . that a true servant of God might consistently be a soldier." Shying from the Gospel admonition to pacifism, the preacher encouraged the congregation to remember Joshua, Gilead, David, and the New Testament figures like Cornelius of *Acts* and the believing centurion at the Crucifixion. As were they soldiers and believers, "so was General Gordon. . . . Destroying the lives of the enemy he knew he was no less in the path of duty than when he was giving his own life or preserving the lives of others. We commemorate then the combination of the noble qualities of the soldier with all the sterling graces of a Christian not so much for the Glory of God, but that we might glorify God in him."[29] Similar services were held at Winchester, Durham, Bangor, Chester, Chichester, Gloucester, Lincoln, Manchester, Rochester, St. Alban's, Salisbury, St. George's Chapel at Windsor Castle, and Northampton.

If Havelock became in the public eye a cartoon image of a "fighting Christian," then Gordon can be seen as nothing less than pure illusion. He became a fighting Christian hero, almost a fighting Christ, without even being much of an orthodox Christian. Although some critics and marginal press entities endeavored to make this point, they had little success. Annie Besant prefigured Strachey's later project by publishing a pamphlet alleging Gordon to be a deviant and hypocrite. She gained no hearing. Other journals like the Baptist *Friend*, the radical *Truth* and the *Weekly Despatch*, as well as the socialist *Commonweal* and the atheist *Freethinker*, did no better in stirring a debate over the nature of Gordon the man.[30] The mainstream press advocates of his cause rolled on.

So, with the aid of press and official church efforts, the hyperbole surrounding Gordon and his life put to pale shame the eulogies over Havelock. During his life, his adventures in China, and his (mixed) antislavery efforts as governor of Sudan and Equatoria (1874–79), Gordon earned a popular acclaim that Havelock could not have dreamed of, much less desired. There were at least three books about a very living Gordon in circulation in 1884,[31] two of which had already been in print some time: The *Ever Victorious Army*, by Andrew Wilson, and *Colonel Gordon in Central Africa*, by Dr. Birbeck Hill. These authors recognized Gordon as the "foremost" expert on irregular warfare and on the continued slave trade in equatorial Africa. The third, a work of Alfred Egmont Hake entitled *The Story of Chinese Gordon*, had already gone into a sixth edition by mid-1884, and was a particular masterpiece of hagiography. Like the eulogies to be delivered over Gordon in February 1885, the *Story* picked up on a perverse impulse at a Christological interpretation of Gordon's life.

Although Hake himself today is obscure, it is important to note that between 1884 and at least 1896 he was the foremost biographer of and an ardent polemicist for Gordon.[32] When Wolseley returned to England, he brought with him journal material Gordon had smuggled out of Khartoum before its fall. He gave those journals to Hake. Within months of the news of Gordon's demise, Hake produced not only the edited journals for public consumption, but also a second installment on the *Story*. This piece magnified the pious Gordon, and insinuated that the Gladstone government had let the General die on purpose. Even the approving critic in the *Saturday Review*, who used the book announcement to bash Gladstone, could not go this far. The *Review* cited Hake as understandably distraught, and added that although the government had fatally blundered, there could not have been a conspiracy.[33]

Like Brock's biography of Havelock, Hake's *Story* was at immediate pains to portray Gordon as a manly, virile agent empowered by Christian faith, in charge of his destiny and humble only before God. Moreover, Hake undoubtedly saw this combination of virility and holiness as the ingredients of personal genius, fame, power, and of the success of Britain abroad. On the very first page the author put Gordon upon the highest pedestal. He began his book

> The history of Christ has been recorded to the end that men might have before them the example of a perfect life. This example Charles Gordon has followed, perhaps as closely as mortal may do. To show his achievement step by step is to place the actions of such a man in a light wherein they may serve as a beacon to others; with this intention it is that the story of Chinese Gordon is given to the world. . . . His story, indeed, is the story of a swordless conqueror: of a true disciple of the Divine Master who laid down His life for humanity; of a complete Christian in thought, word and deed.[34]

From the first and at a time when Gordon was still alive, Hake set a tone of hyperbole in which Gordon's military career equated with evangelism; his war making became crusading, or more, sacrificial struggle for salvation; and his every action would be of the highest philanthropic nature, often inscrutable to ordinary men. Throughout the *Story*, the first volume of which appeared before Gordon even went to Khartoum, Hake built upon the image of the Fighting Christian Hero to give his readers a superman.

After a chapter setting the nature of Gordon's character, the *Story* begins by breezing through his early career with anecdotes like one concerning his first patrol in Crimea. Gordon was to go forward of the French and British lines with a sapper party and complete some rifle pits for the forward allied skirmishers. In some confusion, the party received fire from their own lines. This excited the Russian piquets to fire as well, and in the crossfire, the party panicked and ran for cover. Gordon supposedly stayed out alone and completed the rifle pits himself. The author concluded, "The manner and the circumstances of this, Gordon's first important duty, are in some sort typical of his whole achievement. As will be seen later on, he was frequently fired upon by friends as well as foes, and several of his most notable conquests were made almost single-handed, after those whom he had under his command had mutinied or deserted him."[35] For Hake, it was a theme of Gordon's life that the Great Man never had followers worthy of him. He lacked only a close disciple to deny him three times.

As the title implied, *The Story of Chinese Gordon* concentrated primarily upon the General's years with the EVA in operations against the Tai Ping. This central core of the book was much more the adventure story, and less the saintly hagiography. Of course, in these chapters Gordon never made a mistake. All of his seemingly questionable or ill-planned maneuvers and schemes later proved to have been laid out with incredible foresight and calculation. He was the master of Chinese politics. An astute judge of character, Gordon supposedly discerned the minds of foreign men whose language he could not speak and history and culture he did not know. For Hake, Gordon's spiritual superiority formed the backdrop of his virtue. It was the guarantee that he would never lie or deceive even his enemies. It reassured the reader that even a summary execution of an EVA sergeant, ordered and presided over by Gordon to enforce his command over his striking troops, was wholly justified. The death of the one ultimately spared many more lives, which would have been lost in a full mutiny.[36]

After concentrating on Gordon's years with the EVA and his first governorship of Sudan, Hake's *Story* returned to the theme of heroic spirituality and closed with Gordon in the Holy Lands. Gordon indeed went to Palestine in 1883 on a sort of semiretirement. There he wished to relax, to recharge spiritually. He planned to execute some surveys of Christian holy sites in an effort to support some of his personal archaeological and theological theories he had developed from reading the Bible. Leaving Gordon to this work, Hake thus closed his book,

> As far as may be the story of Chinese Gordon is told. It has proved him a true soldier, a true statesman: a soldier whose aim in war is never the gains of victory, but the riches of peace, whose aim in peace is never loud-voiced glory, but silent self-denial; a statesman without fear and without reproach, whose statesmanship is founded on fearless justice and truth; in one word, a hero, who counts no conquest greater than the conquest of self. . . . A story as of the Temptation in the Wilderness might be told of the moral campaign he has waged upon such of the world's worst citizens . . . as have sought to lure him from his chosen way. . . . Strong in the armor of God, he has fought the good fight, and prevailed.[37]

Immediately after Gordon's death at Khartoum, Hake reissued the *Story* in revised form. This work, entitled *Gordon in China and the Soudan*, was substantially the same as the original story, with two differences. The first, and least important here, was Hake's insistence that the Liberals had always had a vendetta against Gordon, and that the disaster at Khartoum had been no accident. Without giving reasons or proof, Hake nonetheless asserted that Gladstone had willfully left Gordon to die at Khartoum, that somehow sacrificing Gordon fit the political ends of the Liberal government.[38] The second revision to the original manuscript was the inclusion of a chapter titled "God Bless the Kernel," taken from a graffiti message of thanks once scrawled on the garden fence of Gordon's home in Gravesend. During the period 1865 to 1871 Gordon was engineer in charge of the Thames defenses. Living and working in the East End of London, he became familiar with the poverty and degraded conditions of life prevalent there. All his biographers, contemporary and modern, agree that during this time he began to run a one-man mission to the poor, especially young boys, of Gravesend: taking them into his own home, supporting them on a personal dole, holding tutoring sessions for them every night, and securing whenever possible posts for them to go to sea in the navy and the merchant marine.[39]

Hake worked this story to magnify a now-sainted Gordon. The Gravesend days, he wrote, were a time of Gordon's demonstration to the world of his otherworldly superiority. The "Kernel" cared not at all for material wealth. He denied himself food and fine clothing. He rejected offers to attend entertainments and dinners, answering, "Ask the poor and sick; don't ask me who have enough." He spurned awards and professional recognition. When asked how a man might improve himself, he answered that one should sell all one's finery and give the proceeds to the poor. Then, as if to insure no one could miss the Christ analogy, Hake added that Gordon indeed recognized how few people could disdain worldly goods the way he did.[40] This life of charity, chastity, and poverty Gordon punctuated with prayer and fasting.[41]

In death Gordon continued to fuel a blaze of publishing. He was sermonized and eulogized. He became the subject for a number of books and pamphlets, ranging in tone from hero worship to conspiracy theories like Hake's, about the "real reasons" he was allowed to die at Khartoum.[42] Hake was able to compile, edit, and release the Khartoum journals only four months after Wolseley reported Gordon dead. Over ten years later Gordon continued to inspire books on his life, including instructive manuals designed to edify and inspire young men in manly Christianity. In all these works, authors repeated several themes: Gordon as martyr; Gordon as atoning sacrifice so that barbarians might be lifted to civilization; Gordon as consummate Christian.[43]

Yet consider again his earliest exploits, which gained him public recognition. When Gordon assumed command of the Ever Victorious Army, it was already a well established, and notorious, mercenary enterprise funded by Chinese merchants and mandarins fearful of the Tai Ping rebels. The rebels, because of the nominal, if twisted, Christian content of their movement actually drew public support from the observers in Britain who gave the matter any thought. The EVA, on the other hand, aside from being a mercenary army, was corrupt, lustful of plunder, prone to infighting, and in 1863 under the command of two disreputable American military adventurers who had avoided their own country's Civil War. Command of the EVA was hardly then a "respectable" calling. Few of Gordon's brother officers thought so. But the Tai Ping, due to their own infighting and disordered leadership, lost the aura of Christian rebels. Gordon was able to control the troops and officers of the EVA, a fact attributed to his own spartan self-discipline. Because Gordon gained military victories where the EVA had been a military failure before he commanded, he converted his unorthodox service in China into fame and honor.

The differences between Havelock and Gordon reveal clues as

to what had happened to the public face of the British army. Havelock was throughout his career a professional officer. With the possible exception of his two efforts at military history, his career ethic and his religious perspective led him to accept the onerous common duties of his calling with perseverance and resignation. This steadiness of character made him an excellent staff officer and military organizer. Gordon was never any of these things.

For much of his adult life, despite the generous impulses of his personality, a tendency to physical reclusiveness, and his sincere but quirky spirituality, Gordon was addicted to seeing his name in print. The Christian hero, as the image grew out of Henry Havelock, was steady. He accepted responsibility and duty not for the possible rewards or recognition, but because his vocation was God's will. Chroniclers of Gordon, during his life and after it, attributed these ideal traits to their subject, but the real man was far different. Gordon was anything but steady, and God's will or not, he loved recognition and publicity. On all six books of the journal that he ordered smuggled out of Khartoum during the siege he noted, "It will require to be pruned out if published."[44]

Gordon lacked Havelock's steadiness in his personal life as well. Havelock was a family man supreme. He married a pious woman descended from Baptist ministers and missionaries. He raised his own family in accordance with the evangelical outlook imparted to him by his mother and supported by his in-laws. He brought up his eldest son, Henry Jr., to be a professional and pious army officer like himself. Indeed, he and the young Havelock fought together during the campaign to relieve Lucknow and Cawnpore. Havelock the elder was known to his friends and his colleagues constantly to worry over the security of his wife and children. One of the greatest personal motivations in his career was his concern that he provide enough in money and social standing to do well by his family obligations.

Gordon, on the other hand, was completely lacking in this particular avenue to respectability. He had no family to speak of, save his sister Augusta. He never married, nor even courted seriously. He wandered incessantly: to China, to Africa, to the Indian Ocean, to English slums. His only foray into domestic life at all came through his personal ministry to young boys while he was stationed at Gravesend. So in family matters, in the catalog of his personal relationships, Gordon could claim to be exceptional, but hardly respectable.

Theologically Gordon was also very much the outsider, in a

way that Havelock never was. Havelock was raised by a pious Evangelical mother who, while she stressed to him the very personal demands of that faith, also imbued him with a loyalty to his state church. He eventually became a Baptist, but by 1830 this denomination, if possibly unfashionable, was hardly countercultural. He converted to the Baptists only after arduous soul-searching, and only after educating himself in the finer points of theological distinction between them and the Anglicans. Gordon adhered to an eccentric, highly individual, and homespun theology, and while this aspect of his character might appeal to contemporary libertarians, it was hardly calculated to win him official sanction or public respectability.

Gordon never fully accepted (nor perhaps understood) the doctrines of the Church of England. He loved to take Holy Communion, believing that the Sacrament did indeed put him in direct physical contact with God.[45] But, he was tolerant, even admiring of other religious traditions. He believed that God spoke to humanity by means of any number of the spiritual practices which had grown up in various regions of the world. He accepted the preeminence of Christianity among these because he accepted the Incarnation as actual. Yet, for example, he admired many of the Muslims he encountered in Africa because of their piety, their monotheism, their recognition of Christ as a prophet, and their earnestness. "I am sure," he wrote in his Khartoum journals, "it is unknown to the generality of our missionaries in Muslim countries, that in the Koran no imputation of sin is made on our Lord, neither is it hinted that He had need of pardon, and, further, no Muslim can deny that the Father of our Lord was God. . . . As far as self-sacrifice of the body, [Muslims] are far above the Roman Catholics, and consequently above Protestants."[46]

Gordon was convinced of God's immediate presence and interest in his own life. He was "converted," but not in the usual evangelical sense of acute awareness of personal sin. Gordon's religious awakening occurred through a mystical realization, founded upon his own intense study of biblical scripture, that God was resident within him and every person, as manifested in the existence of souls.[47] This "success" in interpreting Scripture for himself led him to attempt several more ambitious schemes of exegesis. While stationed on the island of Mauritius, he decided that his readings in Genesis showed the original Paradise to be there.[48] During the retirement after his first tenure in Egyptian service, he traveled to Palestine in order to confirm some theories of biblical archaeology he had likewise developed. His published work, *Reflections in Palestine, 1883*, demonstrates his heterodox approach to Christian spirituality.

This short work, consisting both of Gordon's amateur biblical archeology and his personal theology, appeared in 1884, the year after his brief retirement. The scope of *Reflections* was broad, beginning with a topographical description of the hills of Jerusalem and the layout of the city. This survey, he believed, justified him in pointing out the similarity between the outlines of Jerusalem and the form a human body, with Golgatha as its head. With the aid of Old Testament prophecy from *Leviticus*, he located the true location of the Cross on the day of the Crucifixion.[49]

So too in *Reflections* he engaged in a unique, personal interpretation of biblical Scripture. The theology he so revealed was unorthodox in its dualism. In a section entitled "Possible Analogy between the First Three Days of Creation and Our Own Lives," he wrote that in history, Satan, through Man, had twice defeated God's purposes at the Fall and the Flood. At the third confrontation, God had, through Man the Incarnation, defeated Satan. This cosmic scheme replayed itself daily within the existence of every soul. Enigmatically he wrote, "We see the constant repetition of the days of creation in our own lives. We see a distinct scheme continually repeated to this great end."[50]

He believed he had uncovered a great cycle of creation, a four-phase cycle of battle between the good and evil in every individual. A person's spiritual life incessantly progressed by means of a dialectic in which the infusion of gathering evil into a soul would force an explosive reaction of guilt, then repentance and good in an ever-ascending pattern that would continue even in heaven. After each episode, the individual would then repose spiritually until the next crisis, and so on.[51] Following the abstract framing of this scheme, Gordon included an interesting, probably biographical, illustration.

> We can see this in ourselves. Take an example such as when we have no changes; we are settled on our lees; we are prosperous, but evil is in us; we are in London, where no call for self-denial directly affects us; all of a sudden we commit some most unmistakable act of selfishness, and we are heartbroken, and all our self-confidence gone; we are *scattered*. Evil has distinctly manifested itself. Light has come, showing us ourselves. We have our attention directed to our selfishness. We make an effort, and separate ourselves from it. A *division* takes place in us, and we are no longer selfish in that form;

> and we are *gathered* together and regain our confidence in ourselves. We settle again . . . and are *scattered*.[52]

Here then are some socially and theologically rather unorthodox sentiments made very public by Gordon himself at a time when the popular press was hungry for "Gordonalia." A theory of eternal becoming and renewal? While various religious groups, including Anglican Evangelicals, might have criticisms of metropolitan life, they rarely forsook the capital as a place void of opportunity for self-denial. It was by no means a consensus among English Protestants that prosperity itself was an evil. And as for the eternal becoming of the soul, that smacked of Eastern mysticism.

So Gordon clearly was not the sort of man from which the public had once created the Christian Warrior, Henry Havelock. Gordon was erratic and showy. He was less than stoic in the performance of duty and in his acceptance of authority. He had little in the way of conventional family ties. His religious views were obscure and eccentric. He lacked even the sharp personal distinction from his enemies. Havelock had confronted his pagan adversaries in India with a clear sense of a cultural and religious clash. In his last campaign, Gordon developed a personal and spiritual admiration for the piety of the Sudanese Muslims, if not for the Mahdi himself.[53]

Yet as witnessed by the popular emotion, the mass of literature and sermons about him, none of this seemed to matter. Despite the complexities of each man, and despite the fact that Gordon's character varied widely from the criteria of the respectable Christian gentleman, the British public saw in Gordon a Havelock. The newspaper accounts of him, the eulogies, and popular comment ignored the idiosyncratic Gordon. They overlooked his admiration of Islam, the fact that he was never confirmed an Anglican or anything else, and his belief that God put the cacao-de-mere fruit on Mauritius as a memorial to Eve's genitals in the former Paradise.[54] The popular acclaim of Gordon would not see his manic restlessness, his nearly suicidal love of battle, or his only superficial knowledge of the cultures in which he was supposedly "expert."[55] Havelock was brave, never truly fearing death because it meant for him union with God. Gordon could be foolhardy and and seemed to crave death. Consider his reliance upon his "magic stick" when commanding the EVA in battle. In those days he never carried a side arm, but would lead his columns of Chinese infantry armed only with a riding crop. This he used to point out tactical objectives as the battle progressed, as well as to slap into action stragglers and those too fond of cover. His EVA soldiers came to believe the crop a talisman that warded off bullets. There is some question as to whether Gordon himself did not come to believe the story. At the storming of Kiangsu, in April 1863, he himself led the third and successful attempt to force a breach in the city walls. Two previous attempts had failed, and his subordinate, a Major Bannon, had been killed. Gordon walked into the breach smoking a cigar and armed only with the "wand of victory," his crop.[56]

Popular biographers and the press made of Gordon a steady, knowledgeable, dutiful commander. They made of him a devout and pious Anglican, if with puritanical tendencies. Gordon's image, and it seems to have been all image, ignored the man Gordon and drew instead upon the substance that was actually much closer to Havelock, a first-generation Christian hero. Nearly all the praises of Gordon, despite the increase in volume and hyperbole, had roots in the approbation of Havelock. Personal traits of Havelock's, which, although they became distorted were based upon some fact, were simply pasted over the real person of Gordon. Where Gordon stood, the public was willing, even expected, to see Havelock.

Indeed, the demand for heroes and the popularity of things military reached entirely new heights in the middle and late 1880s. While soldiering was a recurrent theme in the nineteenth-century music hall, for instance, the 1880s and 1890s were "an absolute peak of music hall consideration of the army."[57] Moreover, music hall military sketches increasingly relied upon sentimental, even noble, common-soldier types rather than on traditional aristocratic heroes.[58] The great popularity of Rudyard Kipling and his soldier tales illustrates the point as well. *Soldiers Three* (1889) and *Barrack Room Ballads* (1892) were tremendous hits that emphasized the humanity and rough-hewn virtue of the common soldier.[59] Kipling "probably drew the most extended and certainly the best known character study of 'British Other Ranks' in English literature."[60]

According to the tastes of the popular entertainment audiences of the eighties and nineties, even the rank and file of the army was believably productive of heroic and virtuous behavior. Audiences across class lines responded warmly to these highly sympathetic portraits of officer and enlisted honor and heroics.[61] This phenomenon was repeated in other fields of popular expression. Theater, particularly melodrama, where military themes had always done well since Waterloo, offered up a wealth of new plays on martial valor in the 1880s and 1890s. As in the music halls, soldierly virtue and common soldier nobility were common portrayals.[62] Gordon characters figured in two smash hits after 1885, *Khartoum* and *The Fall of Khartoum*.[63]

For young boys of all classes, the 1880s and 1890s proliferated with toy soldiers, scale-model war games, books, newspapers, and magazines extolling soldierly virtue and military "Britishness."[64] Proimperialism became a hallmark of British boyhood. In fact, boys could hardly escape "the imperial idea." At "schools, in church groups, in recreational associations" boys were taught to honor the empire.[65] Most importantly, from the 1880s forward, even well after the First World War, there existed a lucrative mass market in juvenile literature heavily biased toward imperial adventure: novels, illustrated periodicals, penny weeklies (both "uplifting" and "the awfuls").[66] This literature cut across all class lines, especially thanks to the effects of education reform begun in the early 1870s. For the more privileged the effect was the same, not only from popular entertainment but from an upsurge in public school militarism after 1880.[67]

Some of this can be explained, or at least made understandable, by the changes in the social and political climate between the eras of Havelock and Gordon. Several aspects of national and international life changed between the time of Havelock and Gordon's day. The British embarked on a new phase of empire in the 1880s. British colonial interests the world over, especially in Africa, faced challenges not only from local battles to maintain and control colonies, but also from the encroachments of these European rivals, particularly France. Within ten years of Gordon's death, the British empire in Africa confronted the interests and colonies of France, Germany, Italy, and lesser European nations.

The European world at home was different too. Already in the 1880s, the United Kingdom struggled to compete with the industrial output of Germany and the United States. France, while no industrial threat, retained its traditional role as adversary and military rival. Germany, after the passing of Bismarck from politics, soon added to and then entirely supplanted the Francophobic entry in the British dictionary of fears. The traditional order on the continent, the balance of powers and the concert of diplomacy, all faded with the nineteenth century. Unsurprisingly, these were the years wherein the Christian crusader image of the British army reached its pinnacle; wherein the average British citizen need only know that the forces of his country were out to work Good. These too were the years during which the improving conditions within the army made such an expectation even possible.

In the 1850s, Havelock as the Christian imperial hero had done much to explain the old empire in India. He reaffirmed, after the deadly farce in the Crimea, British martial values and self-confidence. More than that, he justified British force and aggression by lifting the mundane and grubby demands of power and colonial hegemony into the realm of heaven. He was Cromwell and Wellington, a careful mix of the best of both. Better, he was these two and the son of a businessman, a commoner. His image and his legend explained what the empire was and whose it was, who ought best to run it, and what made it a respectable enterprise.

Simply put, by the 1880s Gordon was a type. The ease with which his Christian hero image supplanted his well-known eccentricities was a measure of how ready and willing was the British public to identify the empire and its agent, the army, with the highest good. By 1885 the army had come a long way indeed from the days of Wellington. In 1815, a beatific vision of the military was impossible based upon Wellington's "band of drunkards and robbers." In 1857, Havelock, far above any other martyr of the Mutiny, achieved hero status heavily dependent upon his remarkable military exploits and his very respectable and very real piety. Moreover, by the time of his death, the public through the debates on Crimea had already begun to recognize the internal changes in the army, changes that would integrate it into civil society.

In 1885, that integration was sufficiently advanced to facilitate the canonization of Charles Gordon with the ease of mass production. The "St. Gordon" figure was a ready tool, a product of over five decades of army reform and three decades of public awareness of it. With this highly evolved myth people now explained why Britain had an empire; why British citizens interfered in events the world over; how good home governments understood these things and bad ones did not; how the "high and mighty" could let a good man down, even to the point of costing him his life; and how that fact meant that the empire, even Britishness itself, had to be for everyone, not just the elite.[68]

Finally, the vision of Gleig, the integration of the army and its tasks into the moral vocabulary of general British culture, had matured. Empire and army were no longer the playground of aristocrats; the gate by which the common people had entered the field had been the moral transformation, imperfect in reality though it yet was, of the army. Now it was a good army, with honorable goals and dedicated servants. It encouraged in men fine qualities like loyalty and even piety. It protected what was best in British civilization and carried those gifts abroad through the medium of empire. It fought fairly, and killed only with justice. It was Christian. Most of all, it was admirably British at last.

Notes

Introduction

1. Olive Anderson, "The Growth of Christian Militarism in Mid-Victorian Britain," *English Historical Review* 86 (1971): 46–72. The other article that historians frequently cite is H. J. Hanham, "Religion and Nationality in the Mid-Victorian Army," in *War and Society*, ed. M. R. D. Foot (London: Paul Elek, 1973), 159–81. Taken together, the arguments of just these two pieces form the foundation of current military-social history, particularly with any reference to the role of religion in the army. No major work on the army is without reference to both these articles.

2. John M. MacKenzie, ed., *Popular Imperialism and the Military, 1850–1950* (Manchester: Manchester University Press, 1992), 1–2.

3. Gwyn Harries-Jenkins, *The Army in Victorian Society* (Toronto: University of Toronto Press, 1977). Also, "The Development of Professionalism in the Victorian Army," *Armed Forces and Society* 1, no. 4 (August 1974): 472–89. See also, W. S. Hamer, *The British Army: Civil-Military Relations, 1885–1905* (New York: Oxford University Press, 1970); and John Sweetman, *War and Administration: The Significance of the Crimean War for the British Army* (Edinburgh: Scottish Academic Press, 1984). All of these works tend to the side of high politics and ministries. On the other side, the following authors have treated religion in the army purely in terms of command and control. See Alan Ramsey Skelley, *The Victorian Army at Home: The Recruitment and Terms and Conditions of the British Regular, 1859–1899* (London: Croom Helm, 1977). See also Edward M. Spiers, *The Army and Society, 1815–1914* (New York: Longman, 1980). The powerful combination of religion and militarism has had a lively exploration in the fields of imperial history. There, however, it is heavily theorized with psychoanalysis, various "constructions," and cultural imperialism.

4. Anne Summers, "Militarism in Britain before the Great War," *History Workshop Journal* 2 (1976): 104–23. Summers indeed argued that religious respectability played a key role in the socialization of the regular army. However, she discounts official government action in the process of military religious reform (109).

5. Anderson, "Christian Militarism," 46–72. Correlli Barnett, *Britain and Her Army, 1509–1970: A Military, Political, and Social Survey* (New York: W. Morrow, 1970). Also, Harries-Jenkins, *Army in Victorian Society*; Spiers, *Army and Society.*

6. Richard L. Blanco, "Attempts to Abolish Branding and Flogging in the Army of Victorian England Before 1881," *Journal of the Society for Army Historical Research* 46 (1968): 137–45. Also, J. R. Dinwiddy, "The Early Nineteenth-Century Campaign against Flogging in the Army," *English Historical Review* 97 (1982): 308–31. Also, Hew Strachan, *From Waterloo to Balaclava: Tactics, Technology, and the British Army, 1815–1854* (Cambridge: Cambridge

University Press, 1985). Also, Hew Strachan, *Wellington's Legacy: The Reform of the British Army, 1830–1854* (Manchester: Manchester University Press, 1984).

7. *House of Commons Parliamentary Papers (HCPP)* 1842 (93), 27. 137, Particulars of the Sum of £11,000 Charged in the Army Estimates for Divine Service in the Army.

8. Ibid.

9. Strachan, *Wellington's Legacy*, 88.

10. *HCPP*, 1848–49 (239), 41.81, Particulars of the Sum of £16,800 charged in the Army Estimates for the year 1848–49. See also, 1857–58, 37.239, Returns for the Distribution of Sums for Divine Service in the Army, 1853–56, and for Religious Books.

11. WO43/819.311–14, 321–24, 332–35.

12. George Robert Gleig, "Moral Discipline of the Army," *Quarterly Review*, 76, (1845): 387–424; also, Strachan, *Wellington's Legacy*, 88–97.

13. *HCPP* 1864, 35.305, Details of Expenditure for Commissioned Chaplains, distinguishing Protestants and Roman Catholics; similar for Officiating Clergy at Home and Abroad; and for Religious Books.

14. *HCPP* 1861, 26.493, Copy of the Warrant appointing Roman Catholic Chaplains to have Rank in the Army.

15. Rev. A. C. E. Jarvis, "My Predecessors in Office," *Quarterly Journal of the Royal Army Chaplains' Department* 3:289–302, 361–82, 444–520; 4:14–77, 320–58; 5:9–29, 95–114, 420–45. Jarvis copied the department's personnel roster for the years 1854 through 1875 into his article; see 5:25–28.

16. These numbers are derived from a survey, Returns for Divine Service in the Army, 1842–1879. The survey is my overview of several Returns.

17. Ibid.

18. *HCPP* 1864 (382), 35.585, Return stating the Numbers and Religious Denominations of all the Soldiers in Her Majesty's Land and Marine Forces; also, 1872 (170), 37.445, Return of Numbers of N.C.O.s and Men in the Army according to their Religious Denominations; also, 1878–79 (159) 43.523,Return of Numbers of N.C.O.s and Men in Army, according to their Religious Denominations.

19. Hanham, "Religion and Nationality," 180–81.

20. Linda Colley, *Britons: Forging the Nation, 1707–1837* (New Haven, Conn.: Yale University Press, 1992).

Chapter 1. The Royal Army Chaplains' Department, 1809–1825

1. Colley, *Britons*, 177–93, 285–308.

2. Tony Hayter, *The Army and the Crowd in Mid-Georgian England* (London: Macmillan Press, 1978).

3. Peter Burroughs, "An Unreformed Army? 1815–1868," in *The Oxford Illustrated History of the British Army*, ed. David Chandler and Ian Beckett (New York: Oxford University Press, 1994), 168–69. See also Blanco, "Attempts to Abolish Branding and Flogging" 137–45; also, Peter Burroughs, "Crime and Punishment in the British Army, 1815–1870," *English Historical Review* 100 (1985): 545–71; also Dinwiddy, "Flogging," 308–31; also E. E. Steiner, "Separat-

ing the Soldier from the Citizen: Ideology and Criticism of Corporal Punishment in the British Armies, 1790–1815," *Social History* 8, no. 1 (1983): 19–35.

4. Spiers, *Army and Society, 1815–1914* (New York: Longman, 1980), 89. See also, Dinwiddy, "Flogging." Both Spiers and Dinwiddy portray the debates about flogging as posing outsider political reformers and a small minority of army officers opposed to the lash versus the High Command of the army and the bulk of the officer corps. See also, Burroughs, "Crime and Punishment," 545–46. Burroughs finds the officer corps of this era to have "evinced an unyielding traditionalism and an unquestioning adherence to Wellingtonian practices. They were more concerned with discipline and order, as the necessary basis of military efficiency and morale, than with the welfare and living conditions of the common soldier, for whom their sympathies were remote and impersonal."

5. Wellington, Wellesley, Arthur, First Duke of *Despatches, Correspondence, and Memoranda*, vol. 5 (London: John Murray, 1880), 594, "Memorandum on Plan to Reduce Flogging," 22 April 1829. Hardinge, Hill, and, until death removed him from command, the duke of York concurred. See also Dinwiddy, "Flogging," 320.

6. Wellington, *Despatches*, 28:37, "Memorandum on Corporal Punishment," 4 March 1832.

7. Paul E.Kopperman, "Religion and Religious Policy in the British Army, c. 1700–1796," *Journal of Religious History* 14, no. 4 (1987): 390–405. Consider the Reverend Peter Vatass, who in over fifty years never once attended the troops supposedly under his care.

8. Ibid., 390.

9. Frederick Augustus, duke of York and Albany (1763–1827). Second son of George III and Queen Charlotte; gazetted to the army as a colonel at the age of seventeen, from which time he maintained a lifelong passion for soldiering. In 1793, George III demanded York lead the British contingent in the Austrian campaign in Flanders, where the duke failed miserably as a military commander. Elevation to the post of commander in chief in 1798 was followed closely by York's second disastrous attempt to lead troops in the field in Holland, 1799. In 1809 he was forced to retire after revelations that York's mistress, Mary Anne Clarke, had been collecting money to influence the duke's decisions regarding postings and promotions; returned to Horse Guards 1811 to remain commander in chief until his death in 1827.

10. Sir John Smyth, *In This Sign Conquer: The Story of the Army Chaplains* (London: A. R. Mowbray, 1968), 30–31.

11. WO43/578.173.

12. Anthony Bruce, *The Purchase System in the British Army, 1660–1871* (London: Royal Historical Society, 1980).

13. WO43/578.173; Smyth, *In This Sign*, 42.

14. WO43/578.174–85.

15. Ibid.

16. One thinks of the famous Ironsides, and Cromwell's frequent prayer meetings with his men and with fellow officers.

17. Jasper Ridley, *Lord Palmerston* (New York: E. P. Dutton, and Co., 1971), 36–40, 81–83. During his time as secretary at war, Palmerston fought a running battle with Horse Guards over the issue of stoppages. Despite legislation against the practice, and despite winning a ministerial decision in 1812 against the commander in chief, Palmerston never succeeded in overcoming army resist-

ance to this particular civilian "interference;" into the 1840s, a private soldier was lucky if he received 1d. of his daily shilling. Stoppages against soldier pay ranged from mess fees, laundry, and haircuts to barrack repair and hospitalization. Soldiers also had to pay for uniforms and kits. Spiers, *Army and Society*, 52.

18. Spencer Perceval (1762–1812), second son of John Perceval, second earl of Egmont. Trinity College, Cambridge; a legal mind of considerable talent and ambition; MP for Northampton from 1796; attorney general, 1802–6; chancellor of the exchequer under Portland in 1807; prime minister in 1809 in a tulmultuous government during the height of the crisis of the Peninsular Campaign; assassinated May 1812.

19. WO43/578.199, Perceval circular memo to commander in chief and secretary of state at war dated 17 January 1809.

20. WO43/578.208–10. Owen received £800 per annum with an additional £100 to hire an assistant.

21. Smyth, *In This Sign*, 34–36.

22. WO43/226.260–61.

23. WO43/226.223.

24. Wellington, *Despatches* 4:67, 30 July 1827; also, 4:106, 4 August 1827. Wellington hoped that, despite government schemes and parliamentary debates demanding the reduction of army manpower, recruiting could continue "quietly." He also wrote an extensive memo at this time that attempted to portray the army as understrength for its colonial and European commitments.

25. Sir Henry Hardinge, First Viscount Hardinge of Lahore, KCB (1785–1856). Gazetted to the Queen's Rangers in Canada, 1799; rose by purchase to rank of captain in the infantry by 1804; Royal Military College, 1806–7; deputy assistant quartermaster general in the Peninsula, where distinguished service earned him promotion to the Portugese staff; combat officer in the Portuguese Brigade, 1811–14, during which time he earned increasing favor from Wellington; liaison staff officer to the Prussians during the Waterloo campaign; MP 1826–34, 1835–44; secretary for war July 1828 to July 1830 under Wellington; secretary for war under Peel, 1841–44; governor general of India, 1844–48. Though entitled to command forces in India, Hardinge voluntarily served as second in command to Gough during the First Seikh War; elevated to peerage 1846; unsuccesful general commanding in chief, Horse Guards, 1854–56. Despite his distinguished prior record, Hardinge was justly and severly criticized for army shortcomings revealed in Crimea.

26. Wellington, *Despatches* 4:321.

27. "Memorandum restricting King's Warrants in cases in which the Paymaster General rejects 'informal Affidavits,'" Hardinge Papers, McLennan Library, McGill University Library Rare Book Collection, file C, folder 3, "Military Chaplains."

28. Alan D. Gilbert, *Religion and Society in Industrial England: Church, Chapel, and Social Change, 1740–1914* (New York: Longman, 1976), chap. 2, "Patterns of Religious Practice, 1740–1914." See also D. W. Bebbington, *Evangelicalism in Modern Britain: A History from the 1730s to the 1980s* (London: George Allen and Unwin, 1982).

29. WO43/537.142–56.

30. Ibid.

31. WO43.537.156.

Chapter 2. The Breakdown of the Old Establishment

1. Robert Hodgson (1773–1844). Peterhouse, Cambridge, B.A., 1795; fellow, 1796; M.A., 1798; D.D., 1816. Dean of Chester, 1816; dean of Carlyle, 1820; various and plural parishes. Hodgson was appointed chaplain general in 1824 upon the death of John Owen. As will become apparent, Hodgson differed radically from his predecessors in his willingness to interject himself into daily army affairs.

2. WO43/535.85.

3. Wellington maintained a personal supervision of army matters through Hardinge, who did not make changes without the duke's explicit approval. Brief letter Hardinge to Hill, Hardinge Papers, file C, folder 4, 13 February 1830.

4. Jarvis, "My Predecessors" 3:289–302, 261–382, 444–520; 4:14–77, 320–58; 5:9–29, 95–114, 420–45. See 3:477. Because of subsequent heavy PRO weeding of War Office papers, Jarvis is sometimes the only surviving record.

5. Letter, Hardinge to Hodgson, 13 November, 1828. Reproduced in Jarvis, "My Predecessors" 3:478. Hardinge estimated the cost to the Chaplain's Department of half pay and widow's pensions to be nearly £5,000. "Memos Relating to Chaplains on Half-Pay, November 1828," Hardinge Papers, file C, folder 3, "Military Chaplains."

6. During the 1830s and 1840s, there was no discussion about Wesleyans, other Methodists, Baptists, or any other "Dissenting" denomination that had troops in the army. Theirs would be a later day. Instead, the issue first appeared in two of its simplest forms: Presbyterians outside the boundaries of Scotland, and the general case of Roman Catholics. Wesleyans did not get capitation grants to remunerate either civilian clergy for services until 1862 or assistant chaplains until 1881. Even then they refused actual commissions on the grounds that such service would compromise them as a "free church." The government recognized Jews as a distinct group in 1889, and allowed a commissioned Jewish chaplain in 1892. Smyth, *In This Sign*, xix.

7. Presumably by this Crea meant to say he was unattached to any parish, not a Congregationalist.

8. WO43/245.10–11. Crea to Palmerston, dated 1 July 1825.

9. Ibid. See also Jarvis, "My Predecessors" 3:465.

10. King's had been a special military hospital, uniquely suspended from regular legal restrictions during the crisis of the Napoleonic Wars because it was budgeted under "Miscelaneous Irish Estimates." King's therefore had quietly maintained a special arrangement for the services of the Catholic priest. During this era the army had adopted a policy of "benign neglect" concerning legal disabilities on Catholics. Untitled memo regarding recapitulation of money formerly paid to Roman Catholic priests, 1844, Hardinge Papers. Quiet was definitely better than open and uniform repeal of anti-Catholic restrictions. Catholic relief in 1778, prompted by the emergency of the American rebellion, occasioned great political unrest in England, including the infamous Gordon Riots of 1780. Robert Kent Donovan, "Military Origins of the Roman Catholic Relief Programme of 1778," *Historical Journal* 28, no. 1 (1985): 79–102.

11. WO43/213.100.

12. WO43/213.101.

13. WO43/740.241.

14. Hodgson to Palmerston, August 1826, in Jarvis, "My Predecessors" 3:466.

15. Hodgson to Palmerston, September 1826, ibid.

16. Jarvis, "My Predecessors" 3:468. Russell to Hodgson, 18 September 1827.

17. Frederick John Robinson (1782–1859), later first earl of Ripon. Although a lackluster prime minister, Goderich was a Whig who got along well with Wellington. The men shared a similar social conservatism and a strong aversion to popular agitations.

18. The government considered the Scots Greys, the Royals (1st), 21st, 26th, 42d, 71st, 72d, 73d, 74th, 78th, 79th, 90th, 92d, and 93d as "Scotch" regiments.

19. WO43/740.242; see also Treasury to Palmerston, 9 November 1827; also, Treasury Circular on Payment of Officiating Clergy, 10 January 1828, in Jarvis, "My Predecessors" 3:471.

20. WO43/740.242.

21. WO43/740.243. In 1843, Hardinge had his office prepare this memorandum summarizing the history of religious regulations, in an effort to sort out what was by then a confusing and arbitrary system.

22. WO43/740.244.

23. Hodgson to Merry, deputy secretary at war, August 1827, in Jarvis, "My Predecessors" 3:467.

24. Ibid.

25. Hanham, "Religion and Nationality," 161, 162–63. See also memo dated April 1829, WO43/355.8–9. The War Office memo considers only the official Scots units. Hanham found that Scotsmen in the army numbered between 13,500 and 17,000 for most of the nineteenth century.

26. Robert Currie, Alan Gilbert, and L. Horsley, *Churches and Churchgoers: Patterns of Growth of Churches in the British Isles since 1700* (Oxford: Clarendon Press, 1977), 25–30. Currie, Gilbert, and Horsley adopted a system under which they defined "active membership" in the Church of England as equal to the communicants at the "great festivals" of the church calendar.

27. Irish immigration explained rising Catholic numbers. The growth of Nonconformity represented the real struggle for the Church of England.

28. Irreligious attitudes of the rankers might be surmised from phenomena such as Wellington's discipline difficulties in the Peninsula or the notorious abuse of alcohol displayed by British troops both in Europe and India in this era. See Alan Swinson and Donald Scott, eds., *The Memoirs of Private Waterfield, Soldier in Her Majesty's 32nd Regiment of Foot* (Cassel: London, 1968), 8, 24, 28–29, 32–34. In 1842 Private Waterfield began Queen's service in India. Both his departure from Portsmouth and his arrival in Calcutta were marked by drunken riots among the men of his unit. He equated heavy drinking with a cavalier attitude to religious morality. See also *HCPP* 1841 (329) 14.239–50. Reports on Corporal Punishment in the Army, Navy, and Marines. In 1838 and 1839, the army in Great Britain prosecuted an average of 715 cases each year for crimes related to alcohol abuse. Taking the colonies and possessions into account, the army prosecuted 1,903 and 2,294 such cases in each year respectively. Total court-martial offences for each year were 6,347 and 8,280 respectively, making alcohol-related crimes 30 percent in 1838 and 28 percent in 1839. Categories of charges included: mutiny, desertion, violence to superiors, disobedience, quitting/asleep at post, drunk on duty, habitual drunk, disgraceful conduct, absent without leave, theft, and miscellaneous.

29. In a welcome revision to older, more methodically sociological schools of interpretation, J. C. D. Clark and Boyd Hilton have persuasively argued for

the determinative influence of denominationalism and theology as such in the politics and economics of Britain at least until the 1850s. Clark concerns himself with politics in the eighteenth century and until 1832. Hilton focuses on economic and political theory in the Victorian era. J. C. D. Clark, *English Society, 1688–1832* (New York: Cambridge University Press, 1985); Boyd Hilton, *The Age of Atonement: The Influence of Evangelicalism on Social and Economic Thought, 1785–1865* (New York: Oxford University Press, 1988).

30. WO43/355.13–14. Hodgson included in a memo on Mitchell's case a second, similar case of Reverend Josias Wilson at Drogheda.

31. WO43/355.18–19.

32. WO43/740.242.

33. Sir Henry George Grey, Viscount Howick, later third Earl Grey (1802–1894). Second son of Charles, second Earl Grey. Trinity College, Cambridge; M.A., 1832; Whig MP for Winchelsea, 1826–30; strong advocate of Catholic Emancipation; strong advocate of Reform; MP for Northumberland, 1831–41; secretary at war under Melbourne, 1835–39; MP for Sunderland, 1841–45, until elevated to peerage on the death of his father; strong advocate of free-trade; secretary for the Colonies under Russell, 1846–52, after which he never held another office. Though lackluster as colonial secretary, Grey is considered to have been an energetic and reform-minded secretary at war. Peter Burroughs, "An Unreformed Army," in *Oxford Illustrated History of the British Army* (New York: Oxford University Press, 1994), 174–76.

34. This determination would also prove a headache. For the time being, army administrators saw only that a troop's religious affiliation should match the church dominant in his nation, i.e., all English soldiers would be assumed Anglican, all Scots, Presbyterian, and all Irish, Catholic, despite the official if not very lively existence of an Episcopalian Church of Ireland.

35. WO43/740.242. See also Howick to Treasury, 6 October 1835, quoted in WO43/356.20–24.

36. The church reinstituted its English hierarchy in 1850 and 1851. This action stirred much controversy but no violent outbreaks. See, G. I. T. Machin, *Politics and the Churches in Great Britain, 1832–1868* (New York: Oxford University Press, 1977).

37. WO43/740.243. see also untitled memo regarding recapitulation of money formerly paid to Roman Catholic priests, dated 1844, Hardinge Papers. As late as 1830, Catholic Irish constituted 42.2 percent of the infantry, though the figure steadily declined for the rest of the century. Hanham, "Religion and Nationality," 178.

38. John Cam Hobhouse, Baron Broughton (1786–1869). Eldest son of of Sir Benjamin Hobhouse, Bart. Early in life educated in Unitarian dissent; Trinity College, Cambridge B.A., 1808; MA, 1811. Close friend of Byron and self-styled radical. Admirer of Bonaparte. MP from 1820. Secretary at war 1832 under Lord Grey. Notable for his aggresive posture favoring army reforms, but stymied by army leadership; resigned secretary at war 1833. Though he served in other cabinet posts, he always refused to return to the War Office after 1833.

39. WO43/740.243. See also WO43/599.7–8.

40. WO43/356.24. Riley asked for £40 per year for special services for troops and for visiting the sick, acts he had performed some time already without any financial aid.

41. WO43/659.302.

42. WO43/740.245. The sophism prevented the government from paying for

priests to say mass. There was an exception made even to this rule. At Dublin an allowance of £60 per year was paid separately from that of £1.1 each for separate services performed by priests at the Arran Quay Chapel.

43. WO43/356.23.

44. WO43/356.26–27.

45. Rowland Hill, first Viscount Hill (1772–1842). Appointed ensign Thirty-eighth Foot in Ireland, 1790, Hill followed a military career the rest of his life. Combat officer in Gibraltar, Egypt; promoted brigadier 1805; brigade then division commander under Wellington in Portugal and Spain, 1808–14; lieutenant general, 1812; peerage, 1814; heroic service as corps commander during the Waterloo campaign earned Wellington's deep regard; promoted to general, 1825; 1828 during Wellington's premiership appointed general commanding in chief, a post he held until shortly before his death in 1842. Called a "Tory of the old school," Hill shared many values and attitudes with the duke of Wellington, his friend and longtime companion at arms. It was only with great reluctance that Hill finally promulgated orders in 1839 allowing freedom of worship to Catholics and Presbyterians.

46. Hill to Howick via the Deputy Secretary at War, 2 April 1836, WO43/659.303.

47. Report by Lord Howick to the Treasury Board and Lord Hill regarding the payment of Roman Catholic and Presbyterian clergy; no date, but probably around early May 1836, WO43/659.300–301.

48. WO43/659.310–11.

49. WO43/659.314. Howick also found it difficult to count Presbyterians, as the returns of the army classed soldiers by kingdom, and as either "Roman Catholic" or "Protestant" without further distinction.

Chapter 3. A Conservative Hiatus: The Career of W. W. Dakins

1. WO43/226.258.
2. Ibid.
3. WO43/226.260–61.
4. WO43/226.262.
5. WO43/226.268–69.
6. Dakins to Palmerston, 20 July 1824, WO43/226.270–71. The argument had been over pay for the period 4 June to 11 July. In 1827 Palmerston did take some pity when budget cuts cost Dakins his sinecure post as chaplain to the commander in chief. The duke of York had retained Dakins at £100. Wellington kept him on, but when the duke resigned rather than work with Canning, Dakins faced the extinction of his extra pay. Palmerston admitted that Dakins was probably underpaid and convinced Treasury to add the £100 to his salary as assistant chaplain general. See WO43/319.50–54.
7. WO43/535.96–97.
8. WO43/535.97.
9. WO43/535.89–91; WO4/347.41.
10. Anthony Ashley Cooper, seventh earl of Shaftesbury (1801–85); Christ Church, Oxford; converted in the mid-1820s to Evangelical practice of Anglicanism from a lukewarm participation in the church; MP from 1826; eschewed a career in high politics in favor of pursuing philanthropic reform; by marriage

in 1830 established familial relations with Palmerston; from 1828 vocal advocate for reform in mental health care practices; 1830s and 1840s Shaftesbury became the nation's leading spokesman for factory legislation; also dedicated himself and his money to supporting reforms for miners and chimney sweeps, in slum conditions, and for the creation of the "ragged schools;" president of the British and Foreign Bible Society, the London City Missions, supporter of the Church Missionary Society, the YMCA; until his death a nationally renowned social and religious activist.

11. William Wilberforce (1759–1833), St. John's, Cambridge; MP for Hull, 1780; from his school years an intimate and ardent supporter of Pitt; during 1784–85 Wilberforce experienced a religious conversion, after which he dedicated himself to an overtly religious life; 1787, obtained a royal proclamation for a society against vice, the "Proclamation Society;" befriended evangelical reformer Hannah More in 1787; from 1791 Wilberforce was a leader in the parliamentary fight against slavery and the slave trade; author of *Practical Christianity* (1797), an international best-seller on vital religion; leader of the Clapham Evangelicals; 1798, cofounder of the Church Missionary Society; 1803 cofounder of the Bible Society; supporter of Catholic Emancipation from 1813.

12. Dinwiddy, "Flogging," 331; Burroughs, "Crime and Punishment," 571. Both authors conclude that the antiflogging crusade, which achieved its ultimate end in 1881, was an affair of "a spirited minority," Lord Dudley Stuart said, quoted in Dinwiddy. Burroughs found army reform a long "uphill struggle against the forces of tradition and complacency."

13. Wellington's list of "antis" also included liberalization of army education, promotion from the ranks into the officer corps, and reform of systems of army punishment (especially flogging). Gleig, in his late memoirs, made a list of Wellington's failures on the score of reforms in the army: degradation of wagon train and the artillery, and an insufficient distribution of infantry battalions at home and abroad, leaving neither colonies nor Britain well protected. George Robert Gleig, *Personal Reminiscences of the First Duke of Wellington, With Sketches of some of his Guests and Contemporaries* (London: William Blackwood and Sons, 1904), 304–5.

14. Wellington's skepticism toward the "improvability" of the army was based in large part upon his experience in the peninsula. During his campaigns there, he was in constant struggle to prevent his soldiers from robbery, rape, and drunkenness. See Wellington, "Supplementary Despatches" in *Despatches, Correspondence, and Memoranda*, vols. 6 and 7, for his repeated orders against such crimes, and in exhortation to officers to control the men.

15. Wellington to Buckingham, 14 March 1831, Wellington, *Despatches* 7:409.

16. "Notes upon Reform," December 1831, ibid. 8:133.

17. It is important to distinguish Wellington the conservative strategist from the ultra-tories he had so alienated when his government sponsored Emancipation. Above all, Wellington by his conservatism aimed at the maintenance of order and the regime. He understood that limited change could be the best means of this. For example, he considered possible alterations in the status of British Catholics as early as April 1825. See Wellington, ii, *Despatches* 2:435; Seventh Duke of Wellington, *Wellington and His Friends, Letters of the First Duke of Wellington to the Rt. Hon. Charles and Mrs. Arbuthnot, the Earl and Countess of Wilton, Princess Lieven, and Miss Burdett-Coutts* (London: Macmillan and Co., 1965), 53. Wellington announces the completion of a "Catholick

[*sic*] Paper" to the Arbuthnots. Crudely Erastian, it nonetheless offered a plan of government sponsorship of Catholic priests and parishes in return for some control in appointing clergy and review of the message preached. Traditional conservatives simply balked at any state concession, no matter how cynical or contrived, to the dreaded Rome.

18. Hayter, *The Army and the Crowd*, 2. Hayter characterizes the era 1714–1820 as the heyday of the mob and as one in which Britain possessed "an almost perversely ineffective system of police." It is his point to show how tightly linked with the magistracy and with deferential social organization was the brute force of the military in keeping civil order. For vivid descriptions of the army's role in carrying out the frequent executions prescribed by the English common law of the eighteenth and early-nineteenth centuries, see, Douglas Hay, Peter Linebaugh, John G. Rule, E. P. Thompson, and Cal Winslow, eds., *Albion's Fatal Tree: Crime and Society in Eighteenth-Century England* (New York: Pantheon, 1975), 89–92, 98–101.

19. The years 1829 through 1856 witnessed only a slow and partial transformation of the domestic role of the army resulting from the introduction of the professional police. For the legislation creating the metropolitan and provincial police forces, see Stanley H. Palmer, *Police and Protest in England and Ireland, 1780–1850* (New York: Cambridge University Press, 1988), 215–77; also Carolyn Steedman, *Policing the Victorian Community: The Formation of Engish Provincial Police Forces, 1856–1880* (New York: Routledge and Kegan Paul, 1984), 2, 3, 25–27. On the incapacity of the early police forces to handle serious unrest, see F. C. Mather, *Public Order in the Age of the Chartists* (Manchester: Manchester University Press, 1959), 12. On the vital nature of army support for the magistracy well after 1829, see Douglas Hay and Francis Snyder, eds., *Policing and Prosecution in Britain, 1750–1850* (Oxford: Oxford University Press, 1989), 10–11; also Steedman, *Policing the Victorian Community* 3–4, 32–38; also Mather, *Public Order* 153. The army officer corps was increasingly impatient with the task of law enforcement. After 1819 officers more vocally criticized that duty. Hay and Snyder, *Policing*, 10; also Mather, *Public Order*, 157, 175.

20. J. C. D. Clark has done the most to illuminate the nature of the English ancien regime, particularly the vital social role and the theology of the state church. See, J. C. D. Clark, *English Society, 1688–1832: Ideology, Social Structure and Practice during the Ancien Regime* (New York: Cambridge University Press, 1885); also *The Language of Liberty, 1660–1832: Political Discourse and Social Dynamics in the Anglo-American World* (New York: Cambridge University Press, 1994). Dedicated in *Language* to unraveling the intricacies of the American rebellion, Clark provides vital insights into the importance of denominationalism and Christian heterodoxy for understanding the disruptions in the English social order, 1790–1832.

21. Geoffrey F. A. Best, *Temporal Pillars: Queen Anne's Bounty, the Ecclesiastical Commissioners, and the Church of England* (Cambridge: Cambridge University Press, 1964), 245–46.

22. Ibid.

23. Best, *Temporal Pillars;* also, Norman Gash, *Sir Robert Peel: The life of Sir Robert Peel after 1830* (London: Longman, 1972); also, G. I. T. Machin, *Politics and the Churches in Great Britain, 1832–1868* (New York: Oxford University Press, 1977); also Gerald Parsons, ed., *Religion in Victorian Britain*, 4 vols. (Manchester: Manchester University Press, 1988).

24. Gash, *Sir Robert Peel*, 100, 103–4; Best, *Temporal Pillars*, 296–99.

25. Smyth, *In This Sign*, 38–39. Wellington's concept of "Methodism" seemed to include any zealous practice of religion.

26. See Donald M. Lewis, *Lighten Their Darkness: The Evangelical Mission to Working-Class London, 1828–1860* (New York: Greenwood Press, 1986); Geoffrey B. A. M. Finlayson, *The Seventh Earl of Shaftesbury, 1801–1885* (London: Eyre Methuen, 1981); also Dinwiddy, "Flogging." All provide fine examples of ongoing social justice and reform work among religiously active Britons in the same era during which church leadership fought Reform and other social issues. Wilberforce and antislavery and Evangelical efforts at factory legislation also illustrate the point.

Chapter 4. The Early Career of George Robert Gleig

1. George Robert Gleig (1796–1888), son of Bishop George Gleig; Balliol, Oxford; resigned his place there in 1811 to join the army; lieutenant of the infantry: Spain, 1813–14, also America, 1814 and 1815; six times wounded in combat; returned to Oxford, B.A. Magdalen Hall, 1818; M.A., 1821; chaplain to Chelsea Hospital 1834; chaplain general to the forces, 1844–75; inspector general of military schools 1846–57.

2. Alan Ramsey Skelley, *The Victorian Army at Home: The Recruitment and Terms and Conditions of the British Regular, 1859–1900* (London: Croom Helm, 1977), 86, 104. Gleig was a controversial figure as inspector general of military schools and quit the post in 1857, remaining chaplain general for many more years. Gleig throughout his career considered himself an expert advocate of educational reform. National Library of Scotland. G. R. Gleig, manuscript autobiography, "Memories of a Long Life of 4 Score Years," ca. 1886, 264–65 National Library of Scotland, Gleig Papers, for his thoughts on parish schools; also "National Education," *Quarterly Review* 82 (1852): 321–57.

3. Obituary, *Times*, 11 July 1888.

4. Elizabeth Longford *Wellington: Pillar of State* (New York: Harper and Row, 1971), 198, 281. During the lifetime of his duchess, Wellington was often not in control of his own social circle, at least not at his estate. After her death, he shied away from a second marriage, perhaps from fear of the social duties, perhaps out of a desire to keep a free hand with the ladies. He always had the habit of cultivating friendships and liaisons with younger women, married or not.

5. The novel, which appeared in 1825, was his first effort at fiction, and served as a sort of companion to his history, *Campaigns of the British Army at Washington and New Orleans* (1821).

6. This honor, allowing Gleig to dedicate a 1845 edition of *Subaltern* to him, marks perhaps the high point of Wellington's relationship with Gleig. After that year issues such as army education and the creation of new chaplaincies intervened between the men. Wellington's last years were ones of coldness and distance regarding Gleig.

7. Longford, *Pillar*, 138, 265. From the first ministry through the Reform fight, Gleig remained an eager client of the duke. At times, Wellington had to squelch the zeal of Gleig to prevent him fomenting counterrevolution in Kent. Ibid., 284.

8. Wellington, *Despatches*, vols. 7 and 8, passim. For example, hearing Wel-

lington's opinion that such activity would incite excess enthusiasm and be unseemly, Gleig stifled the formation of an anti-Reform Conservative Constitutional Society in Kent. Ibid., Wellington to Gleig, 4 July 1831, ibid. 7:466–68. Gleig to Wellington 14 July 1831, ibid. 7:466–68. Gleig constantly queried Wellington on the progress of the debate in Lords, and in return sent the duke intelligence of the county.

9. Wellington, *Despatches* 8:184. Gleig to Harrowby, 31 January 1832, in Gleig, *Personal Reminiscences*. See chaps. 3, 4, 5.

10. Gleig, Manuscript autobiography, 181–82. When Gleig first entered the army against the better judgment of his parents, he was but sixteen years old. He promised his father that, should he return in good health from his military adventures, he would thereafter heed paternal instructions as to his career. In later life he attributed his entire church career to this promise, and believed his true life's calling to have been that of a military officer.

11. Gleig, *Personal Reminiscences*, 25–30.

12. Ibid., 31.

13. Lord John Russell, First Earl Russell (1792–1878). Third son of John Russell, Sixth duke of Bedford; University of Edinburgh; MP for the pocket borough of Tavistock, 1814–18, 1818–20; between 1820 and 1832 a strong advocate of Reform; advocate for repeal of the Test and Corporation Acts in 1828 and for Catholic emancipation in 1829; parliamentary leader for Reform during the crisis of 1830–32; favored easing all social and legal restrictions on Dissenters; opposed to the continued establishment of the Church of Ireland; leader of the Opposition to Peel; entered Melbourne's cabinet as home secretary; opposed to many terms of the establishment of the Church of England; 1836 favored and won commutation of tithes, civil registration, Dissenter marriages solemnized outside the Church of England; anti-Corn Law 1840s; PM, 1846–52; foreign secretary under Aberdeen, then without portfolio, 1852–55; foreign secretary under Palmerston, 1859–65; briefly PM upon Palmerston's death, October 1865 to June 1866.

14. Gleig, *Personal Reminiscences*, 110–12.

15. Ibid., 112–15.

16. In his long life, Gleig achieved a prodigious, if not qualitatively superior, literary output. His bibliography numbers some thirty-one titles, excluding the textbooks he prepared for his army schools. Topics range from ancient and biblical histories to biographies, to military science and history, to sentimental fiction. Many of his works went through multiple editions and printings, including his two biographical studies of Wellington. He finally lost public esteem as an author around the turn of the century.

17. Gleig, *Personal Reminiscences*, 333. For the progress of army education from 1850, see also Skelley, *Victorian Army*, 86–98.

18. Gleig succeeded in reconverting the post to chaplain general in 1846, undoing the work of Hardinge's 1830 reductions. WO4/1035.336. Hew Strachan, *Wellington's Legacy: The Reform of the British Army, 1830–1854* (Manchester: Manchester University Press, 1984), 87.

19. WO43/357.65–66, 84–85.

20. George Robert Gleig, "Moral Discipline of the Army," *Quarterly Review* 76 (1845): 399, 404. It is also possible to glean these opinions from Gleig's voluminous personal correspondence deposited with the National Library of Scotland.

21. Brian Bond, "Edward Cardwell's Army Reforms, 1868–1874," *Army*

Quarterly and Defence Journal (April 1962): 108–17; Harries-Jenkins, "Development of Professionalism," 472–89; Edward M. Spiers, *The Late Victorian Army, 1868–1902* (Manchester: Manchester University Press, 1992), chap. 4, "Officers."

22. For the debate in Lords over the Army Chaplains Bill of 1868, see below, chap. 5.

23. WO43/740.241.

24. *HCPP*, 1842 (93), 27.137, Particulars of the Sum of £11,000 Charged in the Army Estimates for Divine Service in the Army; also, *HCPP*, 1847–48 (239), 41.81, Particulars of the Sum of £16,800 Charged in the Army Estimates for Divine Service for the Army for the year 1848–49; Skelley, *Victorian Army*, 166. Skelley says that spending for religious services for the troops did not really take off until the 1860s.

25. Sidney Herbert, First Baron Herbert of Lea (1810–61). Second son of George Augustus, Eleventh Earl Pembroke. Oriel College, Oxford, 1831; MP for Wiltshire from 1833; Peelite; secretary of the Board of Control during Peel's short administration, 1835; secretary to the admiralty under Peel, 1841; secretary at war, 1845–46; also under Aberdeen, 1852–55; colonial secretary for Palmerston, 1855; exonerated by the Roebuck Commission investigating incompetence in the Crimea; personal supporter of Florence Nightingale; leader of army sanitary reforms, 1856–59; secretary at war under Palmerston from June 1859; peerage 1860.

26. Gleig, "Moral Discipline," 387–424.

27. Gleig to Sidney Herbert, secretary of state at War, memo dated 30 May 1845, WO43/740.248.

28. That remark alone would be sufficient to raise the ire of Wellington and his followers. Longford, *Pillar*, 373–74. Wellington could always be persuaded to reminisce on and propound the lessons of the Waterloo campaign. Phillip Henry, fifth earl of Stanhope, *Notes of Conversations with the Duke of Wellington, 1831–1851* (1888; reprint, New York: De Capo Press, 1973), 221, 244, 245. Assorted conversations from 1840.

29. Gleig, "Moral Discipline," 390.

30. Ibid., 420.

31. Ibid.

32. Gleig to Herbert, memo, 30 May 1845, WO43/740.250–52.

33. Gleig, "Moral Discipline," 417.

34. WO43/740.252. Services were already mandatory, but the "weather discretion" of commanding officers undermined this regulation. Gleig, "Moral Discipline," 413, 414.

35. WO43/740.253.

36. Alan Haig, *The Victorian Clergy* (London: Croom Helm, 1984), 352; also, Best, *Temporal Pillars*; also, Gash, *Sir Robert Peel*.

37. Haig, *Victorian Clergy*, 2–4. Haig demonstrates that in the decade 1835–45 the general body of clergymen in the Church of England experienced a turnover in personnel. Fully 50 percent of these men were younger than forty-five, and most had been ordained only since 1834. For a survey of the thinking and theology behind the Tractarian movement, see Owen Chadwick, ed., *The Mind of the Oxford Movement* (Stanford, Calif.: Stanford University Press, 1961).

38. Haig, *Victorian Clergy*, 352. George Macaulay Trevelyan, *British History in the Nineteenth Century and After, 1782–1919* (New York: Harper and Row,

1937), 281. For a catalog of tendencies of behavior and thought among Victorian clergy, see Brenda Colloms, *Victorian Country Parsons* (Lincoln: University of Nebraska Press, 1977). The lives of these men, and the pace and manner in which they responded to change, represented the much slower, much less dynamic side of Anglican life.

39. Lewis, *Lighten Their Darkness.* Lewis emphasizes the importance of cooperation between Anglican and non-Anglican evangelicals, what he calls "pan-evangelicalism."

40. Gleig, "Moral Discipline," 397–98.

41. English and Welsh soldiers often did not constitute the majority of private troops, even in "English" units. This was especially true of the infantry. See, Skelley, *Victorian Army,* app. 6, tables 6A–2.1 and 6A–2.2; also, Hanham, "Religion and Nationality," app. 1. Hanham offers figures for the entire army, but nonetheless demonstrates the continued importance of Irish enlisted and noncommissioned officers through the 1860s. Through 1868, Irish accounted for 30 percent of the other ranks. Despite the population boom, English and Welsh soldiers did not constitute even 60 percent of the rank and file until 1869.

42. Gleig, "Moral Discipline," 397.

43. Ibid., 422, 423–24. Gleig also made some more conventional arguments concerning the army's role in providing "pioneering missionary" work in India. If the men of the army lived out virtuous lives, then Indians would understand that British administration meant civilization and spiritual redemption for them. More would convert, and the real reason for British successes in India, bringing the region to Christianity, would come closer to realization. Ibid., 406. This argument surfaced again and again during the nineteenth century, but was particularly critical during the Indian Mutiny of 1857. For a discussion of the relationship between empire and missionary endeavor, see Brian Stanley, *The Bible and the Flag: Protestant Missions and British Imperialism in the Nineteenth and Twentieth Centuries* (Leicester, Eng.: Intervarsity Press, 1990). On the duties of a Christian military presence in India, see Stanley, "Christian Responses to the Indian Mutiny of 1857," in *Studies in Church History: The Church and War,* vol. 20, ed. W. Sheils (Oxford: Oxford University Press, 1983), 278–89; Olive Anderson, "The Growth of Christian Militarism in Mid-Victorian Britain," *English Historical Review,* 86 (1971): 46–72.

44. Secretary at war to Gleig, memo dated 2 June 1845, WO43/740.256–57.

Chapter 5. Professionalization at the Royal Army Chaplains' Department

1. Jarvis, "My Predecessors" 5:25–28.

2. There is a voluminous literature on the Crimean War. The British public at the time, however, drew much of its information from the war correspondence of William Howard Russell of the *Times.* His reports did much to stir the popular fury at home over incompetence in the army. Nicolas Bentley, ed., *Russell's Despatches from the Crimea, 1854–1856* (New York: Hill and Wang, 1966).

3. *Times,* 2 November 1854, 9; and 27 November 1854, 8. The first ten of these volunteers were the Reverends E. Owen, C. E. Hadow, E. Eade, E. G. Parker, R. Freeman, H. A. Taylor, W. F. Hobson, W. Whyatt, D. Winham, and G. H. Proctor.

4. C.F. Pascoe, *Two Hundred Years of the S.P.G.: An Historical Account of the Society for the Propagation of the Gospel in Foreign Parts, 1701–1900* (London: SPG, 1901), 736, 742. See also *A Digest of S.P.G. Records* (London: SPG, 1893), 736, 922–23. See also *Times*, 2 April 1855, 10.

5. *Times*, 2 November 1854, 9.

6. *HCCP* 1856–57, Report on the Army before Sebastopol, vol. 9, pt. 1, 171–73, 180–82, questions 3313–24, 3426–28. Direct questions from the committee specifically about chaplains asked of Reverend E. G. Parker, one of the original SPG men sent to the war, tended to concern only the terrible conditions of the winter of 1855–56. Otherwise, committee members used the chaplain as a witness to the sufferings of the troops short of food, medicine, and adequate shelter.

7. The Church Protestant Defense Society, founded March of 1853, "was a response to . . . ritualism and the movement to revive the Convocation." The society was nominally chaired by the seventh earl Shaftesbury and directed by Secretary Taylor. On the whole, the CPDS was but a minor splinter of political anti-Catholicism. It was, however, one of the first groups to begin hounding "ritualists" within the Church of England. John Wolffe, *The Protestant Crusade in Great Britain, 1829–1860* (Oxford: Clarendon Press, 1991), 163, 319.

8. Ibid., 247. Though there was a brief flurry of agitation surrounding the so-called papal aggression of 1850, by 1854 organized political anti-Catholicism was in decline in Britain.

9. WO43/357.65–66.

10. Fox Maule, second Baron Panmure, eleventh earl of Dalhousie (1801–1874). Charterhouse, no university. Served twelve years as an officer of the line, 1820–1832; Liberal Whig MP for Perthshire, the Elgin burghs, and Perth sucessively, 1835–52; secretary at war under Russell, 1846–52; secretary for war under Palmerston, 1855–58.

11. WO43/357.30–31.

12. WO43/357.84–85.

13. Ibid.

14. WO43/357.88.

15. Edward M. Spiers, *Radical General: Sir George de Lacy Evans, 1787–1870* (Manchester: Manchester University Press, 1983).

16. *Hansard Parliamentary Debates*, 3d ser., 11 April 1856, 878–79.

17. Jarvis, "My Predecessors" 5:25–28.

18. *Hansard*, 11 April 1856, 879–80.

19. Ibid., 880.

20. Palmerston during his time at the War Office argued for strict parliamentary supremacy over army command in all matters. He was notorious for stringent economy. Ridley, *Lord Palmerston*, 36–40, 56–57.

21. *Hansard*, 11 April 1856, 881.

22. Smyth, *In This Sign*, 87.

23. *HCCP* 1861, "Copy of the Order or Warrant appointing Roman Catholic Chaplains to have Rank in the Army," 36.493–94. Also, WO43/740.267–69.

24. *HCPP*, "Copy of the Order"; Smyth, *In This Sign*, 113.

25. Memorandum as to the position of such of the Army Chaplains as are Members of the Established Church of England and Ireland, 3, WO33/19.1–9.

26. Ibid., 4.

27. Ibid.

28. Archibald Campbell Tait, later archbishop of Canterbury (1811–82).

Scottish born; Glasgow University, 1827–30; though raised Presbyterian, he aspired to the clergy of the Church of England and successfully entered Balliol, Oxford, in 1830; B.A., 1833; fellow, 1834; tutor, 1835; ordained, 1836; proponent of Reform, 1831–33; opposed to the Tractarian movement, especially after publication of "Tract XC;" headmaster at Rugby, 1842–50; recommended by Palmerston for the bishopric of London, consecrated 1856; advocate of urban mission, he led renewed evangelization efforts in London, 1857–58; presided over sharp controversies caused by the appearance of Darwin's works (which he denied had anything to say about Christianity), and scriptural criticism (in which he defended the right of Colenso, bishop of Natal, to fair trial for heterodox interpretations of the Pentateuch); elevated to Canterbury, 1869; opposed to Irish disestablishment, he nonetheless cooperated with Gladstone on the grounds of political demand; tolerant of High Church clergy; tolerant of relief for Nonconformity, approved the Burial Act of 1880, allowing for Nonconformist burial ceremonies in churchyards.

29. "Memorandum as to the Position," 7. Charles Thomas Longley (1794–1868). Christ Church, Oxford; B.A., 1815, M.A., 1818; B.D. and D.D., 1829; headmaster at Harrow, 1829–36; consecrated bishop of Ripon, 1836; translated to Durham, 1856; elevated to York, 1860; elevated to Canterbury, 1862; condemned Colenso for his heterodox critical interpretation of the Pentateuch; in Lords he was a liberal, but opposed Oxford University Reform (1854), the Divorce Bill (1857), and liberal alterations to the Prayer Book and burial services.

30. George R. Gleig, "Address to the Men of the Royal Army Chaplains' Department, 12 June 1867." Gleig had the address printed and published as a formal statement of RACD policy respecting the Establishment. A copy appears transcribed in Jarvis, "My Predecessors" 4:335–41.

31. Jarvis, "My Predecessors" 4:336. Gleig was arguing in favor of a political subordination of the church to lay authority. In 1867, this issue, which had been part of the Tratctarians' complaint in the 1830s and 1840s, at the heart of Reform troubles in the 1830s, and had recently exercised minds from Palmerston to Gladstone, was still painful. Since 1828, the Church of England had suffered increasing subordination to an increasingly plural and secularized society. Where was the proper emphasis in the phrase "state church?" Perry Butler, *Gladstone: Church, State and Tractarianism: A Study of His Religious Ideas and Attitudes, 1809–1859* (Oxford: Clarendon Press, 1982); Chadwick, *Mind of the Oxford Movement*, introduction, 1–64; Anthony Lentin, "Anglicanism, Parliament, and the Courts," in *Religion in Victorian Britain*, ed. Gerald Parsons, (Manchester: Manchester University Press, 1988), 2:89–105; P. T. Marsh, *The Victorian Church in Decline: Archbishop Tait and the Church of England, 1868–1882* (Pittsburgh, Penn.: Pittsburgh University Press, 1969); E. R. Norman, *Church and Society in England, 1770–1970* (Oxford: Clarendon Press, 1976), 71–122.

32. In 1867, non-Anglicans in England still faced disabilities such as access to university degrees, and the independent practice of rites of passage such as marriage, birth registry, and burial. These were considered hallmarks of the established nature of the Church of England, although they soon succumbed to politics.

33. Jarvis, "My Predecessors" 4:336, 337.

34. Ibid., 338.

35. These were all High liturgical practices considered "Romanizing," and

therefore scandalous to Low and anti–High Anglicans, as well as to Presbyterians.

36. Jarvis, "My Predecessors," 4:339, 340.

37. The full title was *The Church in the Army; a Letter to the Right Honourable Sir J. S. Pakington, Bart., G.C.B., M.P., Secretary of State for War, by an Officer* (London: W. H. Bartlett and Co., 1868). There is a copy in the British Museum Library. It also appears transcribed in full in Jarvis 4:341–51.

38. "Memorandum as to the Position," 7.

39. Disraeli did not leave office until December of 1868. This bill then was not orignally part of the Liberal plan for army reform introduced by Cardwell and the Gladstone government. It later passed as part of that larger package. All bills having to do with the established church were the primary concern of Lords, wherein sat the bishops.

40. *Hansard*, 3d series, 9 June 1868, 1299–1300.

41. Archibald Campbell Tait.

42. *Hansard*, 9 June 1868, 1300–1301.

43. William Thomson (1819–1890). Queen's College, Oxford; B.A., 1840, M.A., 1844; ordained, 1843; first famed as a scholary logician; tutor in logic at Queen's, 1847–55; popular lecturer and preacher; strong advocate of university reform, especially the removal of geographic restrictions for college fellowships; provost of Queen's, 1855–58; established a wide reputation as a reformer and broad churchman; defended Anglican orthodoxy against Darwinism and new biblical criticism; consecrated bishop of Gloucester and Bristol, 1861; elevated to York, 1862; established a general policy of maintaining the national status of the established church by demonstrating the social relevance of the church for industrializing England; dedicated to winning back the northern working classes; supported due process for the Colenso heresy case.

44. Charles Thomas Longley.

45. *Hansard*, 11 June 1868, 1389–93.

46. Ibid., 12 June 1868, 1466–68. See also *HCPP* 1867–68, "An Act to Afford Greater Facilities for the Ministrations of Army Chaplains" (225), 1.17.

47. Memo G. R. Gleig to Sir Edward Lugard, Permanent undersecretary of state for war, July 1868. Reproduced in Jarvis, "My Predecessors," 4:357–58.

48. Jarvis, "My Predecessors" 5:421.

Chapter 6. A Kinder, Gentler British Army

1. Upon taking office in 1844, Gleig's first task had been to establish the arguments favoring an overhaul of and a greater financial commitment to army religion. His first eighteen months in office were absorbed by a public and private campaign to get out his message. See Gleig, "Moral Discipline," 399, 404. Gleig returned to these ideas frequently in his War office memos and his voluminous personal correspondence deposited with the National Library of Scotland.

2. For most of the nineteenth century, these included Brighton, Bristol, Colchester, Chatham, Canterbury, Dover, Deal, Dorchester, Exeter, Hythe, Hounslow, Leeds, London, Maidstone, Plymouth, Portsmouth, Parkhurst, Sheerness, Shorncliffe, Trowbridge, Weymouth, Winchester, Woolwich, Warley, Windsor, and York. For overview essays on the development of the major garrison towns,

see Peter Dietz, ed., *Garrison: Ten British Military Towns* (London: Brassey's Defence Publishers, 1986).

3. By way of comparison, consider some of the recorded facts about the economy and practices of Metropolitan prostitution. There, poverty or entrapment were the most common explanations of a prostitute's life. See Edward J. Bristow, *Vice and Vigilance: Purity Movements in Britain since 1700* (Dublin: Gill and Macmillan, 1977), 57–67; also Ronald Hyam, *Empire and Sexuality: The British Experience* (Manchester: Manchester University Press, 1990), 60–65; Also, Frances Finnegan, *Poverty and Prostitution: A Study of Victorian Prostitutes in York* (Cambridge: Cambridge University Press, 1979). Finnegan, who argues that conditions of prostitution in Victorian-era York were common in other English cities, found that the York prostitutes faced tremendous economic and social pressures forcing them ever farther down the social ladder. Streetwalking, diseases, drunkenness, and early death awaited most prostitutes. Poverty was the dominant factor in the lives of common York prostitutes. During his investigations of London, Henry Mayhew uncovered countless tragedies of prostitution and poverty. These he reported in the *Morning Chronicle* and later collected in his *London Labour and the London Poor* (1851); see also J. M. Golby, ed., *Culture and Society in Britain, 1850–1890: A Source Book of Contemporary Writings* (Oxford: Oxford University Press, 1986). Golby's book is an interesting compilation of contemporary journalism and political comment.

4. Skelley, *Victorian Army*, chaps. 1, 3; Spiers, *Late Victorian Army*, 142–47; and *Army and Society*, 55–67.

5. Monica Charlot, *Victoria, the Young Queen* (London: Blackwell, 1991), 231, 233; also, Robert Rhodes James, *Prince Albert: A Biography* (New York: Albert A. Knopf, 1984), 106–7; also, Stanley Weintraub, *Victoria: An Intimate Biography* (New York: E. P. Dutton, 1987), 642–43. Perhaps it was not so difficult to gain a reputation (deserved or not) for clean living when one succeeded William IV. Certainly it was not so difficult as long as Albert set the tone of the court. After Albert's untimely death in 1861, the neurotic personality of Victoria, especially in the scandal surrounding her relationship with her "highland servant" John Brown, destroyed the reputation of the court for social and sexual correctness. See Theo Aronson, *Heart of a Queen: Queen Victoria's Romantic Attachments* (London: John Murray, 1991), 135.

6. Similar descriptions, and worse, of urban-poor and working-class housing can be found in many sources, such as Henry Mayhew's letters to the *Morning Chronicle*. These later appeared collected and published under the title *London Labour and the London Poor* (1851). Two well-known examples, one of which also spans forward in time into the twentieth century, are found in Friedrich Engels's *Condition of the Working Class in England* (1845) and George Orwell's *Road to Wigan Pier* (1937). See also, E. P. Thompson, *The Making of the English Working Class* (New York: Vintage, 1963), 318–22.

7. Lt.-Colonel Howard N. Cole, *The Story of Aldershot: A History and Guide to Town and Camp* (Aldershot: Gale and Polden, 1951), 70–78; see, Charles Dickens, "Aldershot Town and Camp," *All the Year 'Round* (20 August 1859): 401–8.

8. *HCCP* 1866, "Report on the Late Epidemic of Scarlet Fever among Children in Aldershot Camp" (3708) 17:6, 21. See also, *HCPP*, 1870, "Copy of Report made to the Secretary of State for the Home Department by Mr. Rawlinson, under the Sanitary Act of 1866, after an Inquiry as to the Truth or other-

wise of certain Allegations made by Members of the Local Board of Health for the District of Aldershot, in the County of Hants, as to the alleged Pollution of the River Blackwater by SEWAGE permitted to flow unclarified from the CAMP FARM," 56:568.

9. *HCPP*, "Scarlet Fever," 16. Similar huts set apart for married soldiers were supposed by authorities to house adequately five families each, although in some units ten couples and their children shared one hut. So-called permanent barracks were even more crowded (19). See also Cole, *Story of Aldershot*, 59–62. Unfortunately, these conditions were not unique to Aldershot; army housing in the 1850s and 1860s was universally atrocious. See Skelley, *Victorian Army*, 27–41; also Spiers, *Army and Society*, 55–58, 157–61.

10. *HCPP* 1862, Copies of the Report of General Eyre's Commission on Libraries, Day and Reading Rooms for Soldiers:—and, of Captain Pilkington Jackson's Report to the Secretary of State for War, on the Soldier's Institutes as Aldershot and Portsmouth, 1862 (126) 32.707.

11. Dickens, "Aldershot," 402.

12. *HCPP*, "Copies of the Report," 709.

13. Ibid., 708.

14. Ibid., 709.

15. Hew Strachan, "The Early Victorian Army and the Nineteenth-Century Revolution in Government," *English Historical Review* 85 (October 1980): 783–809. There is little evidence to suggest that any of the army reformers in the era 1815 to 1856 derived much inspiration from the philosophical utilitarians. Instead, men like Jackson acted from the demands of "practical requirements [which] dictat[ed] the evolution of administrative change" (808). Here I am using the term utilitarian in a generic sense.

16. Judith Walkowitz, in her study of the Contagious Diseases Acts of 1864, 1866, and 1869 makes this very point. She concludes that the acts, which provided for police-ordered genital examinations of women suspected of prostitution, were couched precisely in terms of male necessity. Women prostitutes, not male customers, suffered government censure. The acts assumed two different standards of sexual propriety for men and women. Genital inspection of enlisted soldiers failed because of army and government fears that the resistance thus encountered might result in a collapse of troop morale. See Judith Walkowitz, *Prostitution and Victorian Society: Women, Class, and the State* (Cambridge: Cambridge University Press, 1980). Paul McHugh argues from a similar stance that the acts in conception and enforcement were designed to preserve male power and vigor. *Prostitution and Victorian Social Reform* (New York: St. Martin's Press, 1980). A good overview of the place of commercial sex in Victorian society is to be had in E. M. Sigsworth and T. J. Wyke, "A Study of Victorian Prostitution and Venereal Disease," in *Suffer and Be Still: Women in the Victorian Age*, ed. Martha Vicinus (Bloomington: Indiana University Press, 1972), 77–99.

17. *HCPP*, Copies of the Report, 710.

18. Both McHugh and Walkowitz conclude that Victorian era sexual standards and ideology led would-be regulators of prostitution to conclude that since all men had a natural appetite for sex, and since only perverse women would readily provide sex outside of marriage, the general problem of prostitution was to control the population of "fallen women" in such a manner as to reduce the risk of disease. Only later in the nineteenth century, largely thanks

to feminist reformers, did a serious consideration of single-standard morality enter into the public dialogue.

19. In cataloging Victorian attitudes to sex and sexuality, Michael Mason has argued that alongside vehement condemnations of commercial sex (vendors and customers) existed a sentimentalism and sympathy for the plight of the prostitute. This motivated rescue work and personal appeals to prostitutes, a movement that Mason calls "magdalenism." *The Making of Victorian Sexual Attitudes* (Oxford: Oxford University Press, 1994), 82–115.

20. William Acton, *Prostitution* (1857, reprint; London: MacGibbon and Kee, 1968), 56–57. Acton's report first appeared in 1857. That his opinions were influential did not necessarily mean they were accurate. See Finnegan, *Poverty and Prostitution*, 2–11. Until the 1980s, historians of Victorian sex and prostitution labored under an undue influence of Acton's researches, thanks largely to Steven Marcus and his reintroduction of Acton's nearly forgotten works in the 1960s. Steven Marcus, *The Other Victorians: A Study of Sexuality and Pornography in Mid-Nineteenth-Century England* (New York: Basic Books, 1964).

21. For a literary-cultural reading of the Victorian notion of "fallenness," see Amanda Anderson, *Tainted Souls and Painted Faces: The Rhetoric of Fallenness in Victorian Culture* (Ithaca: Cornell University Press, 1993), 2, 7, 13–15, 39–51. Anderson argues that the prostitute skewed important Victorian beliefs about gender roles, and thus even more than being a moral affront was a frightening aberration in Victorian schemes of character and personal agency. The prostitute was at once a "public woman," an aggressive sexual agent, and an object of unregulated lust; she was paradoxically victim and threat, whose existence thus cast doubts on the perceived relationships between environment, character, and individual will. Most observers agreed that women of any class tended to be chaste prior to a fall, but easily became thoroughly degenerate after. Mason, *Sexual Attitudes*, 61–62. Social critics also argued about the potential for pre-marital male chastity, a notion which only gained popularity during and after the 1880s. Bristow, *Vice and Vigilance*, 125–40.

22. Jean-Jacques Rousseau is the modern progenitor of such thinking, but hardly stands alone in the dissemination of the dual sexuality scheme. See Susan M. Okin, *Women in Western Political Thought* (Princeton: Princeton University Press, 1979), Pt. 3, "Rousseau," 99–196. This basic scheme of peculiar female morality dominated European and American thought about women in the nineteenth century. In different forms it appears in the works of such diverse persons as Friedrich Engels, German reformer Louise Otto-Peters, British feminist Josephine Butler, American Susan B. Anthony, even the egalitarian John Stuart Mill, who could not rid himself of notions of the identity of femininity and mothering. See Friedrich Engels, *The Origin of the Family*; for a discussion of "womanly feminism," Karen Offen, "Liberty, Equality, and Justice for Women: The Theory and Practice of Feminism in Nineteenth-Century Europe," in *Becoming Visible: Women in European History*, 2d ed., ed. Renate Bridenthal et al. (Boston: Houghton Mifflin, 1987), 335–74; for Anthony, see E. C. DuBois, ed., *Elizabeth Cady Stanton and Susan B. Anthony: Correspondence, Writings, Speeches* (New York: Schocken Books, 1981); see also John Stuart Mill, *The Subjection of Women*.

23. Acton, *Prostitution*, 65.

24. The following chapter explores the origins of this movement in some detail. Edward Spiers finds that the Christian soldiers' homes movement had

a positive impact on soldier vice. The homes attracted the men, even though they knew proselytizing to be part of the home environment. The extent of the impact he finds "not entirely clear." Spiers, *Late Victorian Army*, 145–46; and *Army and Society*, 66–67. Alan Skelley also finds that the homes were popular, superior to official varieties, and patronized by thousands of the rankers. He is also careful to point out that many men did complain, and avoided the homes, because of the religious atmosphere and the prohibition against alcohol. Skelley, *Victorian Army*, 161, 164. Both conclude that by 1900 the rate of incidence of crimes and injury related to alcohol abuse in the British army had dropped tremendously.

25. For the pervasiveness and content of Victorian domesticity ideology, see, Leonore Davidoff and Catherine Hall, *Family Fortunes: Men and Women of the English Middle Class, 1780–1850* (Chicago: University of Chicago Press, 1987), 108–16. Also Barbara Carrado Pope, "The Influence of Rousseau's Ideology of Domesticity," in *Connecting Spheres: Women in the Western World, 1500 to the Present*, ed. Marilyn J. Boxer and Jean H. Quataert (New York: Oxford University Press, 1987), 136–45.

26. Davidoff and Hall, *Family Fortunes*, 114–18. By the 1850s, evangelical Christian models of feminine virtue (chastity, submissiveness, dependence, home-centeredness) had gained great popularity among the English middle classes.

27. *HCPP* 1867, Report of a Committee Appointed by the Secretary of State for War to Inquire into and Report on the Present State and on the Improvement of Libraries, Reading Rooms, and Day Rooms (2920) 32.776. Jackson's comments here appear in the form of a letter, dated 15 May 1861, to Major General Eyre, commanding the garrison at Chatham.

28. Ibid., 777. Jackson self-consciously asserted his having won over the "respectables" of Gibraltar. Officers, clergy, professionals—these were the classes supposedly most benefited by and most representative of the civilizing effects of religion, decorum, and education. These were also largely the members of the middle classes so dominated by domestic ideology. Davidoff and Hall, *Family Fortunes*, 228–34.

29. *HCPP*, Report of a Committee, 777.

30. *HCPP*, Copies of the Report, 712.

31. Arguing against the desirability of explicit religious instruction in a soldiers' home, Jackson cited a similar facility at Portsmouth that failed, he believed, just because its founders had attempted religious education and evangelization of the men. *HCPP*, Copies of the Report, 716. The house at Portsmouth, established in 1856 during the last year of the Crimean War, was an openly Anglican establishment. Unlike Jackson's homes, this one was under a committee not of officers, but of a mixed group of clergy, officers, and townsmen.

32. Burroughs, "An Unreformed Army?" 168–69. See also Blanco, "Attempts to Abolish Branding and Flogging," 137–45; also, Burroughs, "Crime and Punishment," 545–71; also Dinwiddy, "Flogging," 308–31; also Steiner, "Separating the Soldier," 19–35.

33. Organized efforts at army education dated back to the seventeenth century, but around the time of Crimea a massive campaign began to educate the soldier and his family. Supporters argued that army education would produce more disciplined, more competent soldiers and expose underclass army families to civilizing influences they might otherwise never have encountered. Other

obedience schemes included good conduct pay and badges, fines for drunkenness, reduced recourse to corporal punishment, improved food, and new amusements. See Skelley, *Victorian Army,* 85–89, 92–98, 130–31, 160–63, 182–83, 187–89; also, Spiers, *Army and Society,* 63–66.

Chapter 7. Winning the Troops

1. Anne Summers, "Militarism in Britain before the Great War," *History Workshop Journal* 2 (1976): 104–23. Twenty years ago, Summers also argued that popular British militarism was clearly linked to the efforts of women evangelicals.

2. Stephen E. Koss, *Nonconformity in Modern British Politics* (Hamden, Conn.: Archon Books, 1975), 15; Lewis, *Lighten Their Darkness,* 1–5, 220–23.

3. For the revival of 1859, see James Edwin Orr, *The Light of the Nations: Evangelical Renewal and Advance in the Nineteenth Century* (Grand Rapids, Mich.: Eerdmans Publishing Co., 1965); also, *The Second Evangelical Awakening in Britain* (London: Marshall, Morgan, and Scott, 1949); also, David Hempton and Myrtle Hill, *Evangelical Protestantism in Ulster Society, 1740–1890* (New York: Routledge, 1992).

4. As a woman, obviously not an ordained representative of the Connection, Daniell suffered few of the problems that Reverend William Harris Rule did in bringing an official Wesleyan presence to the army. Despite male censorship of public females in Victorian England, being female, and therefore officially unable to threaten men, could provide strength for public works. "Women manipulated the language of separate spheres; it could be used radically to claim public space, or conservatively to confirm gender stereotyping." Anne Digby, "Victorian Values and Women," in *Victorian Values: A Joint Symposium of the Royal Society of Edinburgh and the British Academy, December 1990,* ed. T. C. Smout (Oxford: Oxford University Press, 1992), 204.

5. On social work as a woman's duty, especially for women somehow deprived of marriage, see Jane Lewis, *Women and Social Action in Victorian and Edwardian England* (Stanford, Calif.: Stanford University Press, 1991), 303; also, chap 1, "Octavia Hill."

6. G. F. S. Daniell, *Aldershot: A Record of Mrs. Daniell's Work amongst Soldiers and Its Sequel, by her Daughter* (London: Hodder and Stoughton, 1879), 7–13. Her interventionist style was a commonplace resort of philanthropic women of her day. For the tradition of "visiting" and "visiting societies," see F. K. Prochaska, *Women and Philanthropy in Nineteenth-Century England* (Oxford: Clarendon Press, 1980), 97–137.

7. Daniell, *Aldershot,* 26.

8. "Perverts to Rome" was the term Miss Daniell commonly assigned to Roman Catholics in her book about her mother's army ministry. Her staunch anti-Catholicism, while common for an 1860s Englishwoman (especially a Wesleyan), potentially limited her ministry given the high percentage (roughly 32 percent) of Irish Catholics in the English infantry at this time. See Hanham, "Religion and Nationality," app. 1. The literature on English anti-Catholicism is, of course, immense.

9. Daniell, *Aldershot,* 32–33.

10. Anthony Ashley Cooper, seventh earl of Shaftesbury (1801–85).

11. Daniell, *Aldershot,* 41–44.

12. Richard L. Bushman has explored the connection between the physical and mental culture of the home in preindustrial domestic life. His concern was to review the architecture of American homes as well as the design of American towns and cities between the colonial era and the turn of the present century. However, since he demonstrated that American notions of refinement emanated from English standards of gentility and civilization, his book offers us a useful comment in this instance. Richard L. Bushman, *The Refinement of America: Persons, Houses, Cities* (New York: Alfred A Knopf, 1992); also Davidoff and Hall, *Family Fortunes*, chap. 8, "'My Own Fireside': The creation of the Middle-Class Home," passim.

13. Bushman, *Refinement*, 100–38; Davidoff and Hall, *Family Fortunes*, 370–74.

14. Bushman, *Refinement*, 118–22.

15. Ibid., xiii; also Davidoff and Hall, *Family Fortunes*, chap. 3, "'The Nursery of Virtue': Domestic Ideology and the Middle Class"; also Pope, "Rousseau's Ideology," 136–45.

16. Daniell, *Aldershot*, 48–50.

17. Eric Hobsbawm, "The Formation of British Working-Class Culture," in *Workers: Worlds of Labor* (New York: Pantheon, 1984), 176–93. This was a contentious assumption for Mrs. Daniell to make. Eric Hobsbawm has argued that certainly after 1848, artisans and the "labor aristocracy" had economic and cultural "respectability." Their sons would therefore have appreciated a parlor, but stayed away from army recruiters in all but desperate circumstances. However, the laboring and poor classes farther down the scale did not benefit from an economic integration into mainstream British society until the early 1880s. Soldiers from these classes, who provided most of the recruits, would know much more about squalid rural cottages and urban slum dwellings than about parlors (181–85).

18. Louise A. Tilly and Joan Scott, *Women, Work, and Family*, 2d ed. (New York: Methuen, 1987).

19. For Victorian notions of women's peculiar qualifications for "home keeping," and also for women's distinct character, see Karen Offen, "Liberty, Equality, and Justice," 337–38. Offen distinguishes between "relational" feminism (which propounded women's unique moral and personal characteristics and excellence) and "individual" feminism (which called for maximal personal liberty); also, Davidoff and Hall, *Family Fortunes*, 114ff. for feminine piety.

20. Daniell, *Aldershot*, 31, her emphasis.

21. Ibid., 56–58.

22. Ibid., 73–74.

23. A third woman, Sarah Robinson, also pursued a national ministry to men in the army and navy, but with less scope and success than either the Daniell or Sandes efforts. In the 1860s, when working for the Daniells, Robinson was dismissed because she insisted on entering bars and brothels in Aldershot in order to seek out rescue cases. Jennie Chappel, *Noble Work by Noble Women: Sketches of the Lives of Baroness Burdett-Coutts, Lady Henry Somerset, Miss Sarah Robinson, Mrs. Fawcett, and Mrs. Gladstone* (London: S. W. Partridge and Co., 1899); also Prochaska, *Philanthropy*, 196–97.

24. Elise Sandes, *Enlisted; or, My Story. Incidents of Life and Work Among Soldiers*, (London: S. W. Partridge and Co., 1915), 12–20.

25. Ibid., 32.

26. Though Sandes focused on rescuing male soldiers, not all opponents of

military vice remained preoccupied with the men; Miss Sarah Robinson, who preached to soldiers from the 1860s through the 1890s, also sought out "dens of vice" to help prostitutes quit that life. By the 1870s, the Daniell mission to Aldershot also sponsored a "home for girls." Prochaska, *Philanthropy*, 191–92, 196–205, 206–7.

27. Sandes, *Enlisted*, 74–75, her emphases. Important activist and social reform-minded Victorian women shared this view. Prochaska, *Philanthropy*, 146–47; Davidoff and Hall, *Family Fortunes*, for the power of "home" over the early-Victorian middle classes.

28. Sandes, *Enlisted*, 147.

29. Edward Spiers finds that the soldiers' homes movement had a positive impact on soldier vice. The homes attracted men, even though they knew proselytizing to be part of the home environment. The extent of the impact he finds "not entirely clear." Spiers, *Late Victorian Army*, 145–46; also Spiers, *Army and Society*, 66–67. Alan Skelley also finds that the homes were popular, superior to official varieties, and patronized by thousands of the rankers. He is also careful to point out that many men did complain and avoided the homes because of the religious atmosphere and the prohibition against alcohol. Skelley, *Victorian Army at Home*, 61, 64. Both conclude that between 1870 and 1900, the heyday of the homes movement, the rate of incidence of crimes and injury related to alcohol abuse in the British army had dropped tremendously. H. J. Hanham describes a veritable boom in the homes movement from the 1860s through 1914. Different denominations, including finally the Church of England, copied the Daniell/Sandes pattern of home at Aldershot and around the empire. Hanham argues that until 1914 such homes were the center of soldier social life, especially for those seeking some respectability. Hanham, "Religion and Nationality," 169–70.

30. For an interesting foray into feminine friendship and bonding, especially among feminist and social activist women in Victorian England, see Philippa Levine, *Feminist Lives in Victorian England: Private Roles and Public Commitment* (Oxford: Basil Blackwell, 1990), chap. 4, passim.

31. Anne Digby argues that Victorian women of the working and middle classes navigated social confines on the sexes without opposing absolutes of "public v. private," "intellect v. intuition," "rationality v. emotionality," "male v. female." Instead they manipulated social typing in a gray world of "the borderlands" of gender. Digby, "Victorian Values and Women."

32. DuBois, *Stanton and Anthony*, 7–8, 10–11; Kenneth Cmiel, *Democratic Eloquence: The Fight over Popular Speech in Nineteenth-Century America* (Berkeley and Los Angeles: University of California Press, 1990), 70–71; Alice S. Rossi, *The Feminist Papers: From Adams to de Beauvoir*, 2d ed. (Boston: Northeastern University Press, 1988), 254–58. The messages the different women might want to communicate, whether "radical" or "respectable," mattered less than the very fact a woman wished to speak in public.

33. Sandes, *Enlisted*, 96–97.

34. Daniell, *Aldershot*, 58–61.

35. This particular trend of disdain for the common soldier originated in the years of the Hanoverian succession, peaked during the impressments of the Napoleonic Wars, and continued for the entire first half of the nineteenth century. See, Wellington *Despatches*. The duke made no secret about his mistrust and scorn for enlisted men; also, Thompson, *English Working Class*, 78, 81. Cobbett and Shelley both championed the rights of the working classes, and

while they could express sympathy for the individual tragedies of laboring sons forced into the military, they also decried the very existence of a loyal standing army and the obedience of soldiers to "Old Corruption." Hodgson thought soldiers ripe for subversion if the world of opinions, religious or otherwise, should become open to them. Segments of the British Nonconformist population rejected militarism until at least the 1880s. For the relationship between the military and Nonconformity, see Hanham, "Religion and Nationality," 159–181.

36. See above, n. 27.

37. Though Sandes began her career independently in Ireland, she nonetheless made Aldershot her eventual headquarters. Between 1856 and 1862, Wesleyan Methodist William Harris Rule, working at Aldershot, pursued formal army recognition of that denomination. He succeeded, but did not have as great a general impact as the women missionaries did on army daily life. Rule sponsored regular church services for the limited numbers of self-declared Wesleyans in the army. As of 1863, there were less than 3,500 Wesleyans in the army. William Harris Rule, *An Account of the Establishment of Wesleyan Methodism in the British Army* (London: T. Woolmer, 1883); also, *Recollections of My Life and Work at Home and Abroad in Connection with the Wesleyan Methodist Conference* (London: T. Woolmer, 1886); also, Hanham, "Religion and Nationality," app. 2.

38. See the frontispiece and appendix of Sandes, *Enlisted.*

Chapter 8. Havelock and the Birth of the Christian Hero

1. As John MacKenzie complained in 1992, little has been done to analyze the place of the hero as such in popular Victorian culture. MacKenzie gave credit to scholars like Olive Anderson, C. I. Hamilton, and Douglas Johnson, but concluded "none of [their] studies has attempted to place the imperial heroic myths in their wider context, nor have they examined the propagation of the myths through journalism and popular literature." MacKenzie and, most recently, Graham Dawson have sought to fill the void. However, they each have relied heavily upon psychoanalytic and gender construction paradigms. It is possible to "overtheorize" historical analysis. My gloss on Havelock and Gordon is an effort to stay closer to the ground. John M. MacKenzie, "Heroic Myths of Empire," in *Popular Imperialism and the Military,* 110. See also Graham Dawson, *Soldier Heroes: British Adventure, Empire, and the Imagining of Masculinities* (New York: Routledge, 1994).

2. Havelock and Gordon were both officers but rhetoric surrounding them easily transferred to the army at large.

3. As a point in contrast, consider the brief popular acclaim of Lord Cardigan, the man who led the infamous Charge of the Light Brigade during the Crimean War. He returned to England a hero, hailed as the good soldier who had nobly suffered the blunders of his superiors. However, this interpretation was baseless, as the ensuing scrutiny and analysis of the Crimean campaign revealed. Cardigan slipped from the pedestal of the hero into the mire of recrimination that spread forth from the parliamentary and public debates about Crimea. It is doubtful that even a glorious death at Balaclava could have prevented the eventual ruin of his reputation. See, Cecil Woodham-Smith, *The Reason Why* (London: McGraw-Hill, 1954).

4. In her article on Christian militarism in nineteenth-century Britain, Olive Anderson also took the case of Hedley Vicars, a young evangelical officer who died in combat in Crimea, to be an archetypical Christian hero. Despite his fame and the prodigious evangelical efforts to promote his example after his death, Vicars's story never captured more of the broad, general public imagination. The same might be said of other Mutiny martyrs like Lawrence or Nicholson. See below, Anderson, "Growth of Christian Militarism." John M. MacKenzie agrees that of the Indian Mutiny heroes and martyrs "only Sir Henry Havelock . . . was elevated to mythic status." "Heroic Myths," 114.

5. Anderson, "Growth of Christian Militarism," 46–72.

6. Ibid., 46–47.

7. For example, H. J. Hanham has demonstrated that throughout the nineteenth century, and right through the period of religious pluralization of the army, Irish Catholic participation in the ranks dropped consistently and drastically. Whereas in 1830 the Irish were 32.3 percent of the total UK population and supplied 42.2 percent of army manpower, by 1891 those figures were 12.5 percent and 14.0 percent respectively. Clearly, economics, the famine, emigration, and Irish nationalism played significant roles. Army leaders could not hope to win the recruiting battle upon the basis of internal reforms alone, and the desire to do so does not explain the choices of actual reforms made. I suspect the rationale to change in the army must have proceeded not only from utilitarian planning, but also from changes in expectations within the army about itself. Hanham, "Religion and Nationality," 159–81. See also Anderson, "Manpower Problems," 526–45; also, Strachan, "Early Victorian Army," 783–809.

8. Stanley, "Christian Responses," 281. Stanley notes that preachers on a national day of humiliation during the Mutiny stressed the need for united prayer for dominion over the heathen.

9. Anderson, "Christian Militarism," 65.

10. Clyde Binfield, "'I suppose you're not a Baptist or a Roman Catholic?': Nonconformity's True Conformity," in Smout, *Victorian Values*, 81–107. Binfield points out the dangers or difficulties of too pat definitions imposed on Victorian social and religious life. This is especially true in the case of a "Nonconformist Conscience," which could handily cooperate in various Tory or Anglican social endeavors without abandoning its self-identification. He reminds us not to mistake helpful abstractions for absolute realities.

11. Two examples: A. B. Evans, *War: Its Theology; its Anomalies; its Incidents, and its Humiliations by Alfred Bowen Evans* (London: Peace Society, 1855); also, *The Soldier and the Christian: Addressed to All Willing to Hear Both Sides, but Especially to Parents about to Choose a Profession for their Sons, by A Clergyman of the Church of England* (London: Peace Society, 1855).

12. I do not endorse the plan of Lytton Strachey (and more recent and more prominent historians) to scuttle heroes. There is no need for character assassination. I want only to get a measure of the distance between these men and their public faces. Even a brief examination of the biographical record of each, or of memoirs or published letters, reveals these men to have been (in distinct ways) sincere and reflective individuals. If Havelock pursued a more theologically orthodox Baptist faith, that does not detract from the personal, and admittedly quirky, spirituality of the more eclectic Gordon.

13. The best modern biography of Havelock is that by Leonard Cooper, although it suffers from a rather journalistic style and a derivative reliance upon

bland military history for the entirety of the sections on the Mutiny. Leonard Cooper, *Havelock* (London: Bodley Head, 1957), 9–13; also, J. C. Pollock, *The Way to Glory: The Life of Havelock of Lucknow* (London: John Murray, 1957). Pollock's book benefits by his recourse to the Havelock family papers. The Havelock Papers reside in the North Yorkshire County Record Office. See also, *Times*, 16 September 1857, 5. The *Times* published a biographical note on Havelock to identify him for the public.

14. *Times*, 16 September 1857, 5. Oftentimes young gentlemen of means abandoned commissions in units soon to be sent overseas. Such officers, not needing to worry about careers or incomes, could purchase into units in Great Britain or sell out completely. Officers like Havelock relied upon these more dangerous foreign service vacancies to progress in their careers. Spiers, *Army and Society*, 19.

15. *Times*, 16 September 1857, 5. Havelock served as a subaltern for twenty-three years without substantive promotion. He achieved his captaincy only in 1838, at the age of forty-three. Five years later, after meritorious combat service during the disastrous invasion of Afghanistan, he was promoted to major. Thereafter, promotions by brevet came frequently. At the time of the Mutiny he held the rank of colonel. Barring the use of purchase, this slow rate of advancement was not unusual. Spiers, *Army and Society*, 20.

16. Anderson, "Christian Militarism," 50.

17. John MacKenzie too has wholeheartedly endorsed the "fanatic" image of Havelock, going so far as to give credence to stories that Havelock regularly baptized troops. Havelock in his own correspondence displayed a most deferential attitude toward the Baptist ministry. He was nervous of having overstepped the proper bounds of a layman simply because he preached sermons on a few occasions. One suspects, upon reading his essay, that MacKenzie himself has done his part to make a (late-twentieth-century) "myth" out of Havelock. MacKenzie, "Heroic Myths," 119–21.

18. Longford, *Pillar*, 372–73; also Spiers, *Army and Society*, 12–13.

19. Such circumstances bred much ill will in regiments. See the editorials by an anonymous "officer of twenty years experience": "Money or Merit?" *All the Year 'Round*, 21 April 1860, 30–32; and, "Pay for Your Places," *All the Year 'Round*, 27 October 1860, 67–69. The officer claimed to have served in no less than three regiments wherein he had seen the careers of meritorious officers destroyed by the system of purchase.

20. "Pay for Your Places," 68.

21. Cooper, *Havelock*, 29. When Havelock first secured the adjutancy to the Thirteenth Regiment of Foot, some officers wrote to Bentinck (who oversaw all such appointments in Bengal) to complain of Havelock's fanatical attitudes and religiously motivated fraternizing with the men. Bentinck ignored the complaints, and the appointment went through, in no small part because the regimental commander, Colonel Robert Sale (see below) liked Havelock and preferred his abilities to those of other possible candidates.

22. Henry Havelock, *Memoir of the Three Campaigns of Major General Sir A. Campbell's Army in Ava* (Serampore, 1828); also, *Narrative of the War in Affghanistan* [sic] *in 1838–1839* (London, 1840). Havelock was also somewhat protected from the folly of his literary pretensions by the fact that both books were total market flops, apparently read only by some irate denizens of the Horse Guards. Cooper, *Havelock*, 26.

23. Presumably he meant merely some signal to call a religious service.

24. *Times*, 26 October 1857, 9. Havelock's Baptist denomination is pivotal here. The gentry and aristocrats who dominated the officer corps would all have a (nominal, at least) alegiance to the Church of England. The Baptists of Havelock's day were dominated by the lower-middle and the artisan classes. Alan D. Gilbert, *Religion and Society in Industrial England: Church, Chapel and Social Change, 1740–1914* (New York: Longman, 1976), 63.

25. At a meeting at Exeter Hall in January 1858, speakers (including John Marshman, Havelock's brother-in-law and later his biographer) repeated the theme of Christian infidelity and resulting punishment in India. They compared mutinous Bengal to relatively quite Bombay and explained the difference by the supposed popular progress and official support of Christianity in the latter. Marshman argued that attempts at "religious neutrality" in Bengal had been misguided, had promoted idolatry, the caste system, and disrespect for a seemingly weak Christianity, and moreover had done nothing to prevent popular unrest. *Times*, 6 January 1858, 8. The Church Missionary Society had been in constant protest against the "neutrality" of the East India Company since 1852, and in the debates of 1858 was a leading voice in favor of government-sponsored Christian education in India. The conflicts of the 1850s constituted the culmination of long-standing complaints against company complacency. Eugene Stock, *The History of the Church Missionary Society, Its Environment, Its Men, and Its Work*, 4 vols. (London: Church Missionary Society, 1899), 215–61.

26. Havelock to J. C. Marshman, n.d. (August 1857), recorded in John Clark Marshman, *Memoirs of Major-General Sir Henry Havelock, K.C.B.* (London: Longmans, 1878), 389. The 1878 edition was a re-release of the the 1867 second edition. The work originally appeared in 1860, two years after Brock's biography of Havelock.

27. *Times*, 30 October 1857, 10.

28. Ibid.; Cooper, in his biography, merely records that Bentinck smiled and said, "The adjutant should not preach." See Cooper, *Havelock*, 29–30. This is also the version recorded by Marshman, *Memoirs*, 45–46.

29. Crossing over between the ranks and the officer corps was not only considered poor form, but also a serious threat to the discipline of the army. Rankers and officers simply did not originate from the same world. Spiers, *Army and Society*, 2–6.

30. These were temporary, sometimes prospective promotions, often given in order to qualify an officer for some position without changing his substantive rank. Marshman, Brock, and Cooper all record the offices and opportunities offered to Havelock, without then abandoning the persecution story.

31. Anderson, "Christian Militarism," 50n. Marshman himself was one of the progenitors of the punishment theory of the Mutiny. Marshman describes Havelock as "'the neglected Lieutenant' [who] rose by national suffrage to the pinnacle of renown." Marshman, *Memoirs*, 448.

32. The classics marked the education of a gentleman; witness the aphorism "Every true gentleman has forgotten much Latin and a little Greek."

33. Cooper, *Havelock*, 10; see also Marshman, *Memoirs*, 3–4. As a counterpoint to Havelock's fondness for his school days, consider the evangelical seventh earl of Shaftesbury (1801–85) who viewed his own education at Chiswick and (admittedly less so) Harrow as a purgatory of torture, corruption, and imprisonment. His views on the dangers of the public school were quite popular among nineteenth-century Evangelicals. Finlayson, *Shaftesbury*, 16–17.

34. Cooper, *Havelock*, 16, 27, 41. Havelock did not become abstinent until 1841, eleven years after his conversion to the Baptists. Even then he did so because he feared wine drinking might induce the "liver-fevers" that troubled his health at this time. He also feared the overconsumption to which rankers in the army were prone, but this was a matter far removed from that of a drink enjoyed between gentlemen.

35. Temperance only began to make inroads on the evangelical self-identification in the 1830s. It was not a dominant theme until after the 1870s. The Wesleyans always suspected temperance to be a potential cult of "salvation by works." Wilberforce drank wine frequently and used opium for a bowel complaint and stress. For the place of temperance among Nonconformity and Evangelicals, see Boyd Hilton, *The Age of Atonement: The Influence of Evangelicalism on Social and Economic Thought, 1795–1865* (Oxford: Oxford University Press, 1988), 270; also, Brian Harrison, *Drink and the Victorians: The Temperance Question in England, 1815–1872;* also, D. W. Bebbington, *The Nonconformist Conscience: Chapel and Politics, 1870–1914* (London: George Allen and Unwin, 1982), 46–51; also J. C. Pollock, *Wilberforce* (New York: St. Martin's Press, 1977), 45–46, 79–82.

36. C.A. Bayly and Eric Stokes, *The Peasant Armed: The Indian Rebellion of 1857* (Oxford: Clarendon Press, 1986), 66–68.

37. The story of this mistake was known in England during the course of 1858. Havelock's campaign was discussed and analyzed, but his character remained immune from recrimination. For a contemporary example, see Robert Montgomery Martin, *History of the Indian Empire* (London: London Printing and Publishing Co., 1858), 419–20.

38. In 1857 telegraph communications with to the east reached only as far as Trieste. News had to travel by dispatch between the subcontinent of India and the Adriatic port.

39. Stanley, "Christian Responses," 278–79. The intensity of national interest was facilitated by the "rapid emergence of a cheap, daily provincial press and the continuing growth of the mass-circulation popular Sunday press" and important technological improvements in overseas communications. Dawson, *Soldier Heroes*, 84–86.

40. Stanley, "Christian Responses," 279–82. The Day of Humiliation occurred on 7 October 1857. Dawson has done an extensive survey of press language and coverage of Havelock prior to news of his death. Dawson, *Soldier Heroes*, 94–104.

41. Telegraphic news of the death reached England 7 January 1858. Mourning Havelock was a national affair expressed in literature, religious services, statues, and public subscriptions for his wife and family. Dawson, *Soldier Heroes*, 79, 80, 114.

42. *Index to the Times of London*, 1857 and 1858, passim.

43. *Times*, 25 September 1857, 10.

44. Ibid., 21 September, 7; 28 September, 7.

Chapter 9. The Hero Becomes an Icon

1. In addition to those discussed in detail there also appeared *The Good Soldier* by the Reverend Owen and *The Christian Soldier* by James P. Grant.

2. Marshman, *Memoirs*. Marshman's book remained popular for many

years, enjoying subsequent editions and reprints until 1909. Pollock, *Way to Glory*, 3.

3. This represented nearly 45,000 copies. Pollock, Ibid. Olive Anderson used Brock only for illustration. John MacKenzie apparently never considered Brock or his book. Graham Dawson discounted Brock's Havelock biography as a "frothy sermon." He focused instead upon a close reading of Marshman, including emotional portrayals of the "domestic Havelock." Dawson, *Soldier Heroes*, 125, 127–50.

4. Charles Birrel, *The Life of William Brock, D.D., First Minister of Bloomsbury Chapel, London* (London: James Nisbet, 1878), 172–74.

5. Ibid., 123–24, 125.

6. Ibid., 225–27, 228. A good sample of Brock's sermonizing is to be had in another biography, by George Wilson M'Cree. This book is less biographical and more in the mode of inspirational literature, and therefore concentrates upon a series of lengthy transcriptions of Brock's sermons and letters. See George Wilson M'Cree, *William Brock, D.D., First Pastor of Bloomsbury Chapel* (London: James Clark and Co., 1876). For theater preaching, see Lewis, *Lighten Their Darkness*, 224–25, 254–55; Gilbert, *Religion and Society*, 190–91. Gilbert finds that 1859 was in the top three of the whole nineteenth century for single-year growth among the Baptists.

7. Bebbington, *Nonconformist Conscience*, 106.

8. Ibid., 106–7. Also, Clyde Binfield, *So Down to Prayers: Studies in English Nonconformity, 1780–1920* (London: J.M. Dent and Sons, 1977), 214–15.

9. Norman, *Church and Society*, 208–10; Gilbert, *Religion and Society*, 194–95; Bebbington, *Nonconformist Conscience*, 30–34. Other issues included marriage and registry of baptism.

10. In 1863, the first in which the army counted non-Anglican and non-Presbyterian Protestants, a census of the army found roughly 3,500 "Other Protestants" out of an establishment of 204,000. Hanham, "Religion and Nationality," app. 2.

11. With the important exception of Wesleyan Methodism. See, Bebbington, *Nonconformist Conscience*, 112–15. For latter-century Wesleyan imperialism, see Stephen Koss, "Wesleyanism and Empire," *Historical Journal* 18, (1975): 105–18.

12. Bebbington, *Nonconformist Conscience*, 106. Binfield, *Down to Prayers*, 214–16. Illustrating the point with the career of George Williams, founder of the international YMCA, Binfield makes the rather fine distinction that many Nonconformists who advocated missionary work were pro-empire, but antiimperial. He must be taken to mean that such persons hoped for missionary success in parts of the world where a British presence might enhance the environment for such work. These same advocate, however, abhorred militarism and expansion by brute force. See also Koss, "Wesleyanism and Empire," 105–18.

13. Or between Nonconformity and a Liberal Imperialism. Bebbington, *Nonconformist Conscience*, 106; also, Stanley, "Christian Response," 288.

14. Marshman was more restrained. While he agreed wholeheartedly that India wanted good Christian rulers, he saw the story of Havelock himself more clearly set in terms of the individual life of the man.

15. Rev. William Brock, *A Biographical Sketch of Sir Henry Havelock, K.C.B.*, 5th ed. (London: James Nisbit and Co., 1858), 6–7.

16. Ibid., 14–15.

17. Ibid., 15.
18. Marshman, *Memoirs*, 446.
19. Brock, *Biographical Sketch*, 23–24.
20. Ibid., 24–25.
21. Ibid., 39. This story was often repeated in the years after the Mutiny and continues to appear in modern literature on Havelock. See also Marshman, *Memoirs*, 24; Anderson, "Christian Militarism," 52; Cooper, *Havelock*, 15. The remark is variously attributed to Colonel Sale of the Thirteenth Foot in 1824, to Sir Archibald Campbell commanding the expedition to Burma in 1825, and to Sir Hugh Gough.
22. Brock, *Biographical Sketch*, 38.
23. Marshman, *Memoirs*, 445.
24. Brock, *Biographical Sketch*, 45. Marshman relays the exact story and quote in his biography, but is at even greater pains to portray Havelock as nonsectarian. See Marshman, *Memoirs*, 34.
25. Brock, *Biographical Sketch*, 46.
26. Marshman, *Memoirs*, 37.
27. Max Warren, *The Missionary Movement from Britain in Modern History* (London: SCM Press, 1965), 45–48. Warren's book is an unabashed apologia for British missionaries but a good one. He takes this scheme of motivation from the work of Johannes Van Den Berg. See Johannes Van Den Berg, *Constrained by Jesus' Love: An Inquiry in the Motives of the Missionary Awakening in Great Britain in the Period between 1698 and 1815* (Netherlands: J. M Kok, 1956). Warren is valuable for his gloss on Van Den Berg, as well as his consideration of years beyond 1815. See also Stuart Piggin, *Making Evangelical Missionaries, 1789–1858: The Social Background, Motives and Training of British Protestant Missionaries to India* (Perth: Sutton Courtenay Press, 1984), 124–55. Piggin includes more cynical motivations, like the desire for prestige, power, and free education. He also acknowledges missionary religious fervor and sincerity and agrees with Warren in rejecting the assertion of Klaus Knorr "that the 'essence' of the modern missionary movement was 'an aggressive cultural imperialism.'" Klaus E. Knorr, *British Colonial Theories, 1570–1850* (London, 1963). Brian Stanley has also rejected the imperial-missionary scheme. His unique contributions include elaboration of the argument portraying missionaries as out of sync with imperialists, as well as his openness about his own Christianity, which brings an "internal" critique to the history of the missions. Stanley, *Bible and Flag*.
28. Even an advocate of "cultural imperialism" theory such as Robert W. Strayer acknowledges that East Africa Company (later British Protectorate) interests clashed with the desires of missionaries to expand missions. "The colonial government [in East Africa] was aware of these separate interests and soon discovered that uncontrolled mission expansion did not serve the ends of orderly administration." Strayer nevertheless maintains that missionary activity, especially in the early stages of a colonial presence in a region, abetted the imperialist domination of local peoples. Robert W. Strayer, *The Making of Mission Communities in East Africa: Anglicans and Africans in Colonial Kenya, 1875–1935* (London: Heinemann Press, 1978), 32–33.
29. Cornelia Witz, *Religionspolitik in Britisch-Indien, 1793–1813: Christliches Sendungsbewusstsein und Achtung Hinduistischer Tradition im Widerstreit* (Religious politics in British India, 1793–1813: The conflict be-

tween Christian missionary consciousness and the toleration of Hindu tradition) (Wiesbaden: Fritz Steiner Verlag, 1985), 132–34.

30. Consider, for two examples, the evangelical argument that mutiny was divine punishment for British dilatoriness in stamping out idolatry; or the rumors that flew around the British side concerning the role that cattle- and hog-lard greasing for rifle ammunition played in starting the revolt. The use of these animal products would of course be an offense to either Hindu or Muslim soldiers in British pay. The real weight of this particular issue in the minds of Mutineers is debatable.

31. Thomas Carlyle, *Oliver Cromwell's Letters and Speeches, with Elucidations*, 4 vols., Carlyle Centenary Series (London: Chapman and Hall, 1897).

32. Ibid. 1:9.

33. J. A. Froude, *Thomas Carlyle, a History of his Life in London*, 2 vols. (London, 1884), 2:420.

34. Bebbington, *Evangelicalism*.

35. Hilton, *Age of Atonement*, ix.

36. Orr, *Light*, 127–31; also *Awakening*, 39–41, 43–45. Hempton and Hill, *Evangelical Protestantism*, 146, 148–60.

37. Steve Bruce, "The Ulster Connection," in *Sermons and Battle Hymns: Protestant Popular Culture in Modern Scotland*, eds. Graham Walker and Tom Gallagher (Edingburgh: Edinburgh University Press, 1990), 231–55. Although Bruce is concerned with discussing twentieth-century sectarianism in Scotland, he devotes the first part of this essay to establishing the long-term ethnic and ecclesiastic links between Ulster and Scotland.

38. Orr, *Light*, 132–37, 138; *Awakening*, 59–74, 76. Among the laity and clergy, the revival wave of 1859–60 also contained elements of strong Sabbatarianism and the rejection of popular amusements like music, dancing, and drinking of alcoholic beverages. Allan I. Macinnes, "Evangelical Protestantism in the Nineteenth-Century Highlands," in Walker and Gallagher, *Sermons and Battle Hymns*, 43–68.

39. Orr, *Awakening*, 78.

40. Orr, *Light*, 140–44; *Awakening*, 90–92.

41. Orr, *Light*, 145–48, 149; *Awakening*, 147–59. Despite local successes, however, neither Finney nor other revival preachers in England succeeded in sparking a general revival of the depth or intensity experienced in Ulster or Scotland. Parsons, *Religion in Victorian Britain* 3:218. Because the English revival of 1859–62 was largely Nonconformist, anticlerical, and lacking in a single notable Anglican champion, John Kent has gone so far as to classify it as "the failure of English revivalism." However, Havelock was a Baptist, and part of his fame rested upon a critique of official complacency in church and state. See John Kent, *Holding the Fort: Studies in Victorian Revivalism* (London: Epworth Press, 1978), 71–131.

42. Orr, *Light*, 149–51. Orr drew these numbers from the evangelical magazine *Revival*. That magazine apparently based its estimates upon the simple formula of multiplying seating capacity by the number of meetings held, assuming 100 percent attendance. Therefore, one must retain some suspicion as to the accuracy of the estimates. Orr, *Awakening*, 97–101. Lewis points out that in the late 1850s men like Charles H. Spurgeon regularly addressed crowds of 6,000 twice each Sunday and drew as many as 25,000 to Crystal Palace services. Exeter Hall, built in the 1830s to house evangelical meetings, seated 4,000. By

the late 1850s, railroads ran special trains to bring provincial travelers to the Exeter "May meetings." Lewis, *Lighten Their Darkness*, 91, 254–57.

Chapter 10. Gordon and the Image of the Christian Hero

1. Charles Chenevix Trench, *The Road to Khartoum: A Life of General Charles Gordon* (New York: W. W. Norton and Co., 1979), 13–14; Anthony Nutting, *Gordon of Khartoum: Martyr and Misfit* (New York: Clarkson N. Potter, 1966), 5.
2. Chenevix Trench, *The Road*, 14–15.
3. Ibid.
4. For the development of and social hierarchy of the Royal Engineers, see Skelley, *Victorian Army*, (London: Croom Helm, Ltd., 1977), 18, 37, 87 (table 2–1), 99–100, 182; also, Spiers, *Army and Society*, 11, 15.
5. Hake, *The Story of Chinese Gordon*, 16–17.
6. Chenevix Trench, *The Road*, 15; Nutting, *Gordon of Khartoum*, 8.
7. Nutting, *Gordon of Khartoum*, 10. Gordon later confessed to friends that he hoped to be killed in the Crimea.
8. Chenevix Trench, *The Road*, 17 (letter quoted).
9. Chenevix Trench, *The Road*, 20–21, 25–26; Nutting, *Gordon of Khartoum*, 11–12.
10. Chenevix Trench, *The Road*, 29–32. Gordon was thirty years old. Nutting, *Gordon of Khartoum*, 37–39.
11. *Times*, 18 May 1863, 6; 26 June 1863, 14; 5 December 1863.
12. *Times*, 16 September 1864. The report originated in July that year, but was delayed by the great distance to London.
13. Ibid. The *Times* China news for 15 September 1864 simply reprinted this *China Mail* coverage of 29 July.
14. *Times*, 28 December 1864, 10. Gordon actually arrived home in January 1865.
15. Bebbington, *Nonconformist Conscience*, 109–10; Ronald Robinson and John Gallagher, *Africa and the Victorians: The Official Mind of Imperialism*, 2d ed., (London: Macmillan, 1981), 24, 46–48; Chenevix Trench, *The Road*, 80, 83, 99–100, 122; Nutting, *Gordon of Khartoum*, 95–96. Gordon was quite often at odds with the Anti-Slavery Society, at least in his own mind, because he believed them to be hopelessly out of touch with actual conditions in the Sudan.
16. Chenevix Trench, *The Road*, 53, 54.
17. Robinson and Gallagher, *Africa*, 134–43.
18. *Times*, 7 August 1884, 5; 28 August 1884, 5.
19. Robinson and Gallagher, *Africa*, chaps. 3–6, passim.
20. Ibid., 140–41, 144, 145.
21. In performing an exhaustive survey of the the metropolitan press for the entire year of 1884, Todd Willy found that while editors of various political stripes contended with each other for the political significance of Gordon, none doubted (or shied from using) the piety and Christianity of the General. See Todd Gray Willy, "The Agitation in Parliament over Charles George 'Chinese' Gordon and His Mission to the Soudan, January 1884 to February 1885" (Ph.D. diss., Speech and Communications, University of Iowa, 1962), chap. 3.
22. *Times*, 22 September 1884, 9.

23. *Times*, 29 September 1884, 9.
24. *Times*, 12 February 1885, 5.
25. *Times*, 23 February 1885, 5.
26. Willy, "Agitation," 312–17. The liberal press of London remained respectful of the heroic aspects of Gordon's character, but tried to mitigate his loss and the fall of Khartoum as unfortunate but not devastating events.
27. *Times*, 14 March 1885, 12.
28. Ibid.
29. Ibid.
30. Willy, "Agitation," 316–17, 318–22, 325–27.
31. Archibald Forbes, the hack military journalist, also published a Gordon book in 1884. He was honest enough to admit in the introduction that his book was a digest of Wilson, Hill, and some of Hake. Forbes wanted only to provide a condensed product for a hot public market. Archibald Forbes, *Chinese Gordon, A Succinct Record of His Life* (London: George Rutledge and Sons, 1884). The Wilson account, much of which was based on Gordon's own journals, exists in a reprint edition that includes the personal notes and textual corrections of Captain John Holland, the man who commanded the EVA prior to Gordon's arrival. Andrew Wilson, *The "Ever Victorious Army": A History of the Chinese Campaign under Lt.-Col. C. G. Gordon, C.B., R.E. and of the Suppression of the Tai Ping Rebellion*, (1868; reprint, San Francisco: Chinese Materials Center, 1977). Wilson's title leaves little doubt as to who figures as the hero in his account.
32. Other accounts of Gordon as hero have attributed primacy among Gordon biographers to better-known figures like F. R. Wingate or Khartoum witnesses like Father Joseph Orhwalder and Rudolf Slatin. John M. MacKenzie, "Heroic Myths of Empire," in *Popular Imperialism*, 128.
33. *Saturday Review* 59, 619. Founded in 1855, the *Review* over its life had maintained a reputation for a moderate conservatism. Stephen Koss, *The Rise and Fall of the Political Press in Britain*, vol. 1; *The Nineteenth Century* (London: Hamish Hamilton, 1981), 88–89, 185.
34. Alfred Egmont Hake, *The Story of Chinese Gordon*, 6th ed. (London: Remington and Co., 1884), 1, 3. The *Story* and its companion volume, *Gordon in China and the Soudan* (1885, 1886; reprint, London: Darf Publishers, 1987), went through many editions and stayed in print into this century. Not for nothing did the iconoclast Lytton Strachey, who did not write *Eminent Victorians* until 1918, select Gordon as one of his victims.
35. Hake, *Story*, 15–16. Hake's work sold especially well in the year that Gordon became trapped at Khartoum.
36. Ibid.
37. Ibid., 406, 407.
38. Hake, *Gordon in China*, 330–32.
39. Chenevix Trench, *The Road*, 56, 57–58; Nutting, *Gordon of Khartoum*, 88–90.
40. Hake, *Gordon in China*, 124.
41. Ibid., 122–23. Chenevix Trench and Nutting both agree that Gordon regulary maintained these practices.
42. The British Museum catalog entry for Gordon is three to four times as long as that for Havelock. I attribute that fact to the increased availability of popular, cheap print media in the ensuing thirty years, but also to the practice

British journalism had gained in the manufacture of the Christian hero and the popularity of the genre.

43. Rev. Stephen A. Swaine, *General Gordon* (London: Cassell and Co., 1890). Reverend Swaine justified his repetition of the Gordon story as the only one prepared especially to educate the young; Colonel Sir William Butler, *Charles George Gordon* (London: Macmillan and Co., 1899). Butler's book originally appeared in January 1889 as part of the English Men of Action series. By 1899 it was into its seventh edition.

44. Major-General Sir Charles George Gordon, *The Journals of Major-General C. G. Gordon, C. B., at Khartoum*, ed. A. E. Hake (London: Kegan Paul, Trench and Co., 1885), 3, 83, 121, 183, 213, 279.

45. Gordon's ideas about the transubstantiation of the Host appear wholly Catholic. See his *Reflections in Palestine: 1883* (London: Macmillan and Co., 1885), 65–68. Gordon saw the Sacrament as "Divine Substance" and an antidote to Original Sin.

46. Gordon, *The Journals*, 19.

47. Of the Creation, Gordon wrote, "He made us in order to have a house to live in. Without us He is houseless; He needs us, and how much do we need Him!" *Reflections*, vi.

48. Chenevix Trench, *The Road*, 171–172. See also, Hake, *Story*, 388. Hake acknowledges only that Gordon made "curious researches concerning the site of the Garden of Eden."

49. Gordon, *Reflections*, 2–3.

50. Ibid., 23–24.

51. Ibid., 25–26.

52. Ibid., 27–28. Gordon's emphases.

53. Gordon thought the Mahdi to be an impostor and hypocrite. See Gordon, *The Journals*, passim.

54. Chenevix Trench, *The Road*, 170–72.

55. There is more than ample evidence of Gordon's longing for death. Nutting, *Gordon of Khartoum*, 83–85, 185–86.

56. Chenevix Trench, *The Road*, 36–37.

57. Dave Russel, "'We Carved Our Way to Glory': The British Soldier in Music Hall Song and Sketch, c. 1880–1914," in Mackenzie, *Popular Imperialism*, 54.

58. Ibid., 58. Russel finds that this trend was marked by the early 1890s. Also, Michael R. Booth, *English Melodrama* (London: Herbert Jenkins, 1965), 93–99. Booth points out that earlier in the century military melodrama emphasized "great leader" characters (Wellington, Nelson, Moore) and spectacle.

59. *Soldiers Three* maintained its popularity well into the age of cinema. Kipling himself believed music halls "the very stuff of social history." He tried to pattern his ballads and poetry after music hall rythms and lyrics. John M. MacKenzie, *Propaganda and Empire: The Manipulation of British Public Opinion, 1880–1960* (Manchester: Manchester University Press, 1984), 40, 90.

60. William J. Reader, *"At Duty's Call": A Study in Obsolete Patriotism* (Manchester: Manchester University Press, 1988), 57. Kipling had soldier stories scattered through many best-selling collections: *Plain Tales from the Hills, Life's Handicap, Many Inventions*.

61. Russel, "'We Carved Our Way to Glory,'" 58–59, 68, 73. "In the final analysis . . . it is undeniable that the music hall's projection of the soldier was

ultimately a positive one and one which helped to raise the army and the common soldier in the public esteem."

62. Booth, *English Melodrama*, 93–95; MacKenzie, *Propaganda and Empire*, 51. Specific wars and crises inevitably boosted the numbers of military shows available in London and on tour (47–50).

63. MacKenzie, *Propaganda and Empire*, 51.

64. Kenneth D. Brown, "Modelling for War? Toy Soldiers in Late-Victorian and Edwardian Britain," *Journal of Social History* 24 (winter 1990): 237–54. Also, Jeff Richards, "Popular Imperialism and the Image of the Army in Juvenile Literature," in MacKenzie, *Popular Imperialism*, 80–90. Patrick A. Dunae, "Boys' Literature and the Idea of Empire, 1870–1914," *Victorian Studies* 33, (1980): 105–21.

65. The Boys Brigade and, in Edwardian years, Scouting, were prime examples of activities that combined youth recreation with imperial education. Hanham, "Religion and Nationality," 172–75.

66. Dunae, "Boys' Literature," 105–6.

67. Geoffrey Best, "Militarism and the Victorian Public School," in *The Victorian Public School: Studies in the Development of an Educational Institution*, ed. Brian Simon and Ian Bradley (Dublin: Gill and Macmillan, 1975), 129–46. Reader, *At Duty's Call*, 84–100.

68. On the power of mythmaking in the Gordon "death saga," see Douglas H. Johnson, "The Death of Gordon: A Victorian Myth," *Journal of Imperial and Commonwealth History* 10, (1982): 285–310. See also MacKenzie, "Heroic Myths," 114–15.

Bibliography

Unpublished Papers

John Rylands Methodist Archives, University of Manchester: William Harris Rule Papers

McLennan Library, McGill University: Sir Henry Hardinge Papers

National Library of Scotland; MSS. 1854, 2840, 2847, 2858–61, Sir George Brown Papers; MSS. 3870, George Robert Gleig Papers

North Yorkshire County Record Office: General Sir Henry Havelock Papers

Public Record Office: WO 4/347–49, 1035; WO 30/93–95; WO 33/19; WO 43, Secretary at War, 'Very Old Series' and 'Old Series'; WO 139/1, 6

Parliamentary Journals and Papers

Hansard's Parliamentary Debates, 3rd Series, 356 vols. (1830–91).

House of Commons Parliamentary Papers

HCPP 1842, vol. 27.137, Particulars of the Sum of £11,000 charged in the Army Estimates for Divine Service in the Army.

HCPP 1847–48 (239), vol. 41.81, Particulars of the Sum of £16,800 charged in the Army Estimates for Divine Service for the Army for the year 1847–48.

HCPP 1848–49, vol. 41.81, Particulars of the Sum of £16, 800 charged in the Army Estimates for the year 1848–49.

HCPP. 1853–54, vol. 59.415, Expenditure of the Sum taken in the Army Estimates for Allowance to officiating Clergymen at Home and Abroad, and for Religious Books.

HCPP 1857–58, vol. 37.239, Expenditure of the Sum taken in the Army Estimates for Allowance to officiating Clergymen at Home and Abroad, and for Religious Books.

HCPP 1859 Session 1, vol. 15.345, Detail of Expenditure for Commissioned Chaplains, distinguishing Protestants and Roman Catholics; similar account for Officiating Clergymen at Home and Abroad; and Religious Books.

HCPP 1859 Session 1, vol. 15.353, Expenditure of the Sum taken in the Army Estimates for Allowance to officiating Clergymen at Home and Abroad, and for Religious Books.

HCPP 1859 Session 2, vol. 17.137, Correspondence during 1858 regarding appointment of Ministers of the Presbyterian Church in Ireland to the Office of Chaplain or Assistant Chaplain.

HCPP 1861, vol. 26.493, Copy of the Warrant appointing Roman Catholic Chaplains to have Rank in the Army.

HCPP 1861, vol. 36.275, Detail of Expenditure for Commissioned Chaplains, distinguishing Protestants and Roman Catholics; similar account for Officiating Clergymen at Home and Abroad; and Religious Books.

HCPP 1861, vol. 36.311, Expenditure of the Sum taken in the Army Estimates for Allowance to officiating Clergymen at Home and Abroad, and for Religious Books.

HCPP 1862, vol. 32.283, Detail of Expenditure for Commissioned Chaplains, distinguishing Protestants and Roman Catholics; similar account for Officiating Clergymen at Home and Abroad; and Religious Books.

HCPP 1862, vol. 32.707, Reports of Captain Jackson respecting the State of Soldiers' Institutes in England; Report of General Eyre's Committee on Libraries and Reading Rooms for Soldiers; Report on Soldiers' Institutes at Aldershot and Portsmouth.

HCPP 1863, vol. 33.463, Reports on Soldiers' Institutes at Chatham and Gibraltar; Correspondence on proposed Institutes at Devonport and Aldershot.

HCPP 1864, vol. 35.305, Detail of Expenditure for Commissioned Chaplains, distinguishing Protestants and Roman Catholics; similar account for Officiating Clergymen at Home and Abroad; and Religious Books.

HCPP 1864, vol. 35.585, Return stating the Numbers and Religious Denominations of all the Soldiers in Her Majesty's Land and Marine Forces.

HCPP 1865, vol. 32.333, Detail of Expenditure for Commissioned Chaplains, distinguishing Protestants and Roman Catholics; similar account for Officiating Clergymen at Home and Abroad; and Religious Books.

HCPP 1872, vol. 37.445, Return of Numbers of NCOs and Men in the Army, according to their Religious Denominations.

HCPP 1876, vol. 42.499, Tabular return of Commissioned Army Chaplains serving in Ireland, and of Parochial Clergy (Episcopalian Protestant) officiating to H.M. Troops in Ireland, their Duties, Salaries, etc.

HCPP 1878–9, vol. 43.523, Return of Numbers of NCOs and Men in the Army, according to their Religious Denominations.

Periodicals

All the Year 'Round

Blackwood's Edinburgh Magazine

Methodist Recorder

Quarterly Journal of the Royal Army Chaplains' Department

Quarterly Review

St. Paul's Magazine

The Times

Contemporary Published Works

Acton, William. *Prostitution*. London, 1857. Reprint, London: MacGibbon and Kee, 1968.

Aitchison, Sir Charles. *Lord Lawrence and the Reconstruction of India under the Crown.* "Rulers of India Series." Oxford: Clarendon Press, 1894.

Dickens, Charles. "Aldershot Town and Camp". *All the Year Round,* 20 August (1859).

Evans, Alfred Bowen. *War: Its Theology; its Anomalies; its Incidents, and its Humiliations.* London: Peace Society, 1855.

Gleig, George Robert. "Moral Discipline of the Army". *Quarterly Review,* vol. 76, (1845).

Martin, Robert Montgomery. *History of the Indian Empire.* 2 vols. London: London Printing and Publishing Company, 1858.

Pascoe, C. F. *Two Hundred Years of the S.P.G.: An Historical Account of the Society for the Propagation of the Gospel in Foreign Parts, 1701–1900.* London: SPG, 1901.

The Church in the Army; a Letter to the Right Honourable Sir J.S. Pakington, Bart., G.C.B., M.P., Secretary of State for War, by an Officer. London: W. H. Bartlett & Co., 1868.

The Soldier and the Christian: Addressed to All Willing to Hear Both Sides, but Especially to Parents about to Choose a Profession for their Sons, by A Clergyman of the Church of England. London: Peace Society, 1855.

Stock, Eugene. *The History of the Church Missionary Society, Its Environment, Its Men, and Its Work.* 4 vols. London: Church Missionary Society, 1899.

Contemporary Biographies and Memoirs

Birrel, Charles. *The Life of William Brock, D.D., First Minister of Bloomsbury Chapel, London.* London: James Nisbit, 1878.

Brock, Rev. William. *A Biographical Sketch of Sir Henry Havelock, K.C.B.,* 5th ed. London: James Nisbit, 1858.

Butler, Colonel Sir William. *Charles George Gordon.* "English Men of Action" Series. London: MacMillan and Co., 1899.

Carlyle, Thomas. *Oliver Cromwell's Letters and Speeches, with Elucidations,* 4 vols. Carlyle Centenary Series. London: Chapman and Hall, 1897.

Chappell, Jennie. *Noble Work by Noble Women: Sketches of the Lives of Baroness Burdett-Coutts, Lady Henry Somerset, Miss Sarah Robinson, Mrs. Fawcett, and Mrs. Gladstone.* London: S. W. Partridge & Co., 1899.

Daniell, G. F. S. *Aldershot: A Record of Mrs. Daniell's Work amongst Soldiers and Its Sequel, by her Daughter.* London: Hodder and Stoughton, 1879.

Edgar, John George. *Heroes of England.* London: J. M. Dent and Sons, 1858.

Forbes, Archibald. *Chinese Gordon, A Succinct Record of his Life.* London: George Rutledge and Sons, 1884.

Froude, J. A. *Thomas Carlyle, a History of his Life in London.* 2 vols. London, 1884.

Gleig, George Robert. *A Narrative of the Campaigns of the British Army at Washington and New Orleans: Under Generals Ross, Pakenham, and Lambert, in the year 1814 and 1815: with some account of the countries visited/ By an officer who served in the expedition.* London: John Murray, 1821.

———. *Personal Reminiscences of the First Duke of Wellington, With Sketches of some of his Guests and Contemporaries*. London: William Blackwood and Sons, 1904.

———. *The Subaltern*. Edinburgh: William Blackwood, 1825.

Gordon, Major-General Sir Charles George. *The Journals of Major-General C. G. Gordon at Khartoum*. Edited by. A. E. Hake. London: Kegan, Paul, Trench and Co., 1885.

———. *Reflections in Palestine: 1883*. London: Macmillan and Co., 1885.

Hake, Alfred Egmont. *Gordon in China and the Soudan*. London: 1885, 1896. Reprint, London: Darf Publishers, 1987.

———. *The Story of Chinese Gordon*. 6th ed. London: Remington and Co., 1884.

Hake, Thomas Gordon. *Memoirs of Eighty Years*. London: 1892. Reprint, New York: AMS Press, 1970.

Havelock, Lieutentant Henry. *Memoir of the Three Campaigns of Major General Sir A. Campbell's Army in Ava*. Serampore, 1828.

———. *Narrative of the War in Affghanistan [sic] in 1838–1839*. 2 vols. Henry Colburn: London, 1840.

Henry, Philip, 5th Earl Stanhope. *Notes of Conversations with the Duke of Wellington, 1831–1851*. 1888. Reprint, New York: De Capo Press 1973.

Lathbury, D. C. ed. *Correspondence on Church and Religion of William Ewert Gladstone*. 2 vols. New York: Macmillan, 1910.

Marshman, John Clark. *The Memoirs of Sir Henry Havelock, K.C.B*. London: Longmans, 1878.

Martin, Robert Montgomery. *History of the Indian Empire*. London: The London Printing and Publishing Company, 1858.

M'Cree, George Wilson. *William Brock, D.D., First Pastor of Bloomsbury Chapel*. London: James Clark and Co., 1876.

Porter, Sir Gerald. *The British Mission to Uganda in 1893*. London: Edward Arnold, Publisher to the India Office, 1894.

Robertson, Field Marshal Sir William. *From Private to Field Marshal*. New York: Houghton Mifflin Company, 1921.

Rule, William Harris. *An Account of the Establishment of Wesleyan Methodism in the British Army*. London: T. Woolmer, 1883.

———. *Recollections of My Life and Work at Home and Abroad in Connection with the Wesleyan Methodist Conference*. London: T. Woolmer, 1886.

Sandes, Elise. *Enlisted; or, My Story. Incidents of Life and Work Among Soldiers*. London: S. W. Partridge and Co., 1915.

Stanmore, Arthur Hamilton-Gordon, First Baron. *Sidney Herbert: Lord Herbert of Lea, a Memoir*. 2 vols. London: John Murray, 1906.

Swain, Rev. Stephen A. *General Gordon*. London: Cassell and Co., 1890.

Swinson, Arthur, and Donald Scott, eds. *The Memoirs of Private Waterfield, Soldier in Her Majesty's 32nd Regiment of Foot, 1842–1857*. London: Cassel, 1968.

Times of London. *Biographies of Eminent Persons*, vol. 3, 1882–1886. Macmillan and Co., London, 1893.

Wellington, Arthur Wellesley, First Duke of. *Despatches, Correspondence and Memoranda*. London: John Murray, 1878, 1880.

———. *Wellington and His Friends, Letters of the First Duke of Wellington to the Rt. Hon. Charles and Mrs. Arbuthnot, the Earl and Countess of Wilton, Princess Lieven, and Miss Burdett-Coutts.* Edited by the Seventh Duke of Wellington London: Macmillan and Co., 1966.

Wilson, Andrew. *The "Ever Victorious Army": A History of the Chinese Campaign under Lt.-Col. C.G. Gordon, C.B., R.E. and of the Suppression of the Tai-Ping Rebellion*. 1868. Reprint, San Francisco: Chinese Materials Center, 1977.

Secondary Works

Books

Anderson, Amanda. *Tainted Souls and Painted Faces: The Rhetoric of Fallenness in Victorian Culture*. Ithaca: Cornell University Press, 1993.

Aronson, Theo. *Heart of a Queen: Queen Victoria's Romantic Attachments*. London: John Murray, 1991.

Ascoli, David. *A Companion to the British Army, 1660–1983*. London: Harrap, 1983.

Barnett, Correlli. *Britain and Her Army, 1509–1970: A Military, Political, and Social Survey*. New York: W. Morrow, 1970.

Bayly, C. A. and Eric Stokes. *The Peasant Armed: The Indian Rebellion of 1857*. Oxford: Clarendon Press, 1986.

Beales, Dereck, and Geoffrey Best, eds. *History, Society, and the Chuches: Essays in Honour of Owen Chadwick*. Cambridge: Cambridge University Press, 1985.

Bebbington, D. W. *Evangelicalism in Modern Britain: A History from the 1730s to the 1980s*. London: Unwin Hyman, 1989.

———. *The Nonconformist Conscience: Chapel and politics, 1870–1914*. London: George Allen and Unwinn, 1982.

Beckett, Ian F. W., and Keith Simpson, eds., *A Nation in Arms: A Social Study of the British Army in the First World War*. Manchester: Manchester University Press, 1985.

Beckett, Ian F. W., and Keith Simpson and John Gooch, eds. *Politicians and Defence: Studies in the Formulation of British Defence Policy, 1845–1970*. Mancherster: Manchester University Press, 1985.

Bentley, Nicloas, ed. *Russell's Despatches from the Crimea, 1854–1856*. New York: Hill and Wang, 1966.

Best, Geoffrey F. A. *Shaftesbury*. New York: Arco Publishing Company, 1964.

———. *Temporal Pillars: Queen Anne's Bounty, the Ecclesiastical Commissioners, and the Church of England*. Cambridge: Cambridge University Press, 1964.

Best, Geoffrey F. A., and Andrew Wheatcroft. *War, Economy, and the Military Mind*. London: Croom Helm, 1976.

Binfield, Clyde. *So Down to Prayers: Studies in English Nonconformity, 1780–1920*. London: J. M. Dent & Sons, 1977.

Booth, Michael R. *English Melodrama.* London: Herbert Jenkins, 1965.

Bourne, Kenneth. *Palmerston: The Early Years, 1784–1841.* London: Allen Lane, 1982.

Bowen, Desmond. *The Idea of the Victorian Church: a Study of the Church of England, 1833–1889.* Montreal: McGill University Press, 1968.

Boxer, Marilyn J., and Jean H. Quataert, eds. *Connecting Spheres: Women in the Western World, 1500 to the Present.* New York: Oxford University Press, 1987.

Bradley, I. *The Call to Seriousness: The Evangelical Impact on the Victorians,* London: Macmillan, 1976.

Brereton, J. M. *The British Soldier: A Social History from 1661 to the Present Day.* London: Bodley Head, 1986.

Brett-James, Antony. *Life in Wellington's Army.* London: George Allen and Unwin, 1972.

Brewer, John. *Party Ideology and Popular Politics at the Accession of George III.* Cambridge: Cambridge University Press, 1976.

———. *The Sinews of Power: War, Money, and the English State, 1688–1783.* Boston: Harvard University Press, 1990.

Bridenthal, Renate, and Claudia Koonz, and Susan Stuart, eds. *Becoming Visible: Women in European History.* 2d ed. Boston: Houghton Mifflin, 1987.

Bristow, Edward J. *Vice and Vigilance: Purity Movements in Britain since 1700.* Dublin: Gill and Macmillan, 1977.

Brown, Richard. *Church and State in Modern Britain, 1700–1850.* London: Routledge, 1991.

Bruce, Anthony. *The Purchase System in the British Army, 1660–1871.* London: Royal Historical Society, 1980.

Bushman, Richard L. *The Refinement of America: Persons, Houses, Cities.* New York: Alfred A Knopf, 1992.

Butler, Perry. *Gladstone: Church, State and Tractarianism: A Study of his Religious Ideas and Attitudes, 1809–1859.* Oxford: Clarendon Press, 1982.

Chadwick, Owen, ed. *The Mind of the Oxford Movement.* Stanford, Calif: Stanford University Press, 1961.

Chandler, David, and Ian Beckett, eds. *The Oxford Illustrated History of the British Army.* New York: Oxford University Press, 1994.

Charlot, Monica. *Victoria, the Young Queen.* London: Blackwell, 1991.

Chenevix Trench, Charles. *The Road to Khartoum: A Life of General Charles Gordon.* New York: W. W. Norton and Company, 1979.

Clark, J. C. D. *English Society, 1688–1832: Ideology, Social Structure and Practice during the Ancien Regime.* New York: Cambridge University Press, 1985.

———. *The Language of Liberty, 1660–1832: Political Discourse and Social Dynamics in the Anglo-American World.* New York: Cambridge University Press, 1994.

Cmiel, Kenneth. *Democratic Eloquence: The Fight over Popular Speech in Nineteenth-Century America.* Berkeley and Los Angeles: University of California Press, 1990.

Cole, Lt.-Col. Howard N. *The Story of Aldershot: A History and Guide to Town and Camp.* Aldershot, Eng.: Gale and Polden Limited, 1951.

Colley, Linda. *Britons: Forging the Nation, 1707–1837*. New Haven: Yale University Press, 1992.

Colloms, Brenda. *Victorian Country Parsons*. Lincoln: University of Nebraska Press, 1977.

Conacher, J. B. *Britain and the Crimea, 1855–1856: Problems of War and Peace*. London: MacMillan Press, 1987.

Cooper, Leonard. *Havelock*. London: Bodley Head, 1957.

Cox, Jeffrey. *The English Churches in a Secular Society: Lambeth, 1870–1930*. New York: Oxford University Press, 1982.

Cunningham, Hugh. *The Volunteer Force: A Social and Political History, 1859–1908*. Hamden, Conn.: Archon Books, 1975.

Currie, Robert, Alan Gilbert, and Lee Horsley. *Churches and Churchgoers: Patterns of Church Growth in the British Isles since 1700*. Oxford: Clarendon Press, 1977.

Davidoff, Leonore, and Catherine Hall. *Family Fortunes: Men and Women of the English Middle Class, 1780–1850*. Chicago: University of Chicago Press, 1987.

Dawson, Graham. *Soldier Heroes: British Adventure, Empire, and the Imagining of Masculinities*. New York: Routledge, 1994.

Dewey, Clive. *The Passing of Barchester*. London: Hambledon Press, 1991.

Dietz, Peter, ed. *Garrison: Ten British Military Towns*. London: Brassey's Defence Publishers, 1986.

DuBois, E. C., ed. *Elizabeth Cady Stanton and Susan B. Anthony: Correspondence, Writings, Speeches*. New York: Schocken Books, 1981.

Fabb, John. *The Victorian and Edwardian Army from old Photographs*. London: B.T. Batsford, 1975.

Featherstone, Donald. *Colonial Small Wars, 1837–1901*. London: David and Charles, 1973.

Finlayson, Geoffrey B. A. M. *The Seventh Earl of Shaftesbury, 1801–1885*. London: Eyre Methuen, 1981.

Finnegan, Frances. *Poverty and Prostitution: a Study of Victorian Prostitutes in York*. Cambridge: Cambridge University Press, 1979.

Gash, Norman. *Sir Robert Peel, the life of Sir Robert Peel after 1830*. London: Longman, 1972.

———, ed. *Wellington: Studies in the Military and Political Career of the First Duke of Wellington*. New York: Manchester University Press, 1990.

Gilbert, Alan D. *The Making of Post-Christian Britain: A History of the Secularization of Modern Society*. New York: Longman, 1980.

———. *Religion and Society in Industrial England: Church, Chapel and Social Change, 1740–1914*. New York: Longman, 1976.

Golby, J. M., ed. *Culture and Society in Britain, 1850–1890: a Source Book of Contemporary Writings*. Oxford: Oxford University Press, 1986.

Haig, Alan. *The Victorian Clergy*. London: Croom Helm, 1984.

Hamer, W. S. *The British Army: Civil-Military Relations, 1885–1905*. New York: Oxord University Press, 1970.

Harries-Jenkins, Gwyn. *The Army in Victorian Society*. Toronto: University of Toronto Press, 1977.

Harrison, Brian. *Drink and the Victorians: The Temperance Question in England, 1815–1872*. London: Faber and Faber, 1971.

Hay, Douglas, and Francis Snyder, eds. *Policing and Prosecution in Britain, 1750–1850*, Oxford: Oxford University Press, 1989.

Hay, Douglas, Peter Linebaugh, John G. Rule, E. P. Thompson, and Cal Winslow, eds. *Albion's Fatal Tree: Crime and Society in Eighteenth-Century England*, New York: Pantheon, 1975.

Hayter, Anthony J. *The Army and the Crowd in Mid-Georgian England*. London: Macmillan Press, 1978.

Hempton, David. *Methodism and Politics in British Society, 1750–1850*. Stanford: Stanford University Press, 1984.

Hempton, David, and Myrtle Hill. *Evangelical Protestantism in Ulster Society, 1740–1890*. New York: Routledge, 1992.

Henderson, Diana M. *Highland Soldier: A Social Study of Highland Regiments, 1820–1920*. Edinburgh: John Donald Publishers, 1989.

Hilton, Boyd. *The Age of Atonement: the Influence of Evangelicalism on Social and Economic Thought, 1795–1865*. Oxford: Oxford University Press, 1988.

Hobsbawm, Eric. *Workers: Worlds of Labor*. New York: Pantheon, 1984.

Howard, Michael. *Studies in War and Peace*. New York: Viking Press, 1959.

Hyam, Ronald. *Empire and Sexuality: the British Experience*. Manchester: Manchester University Press, 1990.

Inglis, K. S. *Churches and the Working Classes in Victorian England*. London: Routledge and Kegan Paul, 1963.

Keegan, John. *The Face of Battle: A Study of Agincourt, Waterloo, and the Somme*. London: Penguin Books, 1976.

Kent, John. *Holding the Fort: Studies in Victorian Revivalism*. London: Epworth Press, 1978.

Knorr, K. E. *British Colonial Theories, 1570–1850*. London, 1963.

Koss, Stephen E. *Lord Haldane, Scapegoat for Liberalism*. New York: Columbia University Press, 1969.

———. *Nonconformity in Modern British Politics*. Hamden, Conn.: Archon Books, 1975.

———. *The Rise and Fall of the Political Press in Britain*, Vol. 1: *The Nineteenth Century*. London: Hamish Hamilton, 1981.

Lehmann, Joseph H. *The Model Major-General: A Biography of Field-Marshall Lord Wolseley*. Boston: Houghton Mifflin, 1964.

Levine, Philippa. *Feminist Lives in Victorian England: Private Roles and Public Commitment*. Oxford: Basil Blackwell, 1990.

Lewis, Donald M. *Lighten Their Darkness: The Evangelical Mission to Working-Class London, 1828–1860*. New York: Greenwood Press, 1986.

Lewis, Jane. *Women and Social Action in Victorian and Edwardian England*. Stanford, Calif.: Stanford University Press, 1991.

Longford, Elizabeth. *Wellington: The Years of the Sword*. New York: Harper and Row, 1969.

———. *Wellington: Pillar of State*. New York: Harper and Row, 1971.

Machin, G. I. T. *Politics and the Churches in Great Britain, 1832–1868*. New York: Oxford University Press, 1977.

MacKenzie, John M., ed. *Popular Imperialism and the Military, 1850–1950.* Manchester: Manchester University Press, 1992.

MacKenzie, John M. *Propaganda and Empire: The Manipulation of British Public Opinion, 1880–1960.* Manchester: Manchester University Press, 1984.

Marcus, Steven Marcus. *The Other Victorians: A Study of Sexuality and Pornography in Mid-Nineteenth Century England.* New York: Basic Books, 1964.

Marlowe, John. *Mission to Khartoum: The Apotheosis of General Gordon.* London: Victor Gollancz, 1969.

Marsh, P. T. *The Victorian Church in Decline: Archbishop Tait and the Church of England, 1868–1882.* Pittsburgh: University of Pittsburgh Press, 1969.

Mason, Michael. *The Making of Victorian Sexual Attitudes.* Oxford: Oxford University Press, 1994.

Mather, F. C. *Public Order in the Age of the Chartists.* Manchester: Manchester University Press, 1959.

Maurice, Major-General Sir Frederick, and Sir George Arthur. *The Life of Lord Wolseley.* New York: Doubleday, Page and Co., 1924.

McHugh, Paul. *Prostitution and Victorian Social Reform.* New York: St. Martin's Press, 1980.

Norman, E. R. *Church and Socity in England, 1770–1970: An Historical Study.* New York: Oxford University Press, 1976.

Nutting, Anthony. *Gordon of Khartoum: Martyr and Misfit.* New York: Clarkson N. Potter, 1966.

Okin, Susan M. *Women in Western Political Thought,* (Princeton: Princeton University Press, 1979.

Orr, James Edwin. *The Light of the Nations: Evangelical Renewal and Advance in the Nineteenth Century.* Grand Rapids, Mich.: Eerdmans Publishing Company, 1965.

———. *The Second Evangelical Awakening in Britain.* London: Marshall, Morgan and Scott, 1949.

Palmer, Stanley H. *Police and Protest in England and Ireland, 1780–1850.* New York: Cambridge University Press, 1988.

Parsons, Gerald, ed. *Religion in Victorian Britain.* 4 vols. Manchester: Manchester University Press, 1988.

Piggin, Stuart. *Making Evangelical Missionaries, 1789–1858: The Social Background, Motives and Training of British Protestant Missionaries to India.* Perth: Sutton Courtenay Press, 1984.

Pollock, John. *Wilberforce.* New York: St Martin's Press, 1977.

Pollock, J. C. *The Way to Glory: the Life of Havelock of Lucknow.* London: John Murray, 1957.

Prochaska, F. K. *Women and Philanthropy in Nineteenth-Century England* Oxford: Clarendon Press, 1980.

Reader, William J. *"At Duty's Call": A Study in Obsolete Patriotism.* Manchester: Manchester University Press, 1988.

Rhodes, Robert James. *Prince Albert: A Biography.* New York: Albert A. Knopf, 1984.

Ridley, Jasper. *Lord Palmerston.* New York: E. P. Dutton and Co., 1970.

Robinson, Ronald and John Gallagher. *Africa and the Victorians: The Official Mind of Imperialism*. 2d ed. London: Macmillan, 1981.

Rossi, Alice S. *The Feminist Papers: From Adams to de Beauvoir*. 2d ed. Boston: Northeastern University Press, 1988.

Skelley, Alan Ramsay. *The Victorian Army at Home: The Recruitment and Terms and Conditions of the British Regular, 1859–1899*. London: Croom Helm, Ltd., 1977.

Smout, T. C., ed. *Victorian Values: A Joint Symposium of the Royal Society of Edinburgh and the British Academy, December 1990*. Oxford: Oxford University Press, 1992.

Smyth, Sir John. *In This Sign Conquer: The Story of the Army Chaplains*. London: A. R. Mowbray, 1968.

Spiers, Edward M. *The Army and Society, 1815–1914*. New York: Longman, 1980.

———. *Haldane: an Army Reformer*. Edinburgh: Edinburgh University Press, 1980.

———. *The Late Victorian Army, 1868–1902*. New York: Manchester University Press, 1992.

———. *Radical General: Sir George de Lacy Evans, 1787–1870*. Manchester: Manchester University Press, 1983.

Springhall, John, Brian Fraser, and Michael Hoare. *Sure and Steadfast: A History of the Boys' Brigade, 1883–1983*. London: Collins, 1983.

Stanley, Brian. *The Bible and the Flag: Protestant Missions and British Imperialism in the Nineteenth and Twentieth Centuries*. Leicester, England: Intervarsity Press, 1990.

St. Aubyn, Giles. *The Royal George, 1819–1904: The Life of H.R.H. Prince George, Duke of Cambridge*. New York: Alfred A. Knopf, 1964.

Steedman, Carolyn. *Policing the Victorian Community: The Formation of English Provincial Police Forces, 1856–1880*. New York: Routledge and Kegan Paul, 1984.

———. *The Radical Soldier's Tale: John Pearman, 1819–1908*. History Workshop Series. London: Routledge, 1988.

Strachan, Hew. *From Waterloo to Balaclava: Tactics, Technology, and the British Army, 1815–54*. Cambridge: Cambridge University Press, 1985.

———. *Wellington's Legacy: The Reform of the British Army, 1830–1854*. Manchester: Manchester University Press, 1984.

Strayer, Robert W. *The Making of Mission Communities in East Africa: Anglicans and Africans in Colonial Kenya, 1875–1935*. London: Heinemann Press, 1978.

Sweetman, John. *War and Administration: The Significance of the Crimean War for the British Army*. Edinburgh: Scottish Academic Press, 1984.

Thompson, E. P. *The Making of the English Working Class*. Vintage ed. New York: Vintage, 1966.

Thompson, Neville. *Wellington After Waterloo*. London: Routledge and Kegan Paul, 1986.

Tilly, Louise A., and Joan Scott. *Women, Work, and Family*, 2d ed. New York: Methuen, 1987.

Trevelyan, George Macaulay. *British History in the Nineteenth Century and After*. New York: Harper and Row, 1937.

Trustam, Myna. *Women of the Regiment: Marriage and the Victorian Army*. Cambridge: Cambridge University Press, 1984.

Vance, Norman. *The Sinews of the Spirit: The Ideal of Christian Manliness in Victorian Literature and Religious Thought*. Cambridge: Cambridge University Press, 1985.

Van Den Berg, Johannes. *Constrained by Jesus' Love: An Inquiry in the Motives of the Missionary Awakening in Great Britain in the Period between 1698 and 1815*. Netherlands: J. M Kok, 1956.

Vicinus, M. ed. *Suffer and Be Still: Women in the Victorian Age*. Bloomington: Indiana University Press, 1972.

Walker, Graham, and Tom Gallagher. *Sermons and Battle Hymns: Protestant Popular Culture in Modern Scotland*. Edinburgh: University of Edinburgh Press, 1990.

Walkowitz, Judith. *Prostitution and Victorian Society: Women, Class, and the State*. Cambridge: Cambridge University Press, 1980.

Warren, Max. *The Missionary Movement from Britain in Modern History*. London: SCM Press, 1965.

Watkins, Owen Spencer. *Soldiers and Preachers Too: Being the Romantic Story of Methodism in the British Army*. London: Charles H. Kelly, n.d.

Weintraub, Stanley. *Victoria, an Intimate Biography*. New York: E. P. Dutton, 1987.

Wetzel, David. *The Crimean War: A Diplomatic History*. East European Monographs Series. New York: Columbia University Press, 1985.

Witz, Cornelia. *Religionspolitik in Britisch-Indien, 1793–1813: Christliches Sendungsbewusstsein und Achtung Hinduistischer Tradition im Widerstreit*, (Religious Politics in British India, 1793–1813: the Conflict between Christian Missionary Consciousness and the Toleration of Hindu Tradition). Wiesbaden, Germany: Fritz Steiner Verlag, 1985.

Woodham-Smith, Cecil. *The Reason Why*. London: McGraw-Hill, 1954.

Wolffe, John. *The Protestant Crusade in Great Britain, 1829–1860*. Oxford: Clarendon Press, 1991.

Articles

Anderson, Olive. "Early Experiences of Manpower Problems in an Industrial Society at War: Great Britian, 1854–56." *Political Science Quarterly* 82, no. 4 (Dec. 1967): 526–45.

———. "The Growth of Christian Militarism in Mid-Victorian Britain." *English Historical Review* 86, (1971): 46–72.

Bebbington, D. W. "Nonconformity and Electoral Sociology, 1867–1918." *Historical Journal*, 27, no. 3 (1984): 633–56.

Best, Geoffrey. "Militarism and the Victorian Public School." *The Victorian Public School: Studies in the Development of an Educational Institution*, ed. Brian Simon and Ian Bradley 129–46 Dublin: Gill and Macmillan, 1975.

Blanco, Richard L. "Army Recruiting Reforms, 1861–1867." *Journal of the Society for Army Historical Research*, 46, (1968): 217–24.

———. "Attempts to Abolish Branding and Flogging in the Army of Victorian England Before 1881." *Journal of the Society for Army Historical Research* 46 (1968): 137–45.

Bond, Brian. "Edward Cardwell's Army Reforms, 1868–1874." *Army Quarterly and Defence Journal* (April 1962): 108–17.

———. "The Late-Victorian Army." *History Today* 11 (1961): 616–24.

———. "Recruiting the Victorian Army, 1870–1892." *Victorian Studies* 5, no. 1 (June 1962): 329–38.

Brown, Kenneth D. "Modelling for War? Toy Soldiers in late-Victorian and Edwardian Britain." *Journal of Social History* 24 (winter 1990): 237–54.

Bruce, Anthony. "Edward Cardwell and the Abolition of Purchase." In *Politicians and Defence: Studies in the Formulation of British Defence Policy, 1845–1870*. edited by Ian Beckett and John Gooch. Manchester: Manchester University Press, 1981.

Burroughs, Peter. "Crime and Punishment in the British Army, 1815–1870." *English Historical Review* (July 1985): 545–71.

———. "An Unreformed Army? 1815–1868." In *The Oxford Illustrated History of the British Army*, edited by David Chandler and Ian Beckett. New York: Oxford University Press, 1994.

Dinwiddy, J. R. "The Early Nineteenth-Century Campaign Against Flogging in the Army." *English Historical Review* 97 (1982): 308–31.

Donovan, Robert Kent. "The Military Origins of the Roman Catholic Relief Programme of 1778." *Historical Journal* 28, no. 1 (1985): 79–102.

Dunae, Patrick. "Boys' Literature and the Idea of Empire, 1870–1914." *Victorian Studies* 33 (1980): 105–21.

Hanham, H. J. "Religion and Nationality in the Mid-Victorian Army." In *War and Society*, edited by M. R. D. Foot. London: Paul Elek, 1973.

Harries-Jenkins, Gwyn. "The Development of Professionalism in the Victorian Army." *Armed Forces and Society* 1, no. 4 (August 1974): 472–89.

Hayter, Tony. "The British Army, 1713–1793: Recent Research Work." *Journal of the Society for Army Historical Research* 63, no. 253 (spring 1985): 11–19.

Howard, Michael. "Wellington and the British Army." In *Studies in War and Peace*, New York: Viking Press, 1959.

Jarvis, A.C.E. "My Predecessors in Office." *Journal of the Royal Army Chaplains' Department* 3 (1932): 444–80, 481–520; 4 (1933): 14–77, 320–58; 5 (1934): 9–29, 95–114, 420–45.

Johnson, Douglas H. "The Death of Gordon: A Victorian Myth." *Journal of Imperial and Commonwealth History* 10 (1982): 285–310.

Keegan, John. "Regimental Ideology." In *War, Economy, and the Military Mind*, edited by Geoffrey Best and Andrew Wheatcroft. London: Croom Helm, 1976.

Kopperman, Paul E. "Religion and Religious Policy in the British Army, c. 1700–1796." *Journal of Religious History* 14, no. 4 (1987): 390–405.

Koss, Stephen. "Wesleyanism and Empire." *The Historical Journal* 18, no. 1 (1975): 105–18.

Lalumia, Matthew. "Realism and Anti-Aristocratic Sentiment in Victorian Depicitions of the Crimean War." *Victorian Studies*, 27, (autumn 1983): 25–51.

Offen, Karen. "Liberty, Equality, and Justice for Women: The Theory and Practice of Feminism in Nineteenth Century Europe." In *Becoming Visible: Women in European History*, 2d ed., edited by Renate Bridenthal, Claudia Koonz, and Susan Stuard. Boston: Houghton Mifflin, 1987.

Pope, Barbara Corrado. "The Influence of Rousseau's Idology of Domesticity." In *Connecting Spheres: Women in the Western World, 1500 to the Present*, edited by Marilyn J. Boxer and Jean Quataert. New York: Oxford University Press, 1987.

Sigsworth, E. M., and T. J. Wyke. "A Study of Victorian Prostitution and Venereal Disease." In *Suffer and Be Still: Women in the Victorian Age*, edited by Martha Vicinus. Bloomington, Indiana: Indiana University Press, 1972.

Spiers, Edward M. "The British Army, 1856–1914: Recent Writing Reviewed." *Journal of the Society for Army Historical Research* 63, no. 256 (winter 1985): 194–207.

Stanley, Brian. "Christian Responses to the Indian Mutiny of 1857." In *Studies in Church History: the Church and War*, vol. 20, edited by W. Sheils. 278–89. Oxford: Oxford University Press, 1983.

Steiner, E. E. "Separating the Soldier from the Citizen: Ideology and Criticism of Coporal Punishment in the British Armies, 1790–1815." *Social History* 8, no. 1 (1983): 19–35.

Strachan, Hew. "The British Army and Society." *The Historical Journal* 22, no. 1 (1979): 247–54.

———. "The British Army, 1815–1856: Recent Writing Reviewed." *Journal of the Society for Army Historical Research*, 63, no. 254 (summer 1985): 68–79.

———. "The Early Victorian Army and the Nineteenth-Century Revolution in Government." *English Historical Review* 85 (October 1980): 783–809.

Summers, Anne. "Militarism in Britain before the Great War." *History Workshop Journal* 2 (1976): 104–23.

Dissertation

Willy, Todd Gray. "The Agitation in Parliament over Charles George 'Chinese' Gordon and His Mission to the Soudan, January 1884 to February 1885." Ph.D. diss. Speech and Communications, University of Iowa, 1962.

Index